Walk with me
I want you to walk with me
We'll travel with the sun
Two becoming one
Together walk through life and love.

Hold my hand
I need you to hold my hand
We'll face whatever comes
Two becoming one
Together stand for life and love.

Take my love
Everything I offer you
We'll love till life is done
Two becoming one
Together drink of life and love.

I know
You know
God knows
how I love you.

Take my love
Let me show you that it's true
I love you.

Palisades.
Pure Romance.

FICTION THAT FEATURES CREDIBLE CHARACTERS AND

ENTERTAINING PLOT LINES, WHILE CONTINUING TO UPHOLD

STRONG CHRISTIAN VALUES. FROM HIGH ADVENTURE

TO TENDER STORIES OF THE HEART, EACH PALISADES

ROMANCE IS AN UNDILUTED STORY OF LOVE,

FROM BEGINNING TO END!

A PALISADES CONTEMPORARY ROMANCE

COMING HOME

BARBARA JEAN HICKS

PALISADES

COMING HOME
published by Palisades
a part of the Questar publishing family

© 1996 by Barbara Jean Hicks
International Standard Book Number: 0-88070-945-6

Cover illustration by George Angelini
Cover designed by David Carlson and
Mona Weir-Daly
Edited by Paul Hawley
Printed in the United States of America

For information:
QUESTAR PUBLISHERS, INC.
POST OFFICE BOX 1720
SISTERS, OREGON 97759

Library of Congress Cataloging-in-Publication Data
Hicks, Barbara Jean.
    Coming home / Barbara Jean Hicks.
        p.   cm.
    ISBN 0-88070-945-6 (alk. paper)
    I. Title
    PS3558.I22976C66   1996
    813'.54--dc20   96-19006
                                                        CIP

96 97 98 99 00 01 02 03 — 10 9 8 7 6 5 4 3 2 1

To all the friends who contributed to this tale,
especially John and Betty Bailey
(and Daisy Mae), Randall Carty, Margie Ellingsen,
Laura Grimes, Chérie Huelshoff,
Stan Thornburg, and Christine Walden.

Thank you for your encouragement,
your stories, and your faith that God
is at work in the world.

Every book is a collaboration…

*I will come to you and fulfill my gracious promise
to bring you back to this place.
For I know the plans I have for you, declares the Lord,
plans to prosper you and not to harm you, plans
to give you hope and a future.*

JEREMIAH 29:10b–11, NIV

Prologue

❧

Two children crouched beneath a lilac bush, peering through its branches at the oldest house on Dearborn Street. They could just see the sagging porch over the bearded grass and white-headed dandelions in the overgrown yard.

Without taking his eyes from the crooked front door, the boy, wiry and tall for his age, stood on his knees and fished a donut from the pocket of his jeans. Breaking it in two, he handed one sticky piece to the carrot-haired girl who huddled next to him. She took it without comment. They waited, munching quietly.

Katie thought the house was scary since old lady Brathwaite had died. Keith thought it was sad. The blue paint was blistered and the porch sagged, and weeds had swallowed up the prize-winning roses. The shades were always drawn across the windows.

Until this morning.

Keith had known something was different on Dearborn Street the moment he woke up. He didn't know what till later, on his way to Katie's house after breakfast, riding the banana seat of his bicycle as a cowboy would his saddle. His favorite possession, even if it *was* secondhand.

He was right in the middle of popping a wheelie when he saw the dusty red pickup sitting in the driveway of the old Brathwaite house. Whipping his front tire around, he skidded to a halt, leaving a black mark on the sidewalk.

His green eyes widened with interest. The shades on the old house were up. The windows were open. The sound of a vacuum cleaner buzzed through the autumn air like a hundred hungry bees. Hopping back on the seat of his bike, he pedaled furiously down the street to tell Katie.

Christine Castle watched Keith and Katie from the window over her kitchen sink, a smile softening the tired lines around her mouth. The two were hiding in the lilacs, oblivious to the fact the bushes had already started their annual shedding of leaves and Keith's turquoise sweatshirt and Katie's tangled mass of orange hair made them as conspicuous through the branches as courting peacocks.

Six-year-old Keith was a never-ending delight to Christine, quick and curious and achingly sweet. She'd worried, as she carried him in her womb, that she would never be able to love him, that he would always remind her of the terror of that rainy Seattle night. The first time she'd held him, every doubt was swept away. Out of the blackest night, God had wrought a miracle. Keith had been born the first day of spring, and every time she looked at him, she found herself thanking God for new life and new beginnings.

The Brannigans had bought a house down the street several years before. Tom and Leigh and their little girl, Katie, had been an answer to prayer; not only did Keith have a playmate, but Christine had someone to count on for childcare. Working two jobs to make ends meet, she had far less time to spend with Keith than she would have liked. Leigh Brannigan, though physically fragile since her midlife pregnancy with Katie, was warm and caring and treated Keith as if he were her own son. Christine would have liked to know her better, but she didn't have much time for neighborly chats over tea.

Katie, younger by a year than Keith, was usually the leader of their backyard adventures. Keith willingly followed, as often as not straight into some mischief Katie had concocted. He played Indian to Katie's chief and soldier to her commandant without complaint.

Leigh Brannigan said that her daughter had been inconsolable last fall when Keith went off to half-day kindergarten without her. Finally Mrs. Brannigan had set up an in-house "classroom" where every afternoon Keith taught Katie what he'd learned that morning. For once, she didn't seem to mind playing the subordinate role.

Even at five and six, the two children discussed every detail of their lives together with almost comical seriousness. Christine loved to listen to them talk. They sang together, too, Katie humming wordlessly, perfectly in tune, while Keith chanted nonsense rhymes like mantras: *Katie-Bug, Lady-Bug, Green Alligatey-Bug, Skeetle-Bug, Needle-Bug, Black Bumblebeetle-Bug...*

Christine grabbed her purse, pulled a sweater from the hall closet, and slipped out the front door. Tiptoeing up behind the children in the lilacs, she bent over, placing a hand on Katie's shoulder and a kiss on top of Keith's head. "Find out all about our new neighbors, Kee," she whispered to her son. "I expect a full report when I get home from work!"

"I will!" Keith whispered back. "See you, Mama." He kissed her on the cheek, grinned his lopsided grin, and turned his eyes back to the house next door.

"Bye, Miz Castle," Katie whispered. "We're spying!"

Christine smiled again as she walked toward the bus stop. She hoped the new tenants of the house next door would be as tolerant as Mrs. Brathwaite had been. The lilacs had been Keith and Katie's favorite place to spy on their elderly neighbor, who had frankly fascinated them. Each time their stakeout ended, they retreated to Christine's front porch, where she listened with amusement to their observations.

Katie: "Mama says Mrs. Brathwaite has a green thumb. But I looked real close and they're both pink."

Keith: "My mama says Mrs. Brathwaite hugs her roses. But I never seen her do it."

"Roses are stickery," Katie commented.

"Mama's nicer to hug," Keith agreed.

Christine had puzzled over this exchange till she remembered an earlier conversation with Keith:

"How come Mrs. Brathwaite's always working in her garden?"

"It gives her comfort, sweetheart."

"What's comfort?"

"Kind of like a hug," she'd said, smiling and giving him one.

When Mrs. Brathwaite died, Christine told Keith she'd gone to live in heaven. "I hope she has a garden," he'd told her solemnly. "So she gets some comfort."

She'd pulled him close, hiding his face from the tears that sprang to her eyes. *God, thank you for this miracle*, she prayed silently. *You have used him for my healing.*

Keith wriggled in her grasp. "You're squishing me, Mama!"

"Sorry, baby. I love you."

"Love you, too!"

I will keep him safe, she vowed. *From all the ugly parts. He doesn't need to know.*

Keith's eyes darted to the colorful assortment of sheets draped over the odd-shaped load in the pickup. "Wonder what's under there?" he whispered, dragging his dark hair out of his eyes.

"Maybe a dollhouse," Katie whispered back.

Keith's hair fell forward again. "Maybe a swing set."

"Maybe a dragon!"

With a disbelieving snort, Keith reached out to widen the peephole between the lilac branches. The sound of bees had stopped. Katie scratched absently at the sunburned skin peeling off her freckled nose. Suddenly her brown eyes widened. She tugged at her friend's sleeve. "Look!"

Keith was already sitting up on his knees, alerted by the squeal of rusty hinges a fraction before Katie's cry. A man opened the front door and pushed a cardboard box against it. He was short and round, and his curly hair and beard were silver-white. He was wearing a red shirt.

Keith and Katie looked at each other, their eyes round as moons. "Santa Claus!" they whispered in awe at the same time.

He walked down the steps, testing each with a bounce of

his knee and then shaking his head. At the bottom of the stairs he shaded his eyes and squinted at the pickup in the driveway. His head swung toward Katie's house and then toward Keith's, his gaze settling exactly where Keith and Katie sat hidden in the lilacs. He raised a hand and waved.

They ducked their heads and flattened into the grass.

"Wow!" Keith breathed. "How did he see us?"

"He sees everything!" Katie whispered back.

"D'you think he's on vacation?"

"Maybe he's moving."

"Then who's doing all the stuff at the North Pole?"

"Mrs. Santa. The elves."

The children were so involved in their discussion they didn't notice that the bearded man was walking toward them through the tall grass. Katie only saw his brown work boots when he squatted down in front of them. Stretching her neck, she looked up into just the kind of eyes she would expect Santa to have, blue eyes that twinkled like stars. Even with his white hair and beard, he didn't look old. Mrs. Brathwaite's skin had been brown and wrinkled as a raisin, but Santa's cheeks were pink and smooth.

Katie scrambled into a sitting position. "Are you going to live in Mrs. Brathwaite's house?"

"If it's all the same to you," he said. His voice was nice.

Katie nodded, awestruck.

"Are you going to have your workshop here?" Keith asked.

He looked surprised. "That's right." Nodding toward the garage, he added, "In there, if I can make 'er seaworthy."

"Wow!" Keith said reverently.

The man scratched his beard. "The two of you my neighbors?"

16

They nodded mutely.

"Well, then! That's just fine. Is your pa home, and might he be willin' to give me a hand?"

Katie stuck a thumb in her mouth and looked at him.

"I don't have a pa, just Mama," Keith said. "My pa died in the war. I wasn't even borned yet." He put out his hand the way Mama had taught him. "My name's Keith. Mama calls me Kee."

The man looked surprised again. He took Keith's hand and shook it vigorously. "Honored, I'm sure. Doc is what they call me. Can't fix broken bones, but I can fix most anythin' else."

"Like broken toys?" Keith asked.

"Could be. Bring 'em on over."

Keith and Katie looked at each other in awe. Santa's toy repair shop, right here on Dearborn Street!

"What about you, young lady?" He addressed Katie respectfully, just as if she were grown up.

She considered him for a moment, then pulled the thumb out of her mouth. "Katie Brannigan," she said, putting her hand out in imitation of Keith. "I don't have a pa, too. Just Mama and Daddy."

As Doc shook her hand, laughing in a nice sort of way, Keith nudged her and whispered, "*Pa's* the same as *Daddy*."

Doc pretended not to hear. "Your daddy will do, Irish," he said, still looking at Katie. "Could you take me to 'im?"

Katie looked at him again for a moment without answering. "He's in A'lanta," she said finally. "Why'd you call me Irish?"

"The red hair and the name," Doc answered apologetically. "Your kinfolk come from Ireland. D'you mind it if I call you Irish?"

Katie's eyes grew wider. She shook her head vigorously.

"Well, then —"

"We could go find Daddy in A'lanta," Katie interrupted. "I'll ask Mama."

Doc laughed again. "That's mighty good of you, Irish, but Atlanta be a little far away. I'll do what I can my own self." He lifted his hand and turned away. "Be seein' you!"

"Be seein' you," they answered in one voice.

Doc tucked his thumbs in the belt loops of his work pants and peered out the window at the children playing in his front yard. Keith picked up an armful of crunchy leaves and sneaked up behind Katie. Arms stretched high in the air, he shouted and showered her with gold and crimson. Laughing, she threw out her arms and whirled around and around and around, her orange curls glinting gold in the autumn sun as it swung out behind her.

Katie must be close to Toni's age, he thought. *My Toni.* A sudden wave of almost overwhelming grief washed over him, pulling him shivering to the floor. He slumped against the wall till it subsided.

He remembered the last time he'd seen Toni as if it had been yesterday instead of two years ago. A beautiful child, a miracle that somehow he'd been part of. She'd been not even two, a baby still: sweet-smelling skin, soft hair, sleepy eyes. Then giggles, and chubby fingers wrapped around his thumbs, and the calling of a name he didn't use anymore: "Papa!"

"It ain't my divorce," he'd insisted to the judge in the custody hearing. "It's hers." He nodded toward Mina without looking at her. "Her thinkin' she don't want to keep our holy vows be one thing. But you can't let her take away my Toni."

Mina hadn't had much to say, only that a girl needed her mama. Doc could see Toni on weekends once a month. It didn't matter that Mina was so angry when she discovered she was pregnant with Toni she'd threatened an abortion. Or that in the six months after the baby's birth, she'd fallen into such a deep depression Doc had quit work to take care of them both. Nothing mattered except that Mina was Toni's mother. That was that.

Beautiful, reckless Mina, barely twenty when they'd married six years ago, half his age, a dewy child next to his middle-aged paunch and the premature silver of his hair. He hadn't had the words to describe the way she made him feel, hadn't dreamed she would even consider his plea to marry him. He didn't know why she'd agreed to be his wife. But almost from the beginning, she was like a wild animal pacing in the cage of their marriage. He'd done everything he knew to please her, and it hadn't been enough.

She'd stood across the courtroom staring out the window as he'd said goodbye to Toni that day, not knowing it was the last time. "See you soon, Half-pint. Don't be forgettin' your Papa." He didn't know Mina had already packed Toni's clothes and bought plane tickets under an assumed name to a city he hadn't been able to find.

Grabbing the window ledge, Doc pulled himself up from the floor. Lots of work to do to make this old Portland house a home. He didn't know when Toni would come back. He just knew, as God was in heaven, that she would.

The wiry boy and the little redhead were still playing in the unmowed grass outside the window. Katie tumbled to the ground and rolled in the leaves, and Keith plopped down on his knees next to her. Doc rubbed his knuckles across his bearded chin. He hadn't known when he bought the old house that children lived on either side. Could it be the great God in his mercy had given him Keith and Katie to love till Toni came home?

He opened the front door and called their names. "Kee! Irish! Would you be wantin' to earn a little Christmas money?"

The children stopped their play and looked across the yard as Doc stepped out on the porch, letting the door slam behind him. The old Brathwaite house didn't look scary *or* sad with Santa sitting on the porch railing. It looked friendly. Keith got up, brushing the leaves from his clothes, and ran to the stairs leading up to Doc's house. Katie followed, unconsciously worrying a loose tooth with her tongue. Keith hung on the banister, his wide grin exposing a gap in his mouth where a tooth had fallen out last week. Katie plopped down on the bottom step.

"I got a quarter from the tooth fairy," he said.

"I'm gonna," Katie said. "When my tooth falls out."

"Well, then! I guess you ain't wantin' the dollar I was fixin' to pay if you helped me pick up them leaves on the lawn?"

Katie jumped up. "I do, I do!"

"Me, too!" Keith chimed in. "Wow, a whole *dollar?*"

Doc scratched his chin. "That's a dollar for the two. Fifty cent a head. It's still worth *two* of them teeth you're talkin' about."

Keith and Katie looked at each other in awe. They were going to work for Santa Claus!

Doc watched the excitement on their faces and felt happier than he had for a long, long time.

One

❦

K eith Castle moved the mouse across the pad, stopped the arrow on "Print," and clicked once. As the inkjet whirred to action, he stretched his spine and walked his long legs up the wall in front of him, rolling the office chair back from his cluttered desk in the process. He sighed in relief. The September Activities Calendar, which should have been sent to the Northeast Neighbors section of the *Oregonian* yesterday, was finally finished.

His whole body felt stiff from bending over the computer all morning. He dropped his legs to the floor and rotated his ankles till he heard the bones crack. Lifting sinewy arms over his head, he joined hands behind his neck, stretching his elbows back as far as they would go. The logo across the front of his black T-shirt tightened across the well-defined muscles of his chest: *Cully Community Center* in a large white half-circle framing a red rose, and underneath, in smaller letters: *Portland Department of Parks and Recreation*.

It was Monday of the last week of summer day camp for the kindergarten-to-third-grade set. Smooth sailing by now, the end of August. His activities director, Rito, and the part-time assistants who'd been at the center all summer could run the day camp without him by this time.

"Hey!" The shout came from the outer office. "Boss-man, we got trouble out here!"

Before Rito had completed the sentence, Keith was out of his chair and through the glass door to the front lawn. Two boys were rolling in the grass on the other side of the parking lot, legs tangled and arms flailing at each other. "The little guy took the first swing," Rito panted as they raced across the park.

The smaller of the boys, slim and dark-haired, appeared to be making up for his lighter weight by throwing twice as many punches as the husky blond who tumbled on the ground with him. Keith grabbed the younger boy around the waist from behind and lifted him off the ground as Rito pulled the older one in the opposite direction.

"Yo' mama!" the husky blond taunted as he struggled in Rito's arms. Keith recognized him as a bully who'd been kicked out of the center more than once. "Yo' mama!"

"You don't know nothin'!" the boy in Keith's grasp shouted. "You shut up about my mama!" He twisted in his captor's arms and turned his fury on the man who held him, almost landing a kick to Keith's bare knee before the man pinned his legs with one strong arm.

"It's okay," Keith soothed. "I'm not going to hurt you." He gestured with a jerk of his head for Rito to take his charge out of sight around the corner of the building.

The child in his arms continued to struggle. "Let me go!"

"I will." Keith kept his voice calm and soothing. "As soon as you settle down." The boy weighed hardly anything.

Couldn't be more than five or six years old, Keith guessed.

Suddenly the child went limp in Keith's arms and started to cry. When Keith shifted him around, the boy involuntarily lifted his arms around the big man's neck and clung to him, shaking with sobs, his face buried in the black T-shirt.

Keith felt a lump rising in his throat. He felt helpless in the face of such sudden, overwhelming sorrow. More than helpless: he felt as if in some obscure way the little boy he held was expressing the last five years of Keith's own sorrow, crying streams of his own unshed tears. He turned away from the watchers who'd gathered around the drama of the fight, afraid of what they might see in his eyes, and walked across the empty baseball diamond, gently bouncing the child in his arms.

When they reached a large oak tree in the center of the park, Keith settled the boy against the trunk and sat down next to him. He fished a wrinkled tissue from the pocket of his shorts and handed it over without comment.

"My name's Keith," he said after a moment. "What's yours?"

The boy snuffled into the Kleenex. "D-Danny," he hiccupped.

"Pleased to meet you, Danny. I don't think I've seen you around here before."

"It's m...my first time. I don't like that boy."

"Why don't you tell me what happened."

"He k...kept buggin' me, sayin' things about my mama." Danny turned his blue eyes, one of them starting to swell shut, on Keith's kind green ones. "B-bad things. He don't even know my mama. She don't even live here."

"Sometimes boys like Jason say things just to see if they

can make you mad, Danny. I guess he did, didn't he?"

"He shouldn't have s…said those things."

"No, he shouldn't have. He was wrong. But it was wrong for you to hit him, too."

"I was just so *m-mad*."

"I know you were."

They sat in silence for a moment while Danny's hiccups subsided.

"You won't tell Grumpy, will you?"

"Grumpy?"

"My grandpa." Danny scrambled to his feet, a look of alarm crossing his tear-splotched face. "He's gonna worry if I'm not waiting by the door!" He seized Keith's hand. "Come on!"

Keith felt such a wave of tenderness at the boy's small hand in his, he hardly knew what he was doing as he rose from the ground and let himself be pulled across the park to the building that housed his office, several meeting rooms, and a new gymnasium.

He loved kids, had always been good with them, but Danny, in the last five minutes, seemed to have grabbed his heart in a way no other child had done. What would it be like, he wondered for the first time in his twenty-six years, to have a child of his own? To have a son of his own blood pulling him across the lawn?

"Hey, Boss-man," Rito greeted him through the sliding window of the office. "Sorry, but Jason got away. Not before I told him not to come back, though." He looked at the boy clinging to Keith's hand and then back at Keith, a question in his eyes.

Keith cleared his throat. Squatting down so that he was at

eye level with the boy, he took both his hands and said gently, "Danny, the rule here is that if you get in a fight, you can't come back to the center for a while. I understand how angry you were at Jason, but it still wasn't right to hit him. I'm sorry, but you won't be able to finish day camp. It wouldn't be fair for me to bend the rules for you. Do you understand?"

Danny nodded sadly.

"I'm sorry," Keith said again, feeling the same sense of helplessness he'd felt when Danny had buried his face in his shirt.

Rito had gone to the freezer compartment of the small employee refrigerator when he saw Danny's eye, which was already turning purple. He handed a bag of ice to Keith, who sat Danny in a folding chair near the front window and showed him how to hold it over his eye.

"Danny Boy? What's this?!"

Danny looked at his lap. "Hi, Grumpy," he said mournfully.

Keith rose from his crouched position and turned slowly. "Doc."

The bearded, white-haired man shifted his concerned gaze from the young boy to the tall man standing next to him. *"Kee?!"* His eyes lit up as he grabbed Keith's hand and pumped it. "I swan, it *is* you! Last I heard you was still playin' ball in Japan!"

"I'm back." Why did he feel so awkward? *Maybe because you've been in Portland for three months and made no effort to contact Doc,* he chided himself. *The man who's the only real father you ever had.*

He cleared his throat. "I'm the center director. Doc — it's

good to see you." Pulling his hand away from the older man's, he nodded at Danny. "Danny's your grandson? Toni's boy?"

Doc turned to look at Danny, the concern returning to his face. "That he is." He focused his attention on the child. "Tell me what's happened, lad."

"I got in a fight, Grumpy," he said sadly, looking at his grandfather out of one eye. Doc reached over and gently removed the bag of ice from the other eye. He winced when he saw it, purple and swollen almost shut.

Keith looked at Danny more closely. He recognized Toni Ferrier now in Danny's deep-blue eyes and the wavy black hair that framed his elfin face. Doc's daughter, Toni, had been Keith's first infatuation, way back in his senior year of high school   an exotic beauty, even at fifteen, with an untamed quality that had fed his adolescent dreams for months. Although he'd never seen her again after he left Portland to play basketball at North Carolina State, he knew that Toni had borne an out-of-wedlock child. Seventeen, she must have been by then. That would make Danny about the right age.

Doc stood slowly, his shoulders slumped. "I'm sorry, Kee," he said to Keith. "I try my best with the boy, but life ain't been easy for 'im. Danny's a good lad, though."

Keith's awkwardness fell away. He reached down and tousled Danny's hair. "I know he is, Doc. His mother's doing a fine job with him."

"Mama don't live with us," Danny volunteered.

Keith shifted uncomfortably at Doc's direct gaze. "The lad lives with me, Kee." He replaced the ice on Danny's eye and moved the little boy's hand to hold it in place. "Things been happenin' since last you lived next door."

They looked at each other without speaking for a moment. Then Keith closed the space between them and put his arms around the older man. "I'm sorry I've been so out of touch, Doc. Things have been crazy for me, too." He patted Doc on the shoulders and stepped back. "Have you had lunch? I can't take much time, but there's a McDonald's around the corner."

"Oh, can we, Grumpy? Please," Danny begged, forgetting his despondency and hopping off the chair.

Keith smiled at the name the boy called his grandfather. "Grumpy" couldn't have been more off the mark for the man he and Katie used to think was Santa Claus.

Katie. The other special person from his past he hadn't looked up since his return to Portland. What was keeping him away?

He couldn't help but see the pleasure lighting Doc's eyes at the invitation to lunch. The look made him feel even more guilty that he hadn't contacted his old friend sooner.

"Will you talk out this fightin' business with your grandpa when we get home?" Doc was asking Danny. "So's we know what to do about it from here on out?"

The boy nodded solemnly. "Me and Kee already talked it out some," he said, picking up on the name Doc had been using.

Doc nodded with approval at Keith. "It's fittin' you and Kee should talk. He an' I've done a fair share o' talkin' our own selves. Did you know Kee lived next door to me when he was no bigger'n you?"

Danny's eyes grew round. "He did?"

"He did."

"Yep," Keith agreed, smiling crookedly at the boy.

Danny grinned back and tugged at his hand. "Let's go!"

"Hang on a minute, Danny." He stuck his head through the open window. "Hey Rito, could you grab the calendar off the printer? I'll take it downtown after lunch."

"Sure thing." Rito slipped the sheets of paper into a manila envelope and passed it through the window.

"Thanks. See you in an hour?"

"Take your time, Boss-man. We're okay here."

Keith and Doc sat at a table outside in the playground area with their hamburgers and fries. Danny had taken two bites of his burger and run off to play.

Keith kept his eyes on the boy as the two men talked. Danny's spirits had certainly improved. "What's happened to Toni, Doc?" he asked quietly.

Doc stirred the ice around in his cola with the straw. "She turned out a wild one like her mama, Kee. It was the drugs and alcohol finally took her down." He paused, then continued sadly. "There was somethin' missin' in my Toni when her mama sent her back. I was too blind to see it. All those years not knowin' if she was dead or alive, I was just happy to have her home."

"Grumpy! Kee!" Danny shouted from the top of the jungle gym. "Look at me!" He let go and swished down the slide, plowing into the sand at the bottom. He jumped up and waved as he headed back to the ladder.

"He's a good lad, he is," Doc said with affection. "He sure has taken a shine to you, Kee. He's pretty quiet, usual. Gets awful moody sometime." He sighed. "Don't always know if

29

I'm doin' right by him. But I'm pleased as punch I'm gettin' to give him all the lovin' care I never got to give his mama."

Toni had been fifteen, a sophomore in high school, when her mother had finally contacted Doc after more than a dozen years of silence. "It's your turn," she'd told him on the phone as if she'd had nothing to do with his absence from his daughter's life. "*You* do something with her!" Within a month Toni was living with the father she hadn't seen since she was two, and her mother had disappeared once again.

Doc's eyes were filmy with unshed tears. "I should've been there while Toni was growin' up."

"Doc," Keith said mildly, "you can't blame yourself for something you had no control over. Her mother kidnapped her! What could you have done?"

"I know it don't do no good wishin' things was different, Kee. But I still wish they was." He took a deep breath and looked Keith in the eye. "Things was real bad between us when I took the lad away from 'er."

"Took him away?"

"Toni wasn't takin' care of 'im. He was just a tiny bit of a thing, not growin', an' mewlin' all the time." Doc turned his eyes back to Danny. "I took the day shift at the college and tried to help out with babysittin' in the evenin's, so's Toni could get the good shifts waitin' tables. But when I found out she left 'im alone a couple times, just a little baby in a crib, I called in the Children's Services." A tear escaped and traveled slowly down Doc's apple cheek. "Broke my heart to turn 'er in. But she was talkin' about takin' 'im to L.A. Who would care about 'im there? I couldn't lose my grandson, the way I lost my Toni."

Keith was silent for a moment. "What about Danny's

father?" he finally asked. "Didn't he have anything to say in the custody hearing?"

"Don't know who he was. Toni never said. Hate to say it, but I have a feelin' she don't know neither. Pretty heavy into partyin' when she got pregnant with Danny, she was."

Danny ran over to their table and grabbed another bite from his burger before taking off again, this time to jump in a plastic bubble and bury himself in a field of red and blue balls. He looked over to make sure the two grownups were watching.

Even as he smiled and waved at Danny, Keith felt his heart growing heavy with grief, hurting for all the pain Doc had endured over the years and for the emptiness of Toni's life and the chaos of young Danny's. He realized his grief was as much anger as sorrow. *God, how could you let this happen to a good man like Doc?* he asked in silent indignation. *To a man who only wanted to do right? It isn't fair!*

He upended the paper cup and tapped the last pieces of ice into his mouth, needing time to settle the disquiet Doc's words had stirred in him. "So what happened to Toni, Doc? Do you see her?"

Doc brightened. "She's doin' real good now, Kee. She's in one of them drug rehab programs. She done it once before, after I got Danny; the courts made her. But it didn't take that time. This time she's in there volunteer. She writes to Danny ever' week. With the help of A'mighty God, I think it'll take this time." He watched his grandson swim through the plastic balls toward the opening in the plastic bubble. "I hope an' pray. I hope an' pray."

Keith didn't respond. He didn't have much confidence in Almighty God these days. Hope and prayer seemed the dreams of fools anymore.

Once again Danny ran to their table, this time settling on Doc's lap to finish the last of his hamburger. He grinned at Keith.

"I have a dog," he announced. "His name is Ruggles."

"I know Ruggles!" Keith said with surprise. "That's the dog your grandpa got when I was in junior high. A long-haired dachshund. He was just a puppy."

Danny shook his head. "Ruggles is a old, old dog," he said.

"Well, he ain't what he used to be." Doc winked at Keith. "But which of us is?"

Keith laughed. "Nothing ever stays the same, does it?"

"I don't know as I'd say *nothin*', but pretty close," Doc said.

They sat in companionable silence for a minute or two.

"How long you been in town, Kee?" Doc asked as he dragged a last french fry through the catsup on his tray. "Can't believe Irish hasn't told me you come home." He put an arm around Danny's waist and pulled the boy against his chest. "Been a godsend with the lad, Irish has. A good friend, ain't she, Danny Boy?"

Danny nodded.

"Us menfolk needs a woman's touch ever' once in a while," Doc added. "There's a big heart in that little gal. Turned into a right pretty thing, too, hasn't she?"

Keith squirmed in his seat like a child caught stealing cookies. "I haven't seen her. Katie doesn't know I'm back."

Doc looked at him in surprise. "I don't mean to be harsh, Kee, but I got to say it. It hurt me an' Irish somethin' fierce when you left the way you did, not tellin' us you was goin' and waitin' half a year's time before you let anyone know where you was."

He rested his bearded chin on top of Danny's head, then added, "I know your mama dyin' weren't an easy thing, Kee, but me an' Irish was your *family*." His eyes were bright with unshed tears. "I'm used to gettin' left, but Irish — well, the heart just went out of that little gal for a spell after you was gone. It weren't a carin' thing to do, Kee. You call her now, won't you?"

"Yes. I'll call her, Doc. I promise."

Two

H i, Em! Cute haircut. Beau still at the garage? Mm-*mmm*, smells good in here!" Katie dropped her briefcase on a chair and reached an arm around her friend's shoulder, pulling her close for a swift, sideways hug. Emily's rounded belly was starting to get in the way of any other kind.

"Hi, yourself! Thanks, yes, and thanks, in that order." Emily pulled her fingers through the short blond wisps of her hair. "You don't think it's too short?"

Katie shook her head. "Makes your baby blues look bigger than life." She lifted her own long hair off her slender neck and pulled it away from her face. Thick and curly, it had darkened with age from an exuberant carrot orange to a luxuriant burnished cinnamon. "What d'you think? Should I go short, too?"

"Right," Emily said, rolling her eyes. "Why don't we just lop it off right now? I'll go get the scissors."

"Okay, okay, I get the message!" Laughing, Katie let the auburn waves fall around her face and followed Emily into the kitchen. "I'll hold off till after dessert, okay?"

The timer on the stovetop buzzed, and Emily reached for a potholder on the white tiled counter. Katie grabbed it from under her fingers. "Here, let me do that. You shouldn't be working like this, in your condition." She opened the oven door, releasing a delicious aroma of chile peppers and cheese as she pulled out the rack.

Emily rolled her eyes again. "You are so bossy! Sometimes I think you think this baby wouldn't have been conceived without you!"

"I *am* the one who introduced you and Beau," Katie answered huffily. She lifted the hot dish to a cooling rack on the counter, inhaling the savory smell. "Wow!" Her pretended injury was forgotten. "Once again you've outdone yourself, Em!"

"It *does* smell good, doesn't it? New recipe from Gram — chicken enchiladas with yogurt sauce. Hope it tastes as good as it smells." Emily glanced at the clock on the microwave. "And I hope Beau gets here before it congeals!"

"As if he's the one who's ever late," Katie teased. Emily was notoriously casual about being on time for anything.

"Very funny." She made a face at Katie and sat down at the kitchen table. "So what's up, girlfriend? You're higher than Mount Hood!"

Sliding into a chair across from her friend, Katie placed her elbows on the table and leaned forward, her brown eyes shining. "I talked to Doc today. You'll never guess who's back in town."

"Keith Castle."

Katie's jaw dropped. "How did you know?"

Emily avoided Katie's eyes. "He came to see Dad when he first got back to Portland. Three or four months ago."

"Three — you mean he was here all *summer*? You knew and didn't tell me?"

"I'm sorry, Katie, really I am. You don't know how many times I've wanted to. But Dad said Keith wanted to be here anonymously for a little while so he could settle in." To Emily's relief, a shrill whistle interrupted their dialogue. She got up to turn off the burner and pour hot water from the teakettle into a ceramic pot. "Earl Grey okay?"

Katie nodded absently, her face troubled. "But Chappie told *you*?"

"Oh, no! Daddy would never breach confidentiality like that. I saw Keith getting into his car at the church parking lot as I drove in. Pretty hard to be anonymous when you're six foot five and look the way he looks." She paused, a glint in her blue eyes.

"Still gorgeous?"

"Made me feel fifteen again! Remember that summer?"

How could Katie ever forget that summer — the last golden summer of her childhood? Even ten years later, the memories were imprinted on her mind. It wasn't just Keith; it was the three of them, she and Keith and Emily, best buddies, together every possible moment. It was Keith's brand-new driver's license and the little red Datsun Doc was helping him buy. It was Cannon Beach and Mount Hood and the Columbia Gorge. It was Tomahawk Community Church, where Emily's father was college minister, and understanding for the first time that God wasn't just "out there," but available to her every day. It was sharing her new faith with Keith and Emily, who'd already made their own commitments. It was sharing dreams and schemes and fantasies.

All but one.

She and Keith had been friends forever, but it took Emily to point out that Keith had excellent boyfriend potential, and though he wasn't right for *he*...

Once the idea was planted in her mind, Katie couldn't let it go. But she couldn't act, either. Afraid of destroying the balance of their wonderful three-way friendship, she insisted to Emily that she and Keith would always be buddies, allies, compatriots — no more. But in secret, she dreamed about him, pined for him in sentimental poetry, wrote love songs she never sang except to herself. Emily hadn't found out for months. Not till after Toni Ferrier entered the picture.

Katie pulled herself from her reverie with difficulty. "So did you talk to him?"

Emily shook her head. "He was preoccupied, didn't notice me." She picked up the teapot and brought it to the table. "But of course I had to ask Dad to be sure it *was* Keith, and then he made me promise not to tell. Forgive me?"

Katie sighed. "At least I know I can trust you with *my* deepest, darkest secrets." She looked bleakly across the table at her friend. *Like the fact that I still get excited about Keith Castle after all these years,* her look said. *After everything that's happened and everything that hasn't...*

Why did she feel so hurt? It wasn't as if she'd expected him to look her up the minute he got back to Portland. Sure, they'd been great childhood friends, best buddies till their midteens. But that had been ten years ago. A decade! So much had come between them in the years after that last perfect summer, the summer she regarded as the end of her childhood: Toni, first of all, and then North Carolina State. Even though a semblance of their old friendship had been restored after Toni, during summers when Keith came back home from school, things hadn't been the same.

And then Keith's mother had fallen ill, five years ago now. Every moment he hadn't been with Christine he'd been with Katie, letting her hold him as he cried. Her heart had ached for him as her arms absorbed his sorrow. Comfort had felt like love; for a few brief days she'd dared to dream again.

His mother died within the week. Katie didn't see him alone again, and after the funeral, without even bothering to say goodbye, Keith had disappeared. Inexplicably, inconceivably, she hadn't heard a word from him since.

The sound of a teaspoon clanging against china brought her back to the kitchen with a start. Emily handed her a steaming mug. She lifted it to her lips, sipping the hot beverage carefully. The sweet, floral aroma of honey dissolving in the freshly brewed tea almost made her dizzy.

"I can't believe he hasn't been in touch with you, Katie. I'm sure he'll call." Emily's tone implied she wasn't as sure as her words indicated. "What d'you think is going on with him?"

"I can't imagine." Katie kept her tone neutral. She lifted her mug again, this time drinking a full swallow of the hot liquid, welcoming the burning sensation as if it might melt the lump in her throat.

She'd understood Keith's need to get away after his mother's funeral, to do his grieving in private. Christine Castle's death had been hard on him, leaving him truly alone. His father had died in Vietnam before he was even born; his mother had never remarried; and if he had grandparents, he didn't know about them.

On the other hand, Katie thought, he had Doc, who had been like a father to him all his growing-up years. *And he had me. Katie-Bug, Lady-Bug, Green Alligatey-Bug....*

Doc had finally heard from him, six months after he'd disappeared. He was playing pro basketball in Italy. He and Chappie heard from him on an irregular basis after that. Doc's last letter had been postmarked Japan. "Say hello to Katie for me," he sometimes wrote. But never a letter with her name on the front, never even a postcard.

"Katie?"

"Wh...? Oh, sorry, my mind was wandering. What was that?"

"I just wondered how things are going between you and Henry now that school is starting up again."

Henry. The truth was, thinking about Henry Gillette made her feel a little guilty, as if she should have known that the two years they'd dated had been more serious for him than they'd been for her. She hoped the fact that she'd turned down his marriage proposal last spring wouldn't affect their working relationship at the small college where they both taught. She couldn't anticipate a time when he wouldn't be a valued friend and colleague.

"I haven't seen much of him yet, but I don't think we'll have a problem. He's a great guy."

"So why'd you say no?"

Katie rolled the wooden dipper in the honey jar and dropped another dollop in her tea. "I never told you about the poem I found when I moved last spring — stuck in that old copy of *Christy* you gave me one summer for my birthday?"

"I don't think so."

"I must have written it when I was sixteen. The year of Toni." Her mouth quirked in a wry smile. "I was inspired by misery that year."

39

She knew the words, quoted them for Emily:

Sometimes —
> *like tonight —*
I can't pretend that I don't hurt for you.

Tears lie so close
> *that the mention of your name*
> *calls them from me*
> *like a trumpet calling bodies*
> *from the grave.*

Touch, trust, tenderness —
> *I need them all —*
But how can I take them from someone I like —
> *when it's you I love?*

Emily's blue eyes were wide. "So Keith was the reason!"

"Knowing I wasn't in love with Henry was the reason," Katie corrected. "I can't say I'm in love with Keith. I can't say I even know him anymore. Maybe it was just the *idea* of Keith I was ever in love with, anyway. It was a long time ago."

Narrowing her eyes skeptically, Emily shook her head. "Keith has never been just an idea to you, Katie."

Katie finished the last of her tea. Setting the mug on the table in front of her, she ran her finger around the edge, staring into the bottom as though the residue of leaves held the answers to her life. "Henry's such a good man, Em. D'you think I made a mistake?"

"Personally? I don't think you should marry anyone unless you're *crazy* in love!"

The screen door to the kitchen banged open. "Crazy in

love?" a deep voice growled. "That's me, babe!"

Katie watched her friend's face soften with happiness at the sight of the burly, curly-haired man entering the room. *One of my better achievements*, she thought smugly. She'd known from the day he'd rescued her by the side of the road in his fancy tow truck that Beau was perfect for her friend. Engineering their first meeting had been a trick, though. "A *mechanic?*" Emily had said. "A *teacher?*" Beau had countered. "Forget that surface stuff!" she'd finally sputtered to each of them in turn. "It's your *hearts* I'm thinking of!" Once they'd met, there hadn't been a question.

Beau swept Emily up from her chair and bent her over his arm, kissing her with theatric enthusiasm. Emily dropped her head back, laughing. "Beau Bradley! In my fragile condition?"

Beau pulled her upright, a crease of concern between his brows. "Forgive me, m'lady! I get so carried away." With his arms still around her, he rained gentle kisses on her forehead. "Crazy in love" was certainly the right description.

Emily was still laughing. "Beau, stop it! We've got company."

"Company? You mean Katie?" He winked at Katie over Emily's shoulder. "Katie's not company, she's family." He kept one arm around Emily and pulled Katie into his embrace with the other.

"And how's my favorite redhead? Breaking hearts again, Katie?"

"Just the one, Beau. And I'm wondering if I shouldn't have given him more of a chance."

"Two years wasn't enough?" He shook her by the shoulder. "Get a grip, Red! You're just feeling lonely. Say, I've got this new guy working for me at the garage…"

Katie snorted and extricated herself from Beau's hug. He was determined to return the favor of his introduction to Emily, but to say he didn't have the knack was an understatement. "Does he wear gold chains and keep his shirt unbuttoned to his navel?"

Beau's laughter boomed in the small room. "So I made a mistake with Dano! Who knew he was a carryover from the seventies? I only see him in overalls. But Billy — I'm willing to bet Billy's more up your alley."

"That's very sweet of you, Beau, but… Let's just say matchmaking isn't your gift and leave it at that, okay?"

"Don't say I never tried to help you," he grumbled.

"How could I? You keep my car in running order, you put up bookshelves, you empty mousetraps —"

Emily cleared her throat loudly. "Okay, you guys. You're worse than my kindergartners to keep on task!" She pointed to both of them. "*Your* mission, should you decide to accept it —"

Beau grinned and picked up the dish from the counter. "Is to make a large-ish dent in this casserole," he finished for Emily. "Let's do it!"

"What do you hear from your folks, Katie?" Emily asked after Beau had said a brief blessing over the meal.

"They're doing okay. The dry heat in Phoenix is helping Mom's arthritis, and her allergies are better, too. But I hate to think of her all alone in a new city when Dad's on one of his trips. I keep thinking I should move down there, work on my doctorate at Arizona State or something so I can be closer."

Katie's parents had made a long-considered move to Arizona several months before for Leigh Brannigan's health. On top of the chronic "female problems" she'd had as long as

Katie could remember, Mrs. Brannigan had severe asthma and a crippling arthritic condition. Nonetheless, the decision to leave Portland hadn't been easy for them to make, or for Katie to accept.

Her father, a manufacturer's rep nearing retirement, still left home on business for days at a time. For many years he'd counted on Katie to watch out for her mother while he was gone. Thomas Brannigan's words to his daughter before every business trip during her childhood were a litany she still remembered: "You're my big girl, Katie. Take care of Mama while Daddy's gone, okay?" Even after he'd stopped saying it out loud, the words echoed in her mind every time he left.

Leigh's severe allergic reactions to an increasing number of environmental substances in Portland's damp climate, along with the crippling pain in her joints, had finally made the decision for them. Katie helped them get the house ready to sell and then, after school was out in June, drove the family car with her father to Phoenix, where her mother flew in the next day. Katie had stayed for a month helping them get settled, but responsibilities at the college kept her from staying longer.

"I'd really be sad if you moved away, girlfriend," Emily said. She had her own opinion about Katie's need to take care of her mother, but she'd never brought the subject up with her friend. Some things seemed better left unsaid.

Beau reached for Katie's plate and then Emily's, serving each a healthy portion of steaming enchiladas. "You going down to visit them for Thanksgiving and Christmas?" he asked Katie.

"Christmas. Not enough time at Thanksgiving." Katie cut

into the casserole and took a bite. "Wow, this is fabulous, Em!"

"Yeah?" Emily patted her belly. "Hope it's not too spicy for Skippy!"

"Skippy?!"

Emily grinned. "Don't worry, it's just temporary. Till we decide on a real name." A sudden thought struck her. "You're going to be here when the baby's born, aren't you?"

"First week of January? No problem. Unless he's early. Shouldn't be, if he takes after you."

"Katie!"

"Sorry." Her impish grin remained unrepentant.

"Careful, or she'll make you sing for your supper," Beau warned.

"Hey, that reminds me — Em, did your dad tell you I'm singing at the Lighthouse again this year? One Friday night a month. You guys will have to come hear me."

"Oh, good!" Emily batted her eyelashes at Beau. "An excuse for my husband to take me out!"

"As if I needed an excuse," Beau said to Katie.

The Lighthouse was a coffee shop near the campus of Columbia River College, where Katie taught music part-time. Emily's father, a college youth minister, had been instrumental in starting a coffeehouse ministry there on the weekends. The Lighthouse was a popular student gathering place on Friday and Saturday nights. With his natural curiosity and authentic respect for others, Mark Lewis created an environment in which questions about faith and spirituality inevitably arose. Students who wouldn't show their faces inside a church for a Sunday service considered him their unofficial chaplain and came to the coffeehouse regularly for espresso, scones, live music, and mostly for "Chappie's" thoughtful responses to their important questions.

"You know you're welcome at my folks' for Thanksgiving," Emily told Katie. "Beau and I will be there, along with the rest of the crew. Aaron's even bringing Gram from San Diego." Emily had six younger brothers and sisters, the four youngest still living at home.

"Thanks, Em. I thought I'd have Doc and Danny over for Thanksgiving dinner. Knowing Doc, they'll go out to a restaurant otherwise."

Emily made a face. "You're right. That would never do. How *is* Doc?"

"He's doing great, considering. Still head of maintenance at the college. I think he'd like to retire, but his pension's not enough for him and Danny both. He can put Danny in the college day-care center after school as long as he's working, too. Danny starts first grade this year, so that will be a help."

"I see the two of them in church every Sunday," Beau said. "Can't believe how quiet that boy sits. It's not natural!"

"He *is* awfully quiet. He seems to have a hard time making friends, which is too bad, 'cause he's a real sweetheart." Katie helped herself to a second serving of buttered corn. "Doc is great with him, but you have to wonder how those first two years affected him. Not to mention the nine months before he was born. From what Doc says, his mother was pretty strung out most of the time."

"Poor Doc," Emily said. "He hasn't had an easy life."

"No, he hasn't, but you wouldn't know it being around him. Doc must be the original Good Humor Man. It was great growing up next to him — like having a grandpa right next door."

"Or a dad," Emily added.

Katie knew she was thinking of Keith. She sent her friend a look that said, *Please, not now.*

"Doc and Danny and I are taking a day hike in the Gorge on Labor Day," she said. "Our 'last hurrah' before school starts. You guys want to come?"

"Thanks, but we have plans," Beau said before Emily could respond. He leaned over and put an arm around his wife. "Breakfast in bed for my lovely lady, and then —" He paused and grimaced in pretended horror. *"Shopping.* We've got to get going on the nursery."

"Really, Beau?" Emily grabbed the hand that lay on her shoulder and squeezed it. "You'll fix breakfast *and* go *shopping* with me?"

"A fate worse than death, I know," he sighed. "But a man's got to do what a man's got to do." He kissed her nose.

Katie felt a sudden touch of envy at Beau and Emily's easy affection. A love match if ever there was one. Best friends, lovers, soon-to-be-parents....

Would it ever happen for her?

Three

❧

Katie pulled her yellow Honda Civic into a faculty slot in the gym parking lot and turned off the engine. Leaning over, she fumbled through the stack of music and papers on the passenger seat beside her. She wished she'd taken time to organize herself the night before, but she'd ended up staying at Beau and Emily's later than she'd planned, watching a video and eating buttered popcorn. "We rented *Amadeus* just for you," Emily appealed when she tried to leave earlier in the evening. The music and drama of Mozart's madly passionate life were too hard to resist, even though she'd seen it several times before.

She leafed through the stack of papers again, looking for one thin packet stapled in the corner, the next-to-final draft of her course outline for the new class she was teaching this term. Dr. Abercrombie, head of the music department, had asked to see it, and she wanted Henry to look it over before she printed up the final copy.

Pulling a sheaf of papers from between a textbook and a folder of sheet music, she checked the title and breathed a sigh of relief: *Music Education in the Elementary Classroom.* She hadn't lost it.

A line of people snaked around the corner of the old brick gymnasium, where registration for fall term had been set up. Katie made her way through the crowd of animated students to the main door. Her disguise must be working, she thought wryly. They were letting her through.

She'd been mistaken for a student at registration last year, so this time she'd come prepared: a little more makeup than she normally wore, in brighter shades; her red hair pinned up in a loose topknot; a black, red, and tan print scarf draped at the neck of her tailored beige suit, gold necklace and earrings, low beige pumps. She looked positively grown up.

It was the last day for new students to register, and Katie had been assigned to cover the music department table with Henry for the afternoon, answering questions about class requirements and advising students as they made scheduling decisions.

The opportunity to teach at Columbia River College for the last year and a half had been something of a fluke. She'd given private lessons to music majors at the college for several years, while she pursued her master's at nearby Portland State University. When a full-time music instructor at the college suffered a family emergency and requested a reduced class load, Katie was offered her general music class, Music for Nonmajors, as a part-time instructor.

Dr. Abercrombie had approached her last spring about teaching an ed class as well. "Without a doctorate?" she'd asked in surprise.

"It's unusual," he acknowledged. "We're in a bit of a spot,

though. Too many students for the teachers we have and not enough to hire a new full-time faculty member. I have every confidence, from the work I've seen you do, that you can handle the class. What do you say?"

"If you really think I can do it… I say yes, yes, yes!"

She'd worked hard all summer preparing for the course. Ordinarily, she'd have gone to Henry for help developing her ideas, but she felt awkward about asking after she'd turned down his marriage proposal. Still, she'd feel more confident about presenting her course outline to Dr. Abercrombie if Henry looked it over first.

"Kate! Over here!" Dr. Gillette waved to her from across the room. He was very handsome in a college professor sort of way: tall and thin, light brown hair and beard, tortoise-shell glasses, a tweed sports jacket worn over a T-shirt and jeans. He'd been on the faculty at Columbia River College for a decade and had in fact been Katie's voice instructor during her undergraduate years. Myra Heimbach, the instructor whose misfortunes had allowed Katie to teach at the college, sat next to him, her round cheeks rosy in the warm gym.

"Hi, Myra, Henry. How's it going?"

"Not as busy today," Myra said, dropping a stack of papers into her briefcase and snapping it shut. "You know freshmen — too dazed to know what's going on, so they don't have many questions. Thank goodness. I got some work done." She squeezed her ample hips between the tables. "Have fun, guys!"

Henry smiled a welcome as Katie scooted behind the table and sat down in the metal folding chair he pulled out for her. "Glad you're a little early. I have a proposal."

She looked at him sharply.

Henry's mouth quirked in a grin. "Bad choice of words," he said, taking her hands between his and holding them for a moment. "Don't worry, my dear, I recognize a solid 'no' when I hear it." A touch of sardonic humor glinted in his eyes.

Katie had worried that she'd broken Henry's heart by turning down his marriage proposal, but lately she wondered if he'd only asked her to marry him because the years were marching on, it was time to get married, and she was the obvious choice. Clearly her rejection hadn't changed the current of affection that ran between them. She was glad for that; he was a valued friend and colleague.

"Henry," she said, laughing, "I hope you know how *dear* you are to me."

He searched her face for a moment. "I do," he said softly. Then shuffling the papers in front of him without looking, he added, "I do need to talk to you about something."

"Likewise," Katie said, tapping the papers on the table in front of her. "I'd love some feedback on my course outline for the music ed class."

"Excuse me…" A young woman's timid voice interrupted. They hadn't noticed her approach.

"Have a seat. What can I do for you?" Katie asked, smiling. Henry sat back as she answered the girl's questions.

When the student rose from her chair, Katie caught the eye of a young man headed uncertainly in their direction and gave him a nod of encouragement. Her freshman year wasn't so long ago that she couldn't remember how overwhelmed she'd felt. "You been here all morning?" she asked Henry.

"Since eight."

"Why don't you go get some lunch? I can handle things for a while."

"Thanks, I'll get a sandwich and bring it back. We can talk then. Get you anything?"

"Please, something cold to drink. It's warm in here." She started to dig in her purse.

"Never mind. I'll take care of it. Want me to look over your outline on the way?"

"Yeah, thanks." She pushed it across the table. "I'd love to hear what you think. But be gentle, okay?"

Henry laughed at her pleading expression. "Relax. Knowing you, it's primo." He picked up the packet as he slid out from behind the table.

Katie smiled at the young man who'd finally made his way across the room. "Hi! How can I help you?"

Keith, inching his way along the registration line for transfer students, had been watching the woman since she'd come through the gym door. He couldn't see her face clearly from this distance, but the brisk energy of her stride had attracted him immediately. Physically she was a small woman, shorter and slighter than many of the students who waited in line with him, but her poise and self-assurance commanded attention. "Presence" was the word that came to mind. She exuded grace and good humor.

He glanced at the sign over the table she was approaching: Music and Music Education. Her hair, pulled loosely up and away from her face, shone like a red cloud under the incandescent globe above her. She greeted the bearded man and portly woman behind the table, and shortly afterward exchanged places with the woman.

Her conversation with the man was spirited. He took her hands between his at one point and held them momentarily as they talked. She threw back her head and laughed. Keith felt a surprising flash of envy for their easy camaraderie, the intimacy of their discourse. They obviously knew each other well and enjoyed each other's company. How long had it been since he'd delighted in someone that way? Enjoyed a friendship so thoroughly?

Since Katie.

He jerked his head around to see who had spoken, but the boy in front of him had his head buried in a book and the two girls behind him were engrossed in their own conversation.

Kate Brannigan.

It took another moment to realize the words were coming from his own mind. He leaned against the wall and closed his eyes. It was true. He'd never had another friend like Katie. What must she think of him, running away after his mother's funeral the way he had, cutting off all contact with everyone who'd ever been important in his life?

Doc's words had cut him to the quick: "It hurt me an' Irish somethin' fierce when you left the way you did, not tellin' us you was goin'....Me and Irish was your *family,* Kee."

He felt a tap on his arm and opened his eyes with a start. "The line's moving," the girl behind him said apologetically. "You okay?"

"Yeah, thanks." He ran his fingers through his dark hair distractedly as he moved forward in the line.

He hadn't meant to hurt anyone; he'd only meant to escape his own pain — the pain not only of his mother's death, but of the truth he'd learned the night she died.

52

Whoever could have known that one long-held secret finally brought to light could so alter one's life? His innocence, his unfailing belief that life was good and God was a God of love — destroyed in an instant. He would never see the world in quite the same way again.

Running away had been pure instinct, not even consciously decided. Returning to his dorm room at North Carolina State in the middle of the final semester of his senior year, he'd stayed only long enough to pack his clothes and few belongings. Then he called the number on the business card he'd been carrying around in his wallet for a year. "Forget college ball. You could be makin' good money in Europe right now!" the agent had told him.

Within a month he was playing basketball in Italy.

Coming home had been instinctive, too. Four years of trying to forget had done nothing to heal his wounds. So here he was, back in Portland, knowing he had a slate of unfinished business but with no idea how to complete it. His college education was the least of it. But it was a start.

He glanced once more across the room. The woman was alone at the table now, her head bent over the paperwork that lay between her and the student across from her. The young man rose, and the woman lifted her head and smiled.

His heartbeat quickened. *It's Katie.*

It was no wonder he hadn't recognized her. The last time he'd seen her, she'd been a kid in a ponytail. She'd grown up in the last five years; this Katie was definitely not a teenager.

The girl behind him touched his arm again, irritated this time. "Come on, it's your turn!"

He looked at her as if through a fog. "Sorry," he mumbled, and took a seat at the table in front of him.

"Kate, this is a wonderful concept! Have you shown this to Abercrombie?" Henry dropped the outline on the table along with a large, plastic-wrapped sandwich and two bottles of water.

"Not yet — I wanted your feedback first."

"It's great!" He slid behind the table and sat next to her. "Music ed classes for elementary teachers usually make me cringe. All that stick-banging and tambourine shaking. Without any *context*. That's what you're providing here — cultural context."

Katie felt the tension in her shoulders relax at his enthusiastic response. Her idea was radical, having her students develop an elementary curriculum with a history of the arts as its backbone, instead of simply inserting the arts into the curriculum if there happened to be time — and money. Recent tax cuts had drastically reduced funding for the arts in public schools.

"It's going to be a lot of work for my students," she said.

"It's going to be an incredibly valuable learning experience for your students," Henry corrected. "I'm excited about the idea, Kate. I think this might be something we could present to Portland Public, maybe for one of the magnet schools to try out. Keep me posted as you get into the term, will you?"

Katie nodded. "I appreciate your support, Henry. Hope Dr. Abercrombie agrees with you."

"Speaking of Abercrombie, there's that little thing *I* wanted to talk to *you* about."

"Oh, right. What's up?"

"The annual Christmas concert."

Katie groaned. "You're thinking about *Christmas?* I'm not even ready for school to start next week!"

"Seems crazy, I know, but it's really not that far away. The new PR man wants to do it up big: 'A Four Corners Christmas,' they're already calling it."

"As in four corners of the world?"

"Right. Christmas music from around the world. And not just a concert, but a sit-down dessert, with traditional Christmas treats from various places, servers in national costumes, that sort of thing."

"Sounds like quite a production."

"Abercrombie's pumped about it. We have a lot of foreign students, and he thinks it's a great way to celebrate the cultural diversity on campus. He asked me to emcee." Henry took a bite of his sandwich, licked his lips, and added, "I told him as long as they served *buñuelos,* I was in."

Katie laughed. "I'll have to see if Mom can find a good recipe in Phoenix and send it so I can make some for you."

"Mmm, tempting. But I've got another idea. I wondered if you'd consider cohosting with me?"

"Henry, what fun! I'd love to!"

"Now why couldn't you have said that when I asked you to marry me?"

Katie looked at him sharply for the second time that afternoon, but saw only mischief in his eyes.

"Henry, I'm going to find you a good woman," she declared. She placed a hand over her eyes and leaned forward, scanning the gymnasium. "Maybe not today, but —"

She stopped abruptly and half-rose from her chair, grabbing the edge of the table with both hands.

"Kate?" Henry's voice questioned.

Sinking back into her chair, she watched the man striding resolutely toward her across the gym. She'd forgotten just how tall six feet five inches was. He looked more muscular than she remembered, strong, toned, fit. His khaki shorts and peach-colored knit shirt emphasized his bronze, sun-darkened skin.

A young woman dropped into the chair in front of her, blocking him from view. "I don't understand this music requirement," she said, pushing the college catalog across the table. "Which classes can I use?"

With effort, Katie pulled her thoughts together and concentrated on answering the student's questions, bending her head over the catalog as much to hide as to point out choices.

"May I help you?" she heard Henry ask.

"Thank you, I'll wait," a deep baritone responded politely.

"She's not in a marrying frame of mind, if you were thinking of asking."

"I was! How did you know?"

Katie sputtered and quickly covered the sound with a cough as the girl across the table looked at her curiously. "Pardon me," she murmured.

"You look like a man with a purpose," Henry said. Was she imagining things, or was there an edge to his voice?

Closing the catalog, she handed it back to the student with a weak smile. "Welcome to Columbia River College. I know you'll enjoy it here."

"Do you suppose she could be convinced to go to dinner?" the baritone voice questioned.

"I wouldn't count on it."

Katie felt a sudden rush of anger. "*Excuse* me!" She jumped up from her chair, her lips compressed and her eyes narrowed as she stared from one man to the other. "D'you think you could stop acting as if I'm not here? Henry, I can make my own decisions, thank you!"

Henry put his hands up in feigned dismay. "Down, girl!"

The look she sent him could have withered a blossom dead on the vine.

"And as for *you* —" She turned her gaze up at the big man across the table and felt her anger melting away. His eyebrows were raised at the inside corners, his eyes twinkled with fun, and a smile quirked at the corners of his mouth.

Hardening her heart, she leaned over the table, resting her weight on her extended arms. "If you think you can trounce in here after five years without so much as a *word* in all that time, and expect me to go out to dinner with you, you've got another think coming!"

Keith's playful expression disappeared. "Katie, please — I know I've been a rotten friend —"

"But sure, I'll marry you," she continued briskly. "I'm free tomorrow morning."

It was very satisfying, having them both stand there with their mouths open, Katie thought smugly. She cocked her head. "Well?"

"Uh — actually I'm busy tomorrow morning, but —"

She sent him a withering glance. "I'm kidding, Castle."

Henry cleared his throat loudly.

"Oh! Sorry, Henry. Keith Castle, Henry Gillette. Keith was one of my early influences," she added flippantly. "Taught me my ABCs."

Henry thrust his hand toward Keith. "*Dr.* Gillette," he said pointedly. "One of Kate's *later* influences. You might say I taught her her do-re-mis."

The two men eyed each other without speaking as Katie rolled her eyes.

Four

They hadn't been able to make dinner work. Or rather, Keith amended to himself, they hadn't been able to make it work soon enough for his taste. He wrapped his large hands around a cup of iced mocha, glancing restlessly down on Pioneer Courthouse Square from his seat outside Starbucks Coffee. A warm wind tempered the heat of the late August day.

He'd been back to Portland for more than three months without even letting Katie know he was home, but now that he'd seen her, two weeks was too long to wait to see her again. Especially after she'd stopped being prickly and admitted she was glad to see him.

Their schedules were completely out of sync. Cully Community Center, the city recreation facility Keith directed, opened at six in the morning for adult exercise classes, and the gym stayed open till ten or eleven at night. More often than not, Keith gave himself the afternoon/evening shift so he could be around when the kids were there. Until now, he hadn't even noticed that the arrangement put a crimp in his social life.

Combining business with pleasure seemed the sensible solution to getting his work accomplished and seeing Katie again. His team at the rec center had brainstormed a series of day hikes for next summer's program, and he needed to scope out the possibilities for a city hike. He'd invited Katie to meet him downtown and walk the route with him.

Pioneer Square was a good place to start a city hike: busy, interesting, within easy walking distance of other downtown sites, and directly on the light rail route both coming and going. The square was crowded with business lunchers from the surrounding retail stores and office buildings, enjoying the fresh air and activity of the city park along with their food.

Keith's fingers tapped nervously on the table as his eyes darted around the square. A trio of dreadlocked drummers was thumping out a syncopated beat on bongos, a kettle-drum, and a tambourine in the small amphitheater below Starbucks. In the middle of the square a group of teenage boys in sagging shorts played hacky-sack, their hands behind their backs as they contorted their bodies to kick the small beanbag around the circle without letting it touch the ground.

On the curved brick stairs of the larger amphitheater sat businesswomen dressed incongruously in dresses and athletic shoes, munching from brown-bag lunches while reading paperback novels. Men with shirtsleeves rolled up and ties loosened and thrown across their shoulders sat on the tiled columns next to the fountain, which cascaded into a pool in the courtyard below, and tried to keep their burritos and bentos, purchased from the carts on the street corners nearby, from dripping onto their slacks.

The sandwiches in Keith's day pack weren't nearly as elegant as dinner at Amadeus in Lake Oswego would have been, but the few evenings he *had* been available to take Katie to dinner, she'd had her own plans. She hadn't volunteered any specifics. He wondered if she and Dr. Gillette had something going on. He hardly seemed her type, but they'd acted more than just friendly as he'd watched them during registration yesterday — tuned in to each other, somehow. And Gillette's cool response to Keith had had all the earmarks of jealousy.

Well, Keith mused, *Gillette would have to be blind and a fool* not to *be attracted to Katie Brannigan.* Katie was, quite frankly, a lovely woman, and an obviously successful professional to be teaching at the college she'd been attending as an undergraduate the last time he'd heard. He'd been surprised and a bit nonplused at how she'd looked in her tailored suit: sophisticated, but utterly feminine. It was going to take some doing to adjust the tomboy image of Katie he'd been carrying around in his mind all these years. He wondered how else she'd changed.

The last time they'd talked, Katie still hadn't had a serious relationship with a man. But that had been years ago. Maybe Gillette *was* her type — how would he know? For all practical purposes, he and Katie were strangers. Meeting her here in the square with a picnic lunch felt more like a blind date than a meeting with an old friend. He wasn't sure he liked the idea.

Catching sight of a slight figure hurrying across the brick courtyard, Keith straightened in the wrought-iron chair, his nervousness dissipating as he watched her stoop to pick up a crumpled sack on the pavement. She hurried across to a garbage can and dropped the litter in. Her hair, plaited into a single thick braid like the one she'd worn in grade school, swung back and forth with the energy of her stride, glinting copper in the late morning sun. She was dressed simply, in khaki shorts, a bright yellow T-shirt, and tennis shoes with yellow socks neatly folded down.

Keith grinned. It was going to be okay after all. This wasn't yesterday's sophisticated, professional Miss Brannigan who'd come to meet him today. This was his old, best friend Katie, the girl next door — well, two doors down, anyway.

His eyes followed her up the brick stairs as she approached their designated meeting place, the bronze "umbrella man" who stood watch over the square. The sculptor had caught a city commuter in mid-stride, holding an umbrella in one hand and raising his other arm in the air as if to stop a bus pulling away from the curb. Katie reached the statue, looked around surreptitiously, then twisted her neck to read the time on the sculpture's watch, as if it could tell her whether Keith was late for their appointment.

His mouth curved in a wider grin. Definitely his Katie.

He rose from his chair, hanging his day pack over one shoulder, and picked his way through the gathering lunch crowd. Katie was sitting cross-legged at the umbrella man's feet, people-watching, when Keith walked up behind her. Peering around the statue, he whispered loudly, "Katie-Bug, Lady-Bug, Green Alligatey-Bug!"

When she looked down at her lap instead of over her shoulder, he felt suddenly uneasy again.

"You're late, Castle."

Her tone of voice raised the hackles on his neck. "It's five after," he protested, moving around in front of her. "Besides, I've been here half an hour, sitting up at Starbucks."

"That's not where we arranged to meet."

He sighed in frustration. "What's the big deal? I didn't remember you were such a stickler for time."

She raised her eyes to his, her chin set stubbornly. "Probably a lot of things you don't remember," she said. "We haven't exactly been communicating."

Keith squatted on the pavement next to her. "Is that what this is all about?" he asked gently. When she looked away without answering, he continued, "Katie, I meant it yesterday when I said I know I've been a rotten friend. I don't want to give you excuses. But I'm trying to make up for it. I wanted to see you again. I want to know about your life. Okay?"

Her chin still resolute, she took a moment before answering. When she finally looked back, her expression was pained and her brown eyes a little too bright.

Doc was right, he said to himself, feeling a pang of remorse. *Leaving without telling Katie hurt her more than I knew. She hasn't forgiven me.*

Katie took a deep breath. "All right, Keith, let's start over. I'm sorry I'm so edgy. You're right, five minutes is no big deal." *But five years... Five years is a big deal*, her eyes seemed to say.

He ran his fingers through his dark hair in a nervous gesture.

"And I *am* happy to see you."

He didn't realize he'd been holding his breath till it rushed out of him in a *whoosh*. He grinned as he rose from his awkward position. "I'm happy to see you, too, Squirt."

The nickname from their junior high days rolled unconsciously off his tongue. "And I may not remember everything, but I *do* remember your temper!"

Katie jumped to her feet, ignoring Keith's outstretched hand. "Well, thank you very much," she huffed. Leaning toward the bronze sculpture, her hands on her hips, she complained to the statue, "First he's late, and then he insults me! Why can't he be more like *you?*"

Laughter sputtered in Keith's throat. This was his Katie! He wanted to grab her and give her a big bear hug, or at least reach over and tousle her hair, the way he used to do, but something told him she wasn't quite ready for that.

They walked down Morrison Street, Keith patient when Katie slowed down to window-shop as they passed Pioneer Place. In front of the maternity shop, she caught him up on Beau and Emily's courtship, marriage, and impending parenthood. As they passed The Museum Company, he told her about his visits to the Sistine Chapel in Rome and the Church of the Sacred Heart, *Sacré Coeur*, on Montmartre in Paris. He didn't add that those visits had been so emotional for him, even as a tourist, that he'd stayed out of churches since.

Keith was aware that though their conversation was lively, it was also holding at a superficial level. He talked about Italy and Japan and playing basketball. She talked about her work and her parents' move to Arizona. A part of him felt frustrated; they'd never been so guarded with each other. But another part of him was relieved. He wasn't sure either of them was ready for anything deeper. Katie had reason not to trust him, and he...

I have reason not to trust anyone, he thought with sudden bitterness. He buried the thought as quickly as it had risen.

64

They had reached Front Street, and Katie was about to hurry across to Waterfront Park on the other side when Keith grabbed her arm and swung her around the corner. "Next stop, Mill Ends Park," he said. "Two more blocks. I figure this will be one of the kids' favorites."

"Mill Ends Park?" Katie looked blank. "Did I miss something while you were gone?"

"You call yourself Irish and you haven't been to Mill Ends Park?" he teased. "Bet you've passed it a million times. Maybe even walked through it."

"What's being Irish got to do with anything?"

Keith shook his head sadly. "Patrick O'Toole would be ashamed."

"Patrick O'Toole?"

When they reached the corner at Taylor and Front, Keith directed Katie's attention to a small curbed oval of soil in the middle of Front Street, marked by a metal post at each end, where a bedraggled bunch of purple flowers swayed in the breeze.

"You're telling me that little piece of dirt is a *park?*"

"And Patrick O'Toole its head leprechaun."

"Mm-hm," she said skeptically.

"You don't believe me?" He pretended injury. "Look here."

He turned her around to read the metal plate attached to a post on the street corner. Twenty years before, Dick Fagen, a columnist for the old Portland *Journal,* had gazed out his office window and seen a hole in the street where a utility pole had once stood. It was through his efforts that the tiny patch of land, twenty-four inches in diameter, had officially become the smallest park in the world. Fagen had also discovered the leprechaun living in Mill Ends and given him authority for its upkeep.

"This Patrick O'Toole isn't doing a very good job," Katie said, shading her eyes. "Looks to me like it needs weeding."

Keith grasped her elbow as the light changed. "Shall we help him out?" he said with a grin.

As they re-approached Pioneer Courthouse Square several hours later, Keith felt happier and more relaxed than he had in years. What had taken him so long to reconnect with Katie? Time had magically fallen away as the afternoon progressed; it almost felt as if the years between their childhood and the present had never happened. He and Katie were kids again, enjoying each other's company without a care in the world.

After pulling the offending weeds in Mill Ends Park, they'd sat on a bench at Salmon Springs and watched the children splashing in the fountain for five minutes before Katie removed her shoes and socks and joined them. At that point, he thought, how could *he* resist?

They dried out in the hot August sun, sharing the walkway along the Willamette River with joggers and in-line skaters. On a bench overlooking the river, Keith opened his day pack, pulling out ham and cream cheese sandwiches on thick slices of French bread; chips and salsa; and two bottles of grapefruit juice.

"Good cook," Katie mumbled around her last bite. Keith raised his eyebrows at the inside corners and said modestly, "I have my specialties."

They wandered along the Willamette to the shops at River Place. "Dessert?" Keith inquired, spotting an ice cream store.

Katie grinned. "Got a donut in your pocket?"

He laughed. "Used to be your favorite, didn't it? Squashed donut á la pocket lint."

Katie made a face. "Kids!"

"Yep. We were *great* at being kids."

They'd strolled up Market Street, licking their ice cream cones, to Ira's Fountain, a city block of waterfalls cascading over concrete columns, and stood behind one of the falls with their eyes closed, feeling the cool mist on their skin. Back toward downtown on Fifth Street, they'd stopped across the street from the statue of Portlandia kneeling above the entrance to the Portland Building and reaching a graceful, muscled arm down in a welcoming gesture. Keith read aloud from the marker describing the creation of the bronze sculpture and her arrival in the City of Roses, and Katie joined him in reading the short poem written in her honor etched in the metal plate.

They'd wandered around Nike Town, as much a sports museum as it was a retail outlet for athletic gear. A group of Japanese tourists were taking pictures of the innovative displays. Katie shook her head. Only in America!

The drummers who'd performed earlier in the small amphitheater in Pioneer Square were gone, replaced by a single musician, a slim, pretty, young African-American woman wearing a batik print cotton dress, her guitar slung over her shoulder.

"It's Sula!" Katie cried. "One of my voice students," she explained to Keith. "Let's get our coffee and go listen."

By the time they'd waited in line for their drinks and walked around the building to the amphitheater below, the audience was whistling and clapping in response to the song Sula had just finished. She smiled and nodded shyly, then began to pick out another tune on the strings of her guitar. Her voice was as sweet and clear as a mountain stream.

"Good for Sula!" Katie whispered to Keith. She caught her student's eye and gave her a thumbs-up sign. Sula grinned with pleasure, her white teeth brilliant in her brown face. "She has as much natural ability as anyone I've ever worked with, but when she started lessons a year ago she had zero confidence. I'm so proud of her for putting herself on stage this way!"

Katie joined in the enthusiastic applause when the young woman finished her song. Sula pulled the guitar strap over her head and held the instrument out in front of her. She was looking straight at Katie.

"Your turn, Soul Sistah," she said. Sula had teased her from day one about having more soul than she did.

"Oh, no —"

"Come on, Miz Bee," Sula coaxed. To the crowd she said, "Don't y'all want to hear some Irish soul?"

Keith raised his little fingers to his mouth and whistled shrilly, which inspired more whistles, as well as cheers and applause. He took Katie's coffee cup and gave her a nudge, and suddenly she was in the middle of the circle with Sula handing her the guitar.

He could practically see the wheels turning in her head as she tried to think of a song. Maybe he shouldn't have pushed her into this, he thought, feeling a little guilty.

"Thank you so much Sula, and thank you Keith. With friends like you…" She grinned at him as the crowd laughed, and he knew it was all right.

She began alternately strumming the guitar and beating her fingers against it in a hypnotic tattoo. "This one's for Sula

68

— some Irish soul," she said.

Katie was definitely on stage, Keith thought, and loving every minute of it. He stretched out his long legs and leaned back on his elbows, but within the first few phrases of her song, a traditional ballad of a brokenhearted lassie and her unfaithful man, he was leaning forward again as if drawn by an invisible string.

She sang with an Irish brogue, her rich contralto resonating with emotion, and there was something fierce about her delivery, something dynamic and vital. He was taken aback by his response to it, a feeling like an electric current running between them.

By the end of the song it was obvious the rest of her audience felt the same thing. He took a deep breath as her final note faded, and it seemed the whole group did the same before bursting into applause.

Katie, obviously energized by her performance, nodded her thanks, her face lit as if from within. He caught her eye, holding her gaze for a moment, thinking how intensely alive she was, how much pleasure she felt in being alive. Katie Brannigan was something special. But hadn't he always known that?

She was still looking at him. "And this —" She held up her hand to quiet the growing crowd. "This is for an old friend who's come home."

It was a simple song with a haunting melody that seemed to creep under Keith's skin and with words that could have been written in his own mind:

The gray dawn comes slowly
While streetlights flicker out
Like candles in the wind.

I've had one too many mornings waking up this way,
So I press my hands against the glass and pray.
I cry out in the silence, yearning to believe.

Her voice sobbed in the silence of Keith's mind. He felt a lump growing in his throat. It took all his strength to hold back the flood of emotions breaking through the carefully constructed box in which he'd buried them, a box built of denial.

Tears flow down like a river, cleanse my heart to see;
And in the stillness of the dawn you come to me.
You hold me in your arms and I am lost in you.

The gray dawn comes slowly
While streetlights flicker out
Like candles in the wind.

He knew without asking that Katie had written the song, that it was an expression of gratitude to the God who had heard her cry and come to comfort her. It was a beautiful song.

He hated it.

The first part was too much like the way he'd felt too often in the last few years. And the second part — well, maybe God *did* come to Katie when she needed comfort. Maybe she had the inside track. But God sure hadn't bothered with Keith. Every time *he'd* cried out in the silence, there hadn't been an answer. God was always off somewhere else when Keith needed comfort.

Katie rejoined him on the steps, her face flushed, in the midst of spirited applause. He took one of her hands in both of his and held it for a moment, feeling close to tears and unable to say anything.

"Keith? What's wrong?"

He shook his head. "Nothing. Katie —"

She looked at him expectantly.

"I've really missed you. I'm so sorry that I —" He paused. "Left you. Lost touch."

Katie laced her fingers through Keith's. "I'm sorry, too, Keith. And I'm really glad you've come home."

After a moment of silence she added, "I've missed sitting with you in church, singing with you —" She grinned. "Picking apart the sermon afterward. Why don't you come on Sunday?"

He tensed. "I don't go to church anymore," he said abruptly, pulling his hands away from hers. He cringed when he saw the look on her face, part hurt, part puzzlement. "Is it a condition of our friendship?"

"No, of course not. Keith, what's *wrong?*"

His expression was grim. "I don't want to talk about it."

She was trying to look indifferent, but her eyes gave her away. "I've got to go," she said, getting up.

"Yeah. Look — I'll call you, okay?"

Five

❧

Keith did call, later the same evening while Katie was at a faculty party. Her heartbeat quickened when she heard his voice on the answering machine beside her bed at midnight.

"Katie? Are you there? If you're home, pick up the phone. Hello? Okay, you must not be there."

Her mouth quirked into a half smile.

"I really had fun today. And I'm sorry I was such a jerk before you left. It wasn't you; it was me. I hope you can find it in your heart to forgive me, because…"

Katie held her breath as his voice on the tape paused.

"You are my sunshine, my only sunshine!" The song, slightly off-key, burst from the box like a woodpecker's quick staccato. *"You make me happy when skies are gray — I was a brat, dear, and I'm so sorry — please don't take my sunshine away!"*

She lay back on her bed with her hands behind her head, her smile full-fledged now. She'd had it in her mind not to forgive him, at least for a while, but who could resist an apology like that?

His message still wasn't over. "There — I've completely abandoned my pride just so you'll forgive me. Please? Call me tomorrow before one. Oh — it's Keith."

She burst into laughter. As though she could possibly mistake him for anyone else!

Just to be ornery, she waited to call him till a few minutes before one the next afternoon, standing at her kitchen table thumbing through the mail. "Hello, Keith."

"Katie-Bug!"

The relief and delight in his voice were so real and spontaneous, it caught her heart by surprise. She sat down with a thump.

"So am I forgiven?" he asked anxiously.

She took her time answering. "You shut me out, Keith."

"I know."

"It hurt."

"I know."

"Don't do it again."

There was silence on the other end of the line before he responded. "I wish I could promise that, Katie," he said softly. "I don't want to hurt you, ever. But I'm human. I know I will."

This time the silence was on her end.

"You're right, of course," she finally said. "I want things to be perfect, and they can't be." She felt suddenly sad. "If you can't promise not to hurt me, can you at least promise to tell me you're sorry?"

"'Love means never having to say you're sorry.'"

Katie snorted. "Not with *this* woman, it doesn't!"

Keith laughed. "I'll never forget seeing *Love Story* with you and Emily and arguing with you about that line till Em

73

finally told us to shut up or she'd never forgive either of us, whether we said we were sorry or not. 'It's a movie, for Pete's sake!'" he mimicked Emily.

"So have I finally convinced you I was right?" Katie demanded.

"Absolutely. Love means saying you're sorry every single time you screw up. I promise."

"All right then. I forgive you."

She laughed as he made a huge production of his sigh of relief.

"So Katie…"

"Hmm?"

"Is it going to be this *messy* every time?"

She laughed again. "Maybe not, now that we've set up guidelines."

"It's a reciprocal process, right?"

"Meaning?"

"Meaning *you* tell *me* you're sorry when you've been a brat."

"A brat? *Moi?*"

She could almost see Keith's grin. "It's really good to be home, y'know?" he said.

"It's really good to have you home, Keith."

"Listen, I've got to get to the center, but when can I see you again?"

"We've been over our schedules for the next two weeks already. It's not going to work. Unless…"

"What?"

"Did you say you have Monday off — Labor Day?"

"Yeah, you were the one with plans."

"Right. I'm spending the day with Doc and his grandson

in the Gorge. Why don't you come along? Doc would love to see you. And you'll like Danny."

"I know. We've met."

Katie was surprised. "Well then?"

"Great! I'd love to join you. Where and when?"

Katie slumped in her chair by the phone for several minutes after hanging up. Her mind whirled. She felt like she was on a roller coaster with Keith, heading for the stars one minute and plummeting toward the ground the next.

Yesterday when he'd been late for their meeting in Pioneer Square, she had truly believed he wasn't coming. Why had she even bothered? She couldn't trust Keith anymore. He wasn't reliable. He didn't care about her.

And then he was there, teasing her out of her peevish mood with his sincerity and good humor. It had been a fairy-tale day, a day bubbling with joy and laughter. Finally he'd told her how much he'd missed her, how sorry he was for losing touch. His regret had seemed so genuine. She'd believed him, was ready to forgive — even without an explanation.

But in the next instant, he was pulling his silent act again. *"I don't want to talk about it."* Period. Finito. End of discussion. After their parting, she'd been sure she wouldn't hear from him again.

Then the message on her machine last night and his unconcealed delight at her call today. Once again he'd apologized for his actions. She was back on the roller coaster. Clearly Keith was going out of his way to let her know he wanted her in his life again. At the same time...

Suddenly it was clear to Katie. He'd apologized for his actions, but it wasn't his actions that hurt — it was his silence. It wasn't the apology she wanted after all; it was the explanation. She wanted to know why.

But Keith was keeping secrets.

It didn't help to tell herself he had every right in the world to have secrets. The fact was, she didn't like it. She felt left out. She and Keith had never had secrets before.

Except for your secret, Katie, an inner voice reminded her. *The feelings you never shared because you thought they would ruin everything....*

She got up abruptly and walked to the window, crossing her arms tightly. *That was different,* she argued with herself. *There was so much at stake....*

But she had no idea what Keith had at stake. Too much, it seemed, to trust her. So she had her secrets, and Keith had his. Maybe someday the truth would be told on both sides.

Doc squinted over his reading glasses at his grandson, who sat on the floor with Ruggles's head in his lap, stroking the long, silky fur on the little dachshund's head. Danny was pouting; Doc had told him Ruggles couldn't come with them on their hike in the Gorge.

"He's too old to be hikin' all day," Doc said.

"He's not as old as you, and you're goin'," Danny countered.

Doc shook his head. "In dog years he's near thirty year older'n me. He'd be gettin' close on to ninety if he was a man. You an' me got to watch out for 'im, Danny Boy. Nobody else goin' to do it."

Danny looked up, a concerned frown replacing his pout. "He'd get real tired, Grumpy?"

"So tired he'd drag around here for days gettin' over it. It just wouldn't be fair to 'im, Danny."

Danny didn't say anything more, just sat on the old braided rug stroking Ruggles's fur. The dog's tail thumped against the floor.

Doc dropped the morning paper on the worn sofa next to him and sat up, absently plumping the pillows he'd been leaning on. He glanced at his watch. Keith and Katie weren't late; he just wanted them to be early.

He got up and wandered around the living room restlessly, straightening the lampshade on an end table, Danny's picture books on the coffee table, the photos on the fireplace mantel.

Picking up the black-and-white studio portrait of Toni, one she'd sent to Danny recently, he studied the flawless image. She was something to make a man's heart stop, he thought, the way her mama was at that age. Her shiny dark hair fell around her face in soft waves; her eyes were thicklashed and luminous, her smile deceptively innocent. Doc didn't know for certain what Toni's life had been like growing up, but he suspected Mina's lifestyle had robbed their daughter of innocence early on.

After Toni's court-ordered rehabilitation, she'd had a year of probation to prove to the courts she could be a good mother to Danny. Doc would have thought she'd stick around for that, but she'd told him disdainfully, "You just don't get it, do you, Pop? I've got to show these people I can earn a living before I can have Danny back." A month later she was in L.A., working for a modeling agency. "I'll be doing TV commercials and print ads," she told him proudly over the phone. "I know I can make it good here. You wait and see."

It wasn't the right place or the right business for a recovering alcoholic and drug addict. She'd quickly fallen back into her old habits, although Doc hadn't caught on for several months.

But God in his mercy had listened to the pleadings of an old man, Doc told himself, his eyes moistening. One of Toni's friends in the business, the photographer who'd done the portrait Doc held, had finally confronted her about her drug abuse and then loaned her the money to check into a clinic in Montana to dry out and get some long-term help. One of these days, Doc vowed, he would thank her friend Georgine face to face.

A rehabilitation program on a ranch in faraway Montana wouldn't have been Doc's first choice for his daughter's recovery, but he was encouraged by her weekly letters to Danny and the brief notes she sent him about her progress, especially when she wrote about her growing spiritual awareness. *I used to think God was for people with no life*, she'd written last week. *Now I know I'm the one who hasn't had a life. So maybe there's something to your God after all, Pop. I'm thinking about it.*

Doc replaced the photo on the mantel and repositioned the framed snapshots on either side of it, one of Danny hanging like a monkey from a tire swing, another of his grandson wearing a cowboy hat and mugging for the camera. Katie's friend Henry had taken the pictures on the Fourth of July a year ago, when the two were still dating and had invited Doc and Danny to Henry's West Hills house to picnic and view the fireworks. Henry had a good eye with the camera, and the camera had almost as much of a liking for Danny as it did for his mama.

Doc felt a bit disappointed that Katie and Henry were no longer dating. He wondered if Keith had anything to do with her turning Henry down, even after all the years he'd been away. Kee and Irish had a special bonding from their years of growing up together, and he'd always suspected she had more feelings for Kee than she let on.

Henry was a good man, though. Irish deserved a good man; in Doc's mind, she deserved the best of everything. Since the first day he'd met her, looking up at him with her thumb in her mouth and her orange hair blowing wild around her freckled face, she'd had a special place in his heart. And he didn't know how he'd have managed his first year with Danny without her help.

The mantel held a small photo of Katie, too, smiling up at him as if she herself, and not just an image, inhabited the frame. Even in a picture, her warmth and vitality shone through. He felt sad that Toni and Irish had never had the chance to grow up together; he thought they might have been good friends. When Toni finally came back to live with him at fifteen, he'd tried to encourage her to spend time with Katie. Toni wasn't interested; she wanted *boyfriends*.

And there was Keith right next door, a high school basketball star, tall and good-looking at seventeen, although still more a boy than a man. He was in and out of Doc's house almost every day, just like he'd been since he was six years old. Once Toni set her sights on him, he didn't have a chance.

Doc had been all for it at first. Who wouldn't want his daughter with such a fine young man as he knew Keith to be? He didn't know till later that Katie felt both Doc and Kee had betrayed her. By the time he realized that Keith meant nothing to Toni anyway, that she wanted someone more "experienced" with girls and was seeing other boys behind his back, Irish and Kee were wounded strangers.

He'd tried to patch things up between them, but Keith had left for college in North Carolina not long after, and Katie didn't come around much with Toni there. On top of everything else, it was turning out to be more than Doc could do to untangle the threads of his and Toni's lost years and weave them back together so their lives as father and daughter made sense. He never really did get Toni back.

Turning around, Doc gazed at Danny, still sitting quietly on the floor, petting Ruggles. People seemed to have a predilection for wanting what they didn't have, he thought, no matter how good the gifts God gave them. *I love you, Danny Boy*, he said silently, a lump in his throat.

He coughed and said aloud, "Who's my best boy, Danny?"

Toni's son looked up with a wide grin. "Me!"

"An' who is it loves you somethin' fierce?"

"You do, Grumpy!"

"That I do, Danny Boy. That I do."

A flood of memories swept over Keith as he turned onto Dearborn Street and saw the three houses lined up next to each other. The two-story house where Katie had grown up was on the corner, the french windows of the enclosed front porch glinting in the morning sun. The porch had been a favorite rainy-day playroom when he and Katie were children: sometimes a jungle, sometimes a classroom, sometimes a distant planet.

Doc's house stood in the middle, looking tired and run-down, the way it looked in his earliest memories when old Mrs. Brathwaite had lived there. Keith frowned. It wasn't like Doc to let his house go. But then, he was close to sixty now, still working full-time and taking care of a young child, too. Probably didn't have much time for shoring up the sagging roof over the porch or painting the peeling trim.

On the other side of Doc's, almost hidden behind the tall pines in the front yard and the blackberry vines tangled in the lilac bushes, was the little shingled house, not much more than a cabin, that Keith and his mother had shared. A small brown child furiously pedaled his tricycle up and down the walk; an older girl sat on the front stoop, intent on the book in her lap.

Keith parked his truck across the street and sat for several minutes, his eyes picking up every detail, every difference and every similarity to the neighborhood of his memory. He could see a garden between the houses, the beans hanging from their trellis of poles and strings, and the tall corn rustling in the breeze.

Doc's corn patch had been a favorite place for him and Katie to play. Barefoot, they'd creep silently between the shady rows of green on summer mornings, stalking fat earthworms for Doc to use as fishing bait. A nickel apiece he'd paid them. Keith would squat between the rows, digging his toes into the soft earth still damp from the night's watering, his arms pulled in close to his body so he wouldn't break the stalks or disturb the young ears of corn. Sometimes a drooping leaf would tickle his nose and make him sneeze.

The world was cool and green and peaceful under the cornstalks....

A movement at Doc's front window caught Keith's eye.

His old friend was waving through the glass. He raised an arm in response. By the time Keith had slammed the door of the Montero behind him, Doc was on the front porch wearing a pleased smile and Danny was skipping down the steps, swooping a balsa airplane side to side.

Keith and Katie had thought Doc was Santa Claus when he'd first moved into the house next door. Secretly, Keith had continued to wonder for a long time, even after he'd openly scoffed at the whole idea of Santa. Mostly, Doc was the grown-up who was always there for his young neighbors. Keith had no father and a mother who worked two jobs; Katie had a fragile mother and a father gone away on business more often than he was home.

It was Doc who took them fishing, Doc who taught them to swim, Doc who gave Keith his first basketball and Katie her first guitar. He didn't have much book learning, but he knew about the stars and about trees and flowers and animals. He knew how to wonder, and he knew how to listen. Danny was a lucky boy to be growing up under Doc's wing. Keith knew.

"Hi, Kee!"

"Hi, Danny!" He swept the boy up and swung him once around before setting him back on the ground, laughing breathlessly. "Did your grandpa tell you I used to live in the house next door?" he asked, pointing.

Danny nodded. "That's Macon's house. He's just a little kid, but I'm real nice to him."

Keith grinned crookedly. "I'll bet you are. You're a nice boy, Danny."

He glanced at the mossy roof of the house next door, barely visible over the brambles. He hadn't been on

Dearborn Street since the day of his mother's funeral, when he'd hurriedly packed the clothes he'd brought with him and called a taxi for the airport.

The estate wouldn't have been much to settle — his mother had never been able to afford much, and he was the only heir — but even that he hadn't wanted to deal with. He'd left instructions with Chappie to contact an estate attorney who was the father of a high-school classmate and have him deduct his fees from the sale of the house and its contents. What little was left, Chappie had offered to wire him overseas. Keith was in Japan by that time and making decent money playing basketball. He instructed the minister to donate the amount instead to the Women's Crisis Center in his mother's name. The action brought him a strange kind of comfort, something he hadn't felt much otherwise in the last five years.

Until now, he thought. Being here on Dearborn Street, remembering. Seeing Doc and Danny. Looking forward to a day in the Gorge, one of his favorite places on earth. Spending time with Katie. Except for a few brief moments entirely his own fault, the day he'd spent with Katie last week had been comforting in a way Keith knew only from long ago. She was so familiar, even after all these years, so much a part of his memories of a childhood probably happier than most....

A loud honk interrupted his thoughts. He and Danny both turned and waved as Katie pulled her yellow Honda into the driveway. She jumped out of the car, her braid swinging, looking young and carefree in short denim overalls with an apricot-colored tank top underneath.

Danny ran over for a hug, then continued clinging to her

hand as Keith placed an arm around Katie's shoulder and gave her a quick squeeze.

Doc watched from the porch, his pleased smile still in place.

"Come on, you guys!" Danny pulled at Katie's hand impatiently. "Grumpy and I been waitin'!"

Six

❧

Doc's pickup didn't have room enough for all four of them in the cab, and Keith declared he wouldn't be able to fold himself small enough to fit in Katie's Civic, so they all piled into Keith's Montero. Katie eyed the height from the ground to the cab with uncertainty as Keith moved the front passenger seat forward. Then she felt his large hands on her waist, lifting her as easily as if she were a child. A small thing, but the gesture made her feel cared for. She smiled without turning around.

She buckled Danny in next to her as Keith helped Doc into the front seat, and before long they were on the freeway headed east. Leaving the interstate at Troutdale, Keith followed the historic Columbia River Highway along the Sandy River and then up the hill through the small community of Corbett.

Across a field of grasses shimmering pale gold in the wind, Katie suddenly caught sight of Crown Point in the distance. The promontory above the Columbia River marked the west end of the Columbia River Gorge.

Over the centuries the river had cut deeper and deeper through the volcanic rock of the Cascade Mountain Range to form a spectacular canyon almost a hundred miles long. At its west end, a series of breathtaking waterfalls, most of them visible from the historic highway, fell over the edge of the cliffs from the streams feeding into the river below. Hiking trails traversed the hills and canyons from one end of the Gorge to the other, giving city dwellers access to the wilds only forty-five minutes from their downtown offices.

The narrow highway, built in the early nineteen hundreds to pave a way to the natural beauties of the canyon, had its own beauty as well. The series of lookouts along the route featured walls, walkways, and other structures of intricate stonework. Elegant arched bridges and viaducts spanned the deep chasms.

Danny's eyes widened as they pulled into the parking lot of Vista House at Crown Point. He was looking at a domed, circular building, constructed entirely of huge gray stones, with arched, leaded glass windows and a parapet around the roof. "A castle!" he breathed.

The warm wind was so strong Danny had to grab hold of Doc and Katie to keep from being blown over. "It's real *blustery!*" he said. "Like in Christopher Robin."

"The Gorge is famous for being blustery, Danny," Keith told him. He picked up the little boy and held him tightly, pointing upriver. "People come here from all over the world to windsurf." He nodded at the brightly colored sails racing along the river, looking like toys from their position high on the hill. Katie watched as a bright orange sail swooped and fell over, its rider splashing around for a moment before grabbing hold of his board and tipping it upright again.

"Looks like fun," she said. "What d'you think, Danny?"

"Don't you be puttin' ideas into his head, Irish!" Doc intervened before Danny could say anything.

Inside Vista House, they plotted their day in the Gorge on the large relief map on the first floor. Keith lifted Danny over the table map so he could reach down and trace the hills and valleys with his fingers.

They climbed the narrow steps curving to the roof and gazed up and down the river, shining in the morning sun. Keith pointed out a hawk gliding high above the cliffs, and the four of them watched its graceful flight for several minutes. The wind and the sails and the swooping bird exhilarated Katie. "I've always thought I could fly, if I just *believed* in it hard enough," she said, leaning over the edge of the parapet.

Suddenly Keith and Doc were gripping her arms on either side, as though afraid she might jump over the wall. "D'ruther you didn't try, if you don't mind!" Doc said. "Thought once off my porch roof was enough for you, gal."

"No, it was enough for *me*," Keith interjected. "*I'm* the one who broke my arm."

Katie groaned. "Am I ever going to live this story down? I still remember Daddy's lecture after that particular adventure." Gentle rebuke had been her father's discipline of choice, and it was usually effective. She loved him and had always tried to please him. "No man is an island, Katie," he told her when her mischief got out of hand. "Everything you do affects other people. You are your brother's keeper."

"Katie was a *wild* girl, Danny," Keith told him solemnly. "You're lucky she doesn't live next door anymore."

"I seem to remember a certain boy in the neighborhood

with wild ideas of his own," Katie huffed.

He let go of her arm and tugged at her ponytail. "I think you remember wrong, Squirt. *I* was just an innocent, pulled unwittingly into your schemes. A Hobbes to your Calvin, if you will."

Katie flipped her ponytail away. "An *innocent...unwittingly...*" she sputtered. "How can you listen to this without defending me, Doc?" she appealed.

Doc scratched his beard. "Sorry, Irish, but I gots to agree with Kee. You was the ringleader most times, as I recall."

Keith grinned. Katie stuck out her tongue. Doc shook his head, and Danny giggled.

They stopped next at Latourell Falls, hiking down from the road for a closer view. Yellow lichen and shelf-like mushrooms clung to the cliffs, and maidenhair ferns grew from cracks in the rocks. The stream fell straight over a high cliff into the pool below. Katie closed her eyes and felt the spray on her face for a moment before Danny tugged at her hand. She followed him along the path that led under the graceful concrete arches of the bridge to an open, grassy park, and then up a series of stone stairs back to the highway.

As they crossed the bridge over the ravine, they were at treetop level. Katie felt a little dizzy looking down on the dense, spreading crown of a white oak, one side of its trunk blanketed with green velvet moss. Or was it Keith standing next to her at the railing with one hand tousling Danny's hair and the other resting lightly on her shoulder that made her feel dizzy?

At Shepperd's Dell, Danny led the way down a set of stairs beside a beautifully crafted stone wall, its curved top blanketed heavily with moss. Dandelions shared soil between the rocks with the delicate star-shaped blossoms of miner's lettuce and a scattering of other wildflowers, tiny blossoms of lavender, yellow, and white. Keith stopped Katie with a hand on her arm and pointed silently to a serene meadow through the arches of the highway overpass. One yellow-leafed tree stood out against the lush green of the wetlands. Katie smiled, thinking how like him it was to share the beauty of the scene.

After a picnic lunch in the woods at Bridal Veil Falls State Park, Keith led the way along a steep, rocky trail to the creek, its water so clear Katie could delineate the individual stones in its bed. Crossing a rough wooden bridge, they climbed to a deck overlooking the falls, which spilled over one high cliff onto a ledge before spilling again into a shaded pool.

Katie leaned against the deck railing with Doc, mesmerized by the play of the water, while Keith and Danny scrambled over the boulders below to get closer. The place had been well named: where the water bounced off the ledge between the two falls, a filmy white mist stirred like a gossamer veil in the wind. Sunlight filtered through the canopy of green overhead. Katie couldn't remember the last time she'd felt so at peace.

"'The children of men shall drink of the river of God's pleasures...'" Doc said in a quiet voice.

Katie smiled contentedly. "You feel it, too, Doc. Why is it so much easier to believe that 'all's right with the world' when you're in a place like this?"

"Can't say as I know for sure," Doc answered slowly, "exceptin' it's the world o' God's makin' instead o' man's fiddlin'."

Keith and Danny were scrambling back over the rocks. "Hey, Grumpy!" Danny called. "Kee says Mama's been here!"

Doc scratched his head in puzzlement.. "I don't remember Toni ever bein' much int'rested in the out-o'-doors, Kee," he said as the two climbed up the stairs to rejoin them on the deck. "You sure she been here?"

"Let's see," Keith mused, looking down at the wooden rail as he ran his hands along it. Katie noticed for the first time that the railing was rough with carvings, names, and initials chiseled into the wood with countless pocketknives. Keith stopped just short of where she stood with Doc. "Here it is, Danny!"

He lifted Danny to the railing and held him there as the boy traced the letters and sounded out the words carved into the wood. Katie's heart sank.

"Kei — th plus To — ni. Toni! That's my mama!"

"That's right. I brought your mom here a long time ago, when she was only fifteen years old." He set Danny back down. "So what do you think about that?"

"Was mama your girlfriend?" he asked curiously.

"I guess you could say she was, for a little while," Keith answered. "Then I went away to college and never saw her again."

"How come?"

Keith shifted uncomfortably. *Well, what did he expect?* Katie thought irritably. *He'd brought up the subject. Danny was bound to be curious.*

"It just didn't work out, Danny. That's all."

The knot of irritability in Katie's stomach dissolved into a dull ache. Keith sounded so *sad*. Was he still carrying a torch for Toni, after all these years? It seemed incredible, until she asked herself why Keith's feelings for Toni should bother *her*, after all these years. The contentment she'd felt just a few short moments ago already seemed a distant memory.

"We'd better get going — still lots of good things to see," she said with a false edge of brightness. "Danny, want to lead the way?"

"Yeah!" he whooped. "Come on, Grumpy!"

Katie was quiet on the short hike back to the parking lot and the drive to their next stop, Wahkeena Falls. She was glad for the variety of distractions there: a little gray mouse with white feet Danny spotted scurrying into the salal off the path; a pretty stone bridge across the creek where Katie stood with her back to the falls, looking through the trees toward the river, where a white-sailed boat skimmed the waves in the distance. She purposely stayed behind when the others climbed the path to a wooden bench overlooking the waterfall, leaning into the spray at close range instead. The mist felt cool and refreshing on her bare arms and legs.

"Katie!"

She looked up to see Keith gesturing wildly for her to join them up the hill. Danny was lying on his stomach on the paved walkway, peering over the edge, and Doc had craned his neck in the same direction. Reluctantly she started up the path.

"Kneel next to Danny," Keith whispered, "and look in the alcove under the asphalt."

A tiny chestnut-colored chipmunk with a sleek black tail and three black stripes down its back sat in the hollow, not stirring, its bright, beady eyes watchful. Katie held her breath, afraid even the slightest movement might scare the little animal away. Lifting her head slowly, she glanced at

Danny and smiled. His delight was almost palpable.

Suddenly the chipmunk scuttled out from under the walkway and into the bushy Oregon grape at the side of the path. Danny lay where he was a minute longer, hoping the creature might return. Only Doc's promise of an ice cream cone at Multnomah Falls, a few more miles up the road, finally persuaded him to abandon his watch and accompany them back to the Montero. Even then he lagged behind, glancing over his shoulder to see if he might catch one last glimpse.

Katie pulled a cropped cotton sweater over her tank top as they continued their drive along the old highway, unsure whether the chill she was starting to feel came from the shady road, the spray of the falls, or some indefinable place inside her. She was glad no one seemed to have noticed her change of mood.

Multnomah Falls was Oregon's most popular tourist attraction, and on this last day before school started at most Portland schools, it seemed every school-age child was visiting, along with parents, grandparents, aunts, and uncles. The most spectacular of the falls in the Columbia Gorge, and the only one visible from the interstate as well as the Gorge highway, Multnomah Falls plummeted a total of six hundred twenty feet, straight down a sheer cliff into an upper pool and then over a second, shorter cliff into a lower pool. No matter how many times Katie saw it, the view always took her breath away.

With the roar of the falls in the background, Danny waited patiently in line with Keith for his ice cream while Doc and Katie rested at a table outside the snack bar. The beautiful old stone building at the base of the falls also housed a gift store and a restaurant. Katie wondered if Keith remembered bringing her and Emily here in his little red Datsun with his brand new driver's license on his sixteenth birthday. They'd sat upstairs in the elegant wood and stone dining room next to a window looking out on the trees, eating huckleberry pie and drinking coffee and feeling very grown up.

Katie leaned back in her chair, pushing the sleeves of her sweater up to her elbows. *Or,* she wondered, *was Keith's memory reserved for more romantic liaisons, like his visit to Bridal Veil with Toni?*

"Here's yours, Grumpy," Danny announced, thrusting a cone with a tall swirl of vanilla ice cream at Doc.

Keith handed Katie a napkin-wrapped cone and nodded toward the stairs behind them. "Want to go sit where we can see the waterfall?"

They tramped up the stone steps, which led to a crowded viewing platform directly across from the lower part of the falls and overlooking the lower pool. Katie, bringing up the rear, nearly tripped over Danny when he suddenly stopped dead in front of her.

"Grumpy!"

Doc and Keith, several steps ahead, turned around to see Katie steadying herself against Danny, who was staring with wonder at an old-fashioned lamppost looking very out of place among the trees.

"Are we in *Narnia?*" he asked, his voice muted with awe.

"I swan, Danny Boy," Doc answered in surprise. "If it ain't just like the one in the woods t'other side of the wardrobe!" Doc had been reading *The Lion, the Witch, and the Wardrobe* to his grandson at bedtime. Obviously, Danny had been listening.

"You like the Narnia books, too?" Keith asked Danny. "They used to be our favorites when we were growing up." He startled Katie by putting an arm around her shoulder to include her.

Keith took Danny down to skip rocks across the lower pool, while Katie kept Doc company watching from above. When they returned, Keith tried to coax Danny into climbing the switchbacks to the high bridge platform across from the upper falls, but the long day was beginning to take its toll on him.

"I'm gettin' a mite tired my own self, Kee," Doc admitted. "Maybe we'd best be gettin' on if we's goin' to see Oneonta and Horsetail before the day's out."

Keith looked crestfallen.

"You got some special reason to go up there?"

"Sentimental reasons. Katie and Em and I walked up to the bridge on my sixteenth birthday and climbed over the rocks to the pool. I haven't been there since."

Katie looked at him with surprise. So he did remember, and it meant something to him....

Doc pulled Danny down to his lap. "Why don't you two go on up while me an' the lad rest here a bit?"

At the top of the paved walkway, the bridge was even more crowded than the lower platform had been. In the midst of the throng, a wedding party stood before the falls, having pictures taken. "I think I would have chosen a more private spot," Keith muttered, grabbing Katie's hand and pulling her across the bridge through his wake. There certainly were advantages to being six feet five inches tall, Katie mused.

On the opposite side of the bridge, the main trail continued up the hill to the left, and a narrow path to the right led down to the deep pool into which the upper falls splashed.

Keith eyed Katie. "You game for some rock climbing?"

"Sure. Wouldn't even mind getting my feet wet."

He grinned. "Now why doesn't that surprise me?"

A family with four small children was scrambling up the path, leaving the rock-strewn poolside empty. Keith stepped back to let them pass, one arm stretched out in front of Katie in a protective gesture.

The next few moments were a blur in Katie's mind. She heard a sound like the crack of ice underfoot, and suddenly she was pressed into the cliff face with Keith's body over her. The crowd's collective gasp turned to shouts and screams as rock chips rained down around her and she heard a splash larger than she ever could have imagined. An instant later a giant wave pummeled her against the cliff, soaking her to the bone. Her knees collapsed in terror and she would have slid to the ground except for the pressure of Keith's body against her.

"Keith!" she cried into his shirt front, trying to struggle away from him.

"Stay still!" he commanded, as if she could do anything else.

They learned later that a massive chunk of rock, nearly the size of a city bus, had broken away from the cliff face behind the falls and tumbled into the pool below. Everyone on the bridge, a full ninety-five feet away, was drenched. A few people suffered minor injuries from flying rocks, and a few more in the general panic that ensued as people tried to get off the bridge, but in the end no one was seriously hurt.

None of the foursome knew that at the time, of course.

Keith and Katie spent two fretful hours wondering if Doc and Danny had experienced any of the fallout from the slide. It took them that long to get back across the bridge, down the path, and through the throng of spectators, victims, and emergency medical personnel who'd been called to the scene.

Katie didn't cry until she spotted Doc and his grandson, dry and in one piece, wandering from one team of EMTs to another with anxious expressions on their faces. She discovered later they'd been in the gift shop away from any danger when the slide had occurred.

"Doc!" she cried, tears streaming down her face as she ran to him and threw her arms around him. Danny put his arms around her waist and clung to her.

"Irish! Kee!" Doc's cheeks, too, were wet with tears of relief. "We been so worried!" Keith joined the joyous group hug and the four clung to each other. Katie couldn't stop crying.

"Are you really okay?" Keith asked uneasily when they stepped back.

She hiccupped and nodded. "Just a few scrapes where *somebody* pushed me into the dirt," she said with a weak grin, swiping a hand across her eyes. Seeing a smudge on the side of his forehead, she reached up to wipe it away.

"Keith! That's dried blood!"

"Really?" He touched the spot and winced. "I did get a little banged up," he admitted. "I'm sure it's nothing serious."

"Let someone qualified determine that," a park employee who had overheard him interrupted. "Follow me."

The EMT agreed with Keith's assessment but offered to transport him by ambulance to a hospital emergency room, as a number of victims had been.

"Thanks, but no," Keith said. "I feel fine."

Katie gave him a worried scowl. "Don't look at me like that, Squirt," he grinned. "I'm a big boy. I can take care of myself."

Doc insisted on driving home, and Keith didn't argue. He stretched out in the front passenger seat with his eyes closed, listening to Katie behind him singing softly to Danny as the little boy rested his head against her shoulder.

When Doc glanced around a few minutes later, Katie was looking vacantly out the front window, still humming quietly. Keith and Danny were both fast asleep.

The shakes didn't set in for Keith till later that night, after Doc had dressed the shallow cut on his head and coaxed him and Katie into having a bowl of chicken soup. He'd gone home to soak in the whirlpool tub and then wrap up in a bath sheet hot from the dryer.

Clicking on the ten o'clock news, he leaned into the pillows stacked against the headboard of his bed. He hardly heard the newscaster's comments as he zeroed in on the side-by-side video shots of Multnomah Falls, before and after.

A large, pale scar on the side of the cliff indicated where the chunk of rock had split off. And a mountain of boulders covered the spot where Keith and Katie would have been standing if they'd stepped onto the narrow path to the pool two minutes earlier.

Seven

❧

The incident at Multnomah Falls brought Keith to two realizations. One, he cared a great deal about Katie. If he had a best friend, she was it. Their relationship had always been straightforward, their connection not only stimulating, but clean and uncomplicated as well. She'd always been there for him; the fact that they'd drifted apart in high school and after he'd gone away to college was his lapse, not hers. And the last five years — well, somehow he'd make them up to her.

No one had shared as much of his life or knew him better, except perhaps Doc, whose friendship was complicated by the older man's position in his life as a father figure. Katie was the one he'd gone to first when his mother had fallen ill — before Doc, before Chappie. Unconsciously he'd known she would be the one best able to comfort him.

For the first week after the slide, Keith checked in with Katie every day, either popping into her classroom or calling to see how she was. Without conscious planning, they fell into a regular habit over the next few weeks of sharing lunch in the school cafeteria the two days he had classes on campus. She introduced him to her favorite students and to other faculty and took him by to see Emily and meet Beau. For years now, he'd been something of a loner, but his reclaimed friendship with Katie was making him feel more connected to the world.

Keith's second realization affected him even more profoundly. He began to seriously take stock of the unfinished business in his life. He and Katie had been two minutes away from losing their lives. Katie might be ready to meet her Maker, but Keith knew with certainty that he was not.

Katie, balancing precariously on the top step of the ladder, reached for the last strip of wallpaper border, positioned it below the ceiling, and smoothed it into place.

"Perfect!" Emily breathed, clapping her hands and turning around in a circle to view the whole of their handiwork. She turned down the volume on the oldies station they'd had at full blast while they worked. "Thanks for your help, girlfriend. Beau had a fit about me getting up on that ladder in my 'delicate condition,' as he calls it."

"As well he should, Mrs. Bradley," Katie answered with mock severity as she climbed down to join her friend. "You've got to take care of yourself, not to mention Skippy." She joined Emily in her survey of the room, nodding in approval at the results of their work.

Beau and Emily had agreed they didn't want to know the baby's gender till Skippy was born, so they'd chosen bright primaries for the nursery instead of the traditional pink or blue. Beau had painted the louvered closet doors banana yellow, the casement windows bubblegum blue, and the door to the hall-way tomato red, picking up the colors in the wallpaper.

A grid of country roads crisscrossed the white walls, with Grandma Moses villages set at the crossroads and farmhouses perched on the hillsides between. Apple orchards, haystacks, and bridges arching over winding streams dotted the land-scape. A procession of farm animals, from tiny chicks to big draft horses, marched around the border below the ceiling.

"A fine room for a city child," Katie teased. "Trying to cash in on Beau's country roots?" Beau had grown up an east-ern Oregon farmboy, but his interest in the machinery his father used to run the farm had quickly eclipsed his interest in crops and livestock. As soon as he'd discovered cars, the idea of farming had lost its appeal. He still drove the first car he'd ever restored, a white '65 Mustang convertible he called Sally.

Emily rolled her eyes. "Beau wanted to go for the city scene, with a bunch of trucks rumbling around the ceiling! I said Skippy would get plenty of *that* without having it on the walls of the nursery, too."

She bent to roll up the unused wallpaper and slip it back into its plastic package. Katie picked up the tray of water they'd used to dampen the prepasted wallpaper and carried it down the hallway to empty it in the tub.

"Want some sun tea?" Emily called after her. "I should have a batch ready on the back porch. Maybe Beau will take a break from the lawn and join us."

"Sure," Katie called back. "We deserve it!"

Emily popped her head around the doorway. "I think we deserve more than a glass of iced tea. How about a slice of cheesecake left over from dinner last night?"

"As long as it's a thin piece."

"As if you needed to worry." Emily looked with envy at Katie's trim figure and rubbed a hand over her rounded tummy. "Think I'll ever get my girlish figure back?"

"You'll be so busy chasing that kid around you won't have an ounce of fat," Katie assured her.

"Well, that's encouraging," Emily laughed.

A few minutes later they were settled on the stairs of the back porch, drinking sun tea mixed with a little peach juice and eating not-so-thin slices of cheesecake. Katie's willpower went out the window when it came to Emily's cooking.

Beau had declined his wife's invitation to join them. "Thanks, hon, but I want to get the front yard finished and get cleaned up before your dad comes by for our tennis game."

"It's great that Beau and Chappie get along so well, Em," Katie said as Beau finished cutting the last swath of grass in the large backyard.

Emily nodded, waving at her husband as he switched off the lawnmower and mopped his brow with the sleeve of his T-shirt. A moment later he wheeled the mower past them on his way to the front yard, raising his eyebrows at their plates of dessert. "Don't say a word," Katie told him. "We've already worked it off."

His eyes narrowed. "You didn't let Em get up on that ladder, did you?"

"Of course not! I take care of my friends, Beau."

Emily's face reddened. "I am fully capable of taking care of myself," she said crossly.

Beau held up his hands. "On that note, I'm off to the hinterlands."

"Oh, Em, am I being bossy again?" Katie asked as Beau disappeared around the corner of the house.

"Yeah." She sighed. "And I'm being grumpy. Sorry."

"Me, too. I've just always been the one in charge, you know? It's a hard habit to break."

The buzz of the lawnmower started up again in front of the house. Katie and Emily sat for a few minutes in companionable silence, eating cheesecake and basking in the warm September sun.

Emily looked at her friend sideways. "We haven't had much time to talk since school started," she said. "How are things going, girlfriend?"

"You first," Katie countered, her heart sinking. The truth was, she hadn't made much effort to talk to Emily since school had started. And she'd managed to put off any serious conversation while they worked on the nursery today by tuning in the oldies station and singing along. There was no question Emily would want to know about Keith, and Katie wasn't sure she knew what to say. "Are you keeping up with your kindergartners okay?" she asked.

Emily sighed and ran her fingers through her short blond hair. "I'm a lot more tired than I'd normally be," she admitted. "I haven't told Beau. I'm afraid he'd worry." Emily was planning to teach up until winter break, two weeks before Skippy was due, so she could take a longer leave after the baby was born.

"You have sick days you can take if it gets too bad, don't you?" Katie asked, a concerned frown creasing her brow.

"Quite a few, actually. But it's so much work getting ready for a substitute teacher, it hardly seems worthwhile sometimes."

"It's worthwhile, Em. If you need a day off —" She stopped herself, realizing she had been about to issue a command once again. "I hope you'll take it."

Emily nodded. "So what's up with *you?*"

"Good stuff. Really good." Katie took a bite of cheesecake and withdrew the fork slowly from her mouth to get all the crumbs. "I have the best group of students I could ask for in my new ed class. I worried they'd rebel at the big project I've assigned, but they're enthusiastic — so far."

"They catch it from you. How are *other* things going?" Emily prompted.

"Fine. Henry's been great to work with, no tension at all between us." *Except when Keith is around,* she added to herself. His response to Keith still puzzled her. It was clear Henry wasn't pining for her, but for some reason Keith seemed to get the professor's hackles up. "Did I tell you we're going to emcee the Christmas concert together? Abercrombie's planning quite the production."

"Sounds fun. So how are *other* things going?"

"Emily, if you want to know what's going on with Keith, why don't you just ask?" She wondered if she sounded as exasperated as she felt.

"I was trying to be subtle," Emily pouted. "Okay, so how are things going with Keith?"

It's just a simple question, Katie told herself. *Give her a simple answer*. "He seems to be enjoying school," she answered noncommittally. Then, grinning, she added, "And vice versa — I'm sure three quarters of the girls on campus have crushes on him." *Who wouldn't?* she thought.

"Oh? And what about him?" Emily waggled her eyebrows. "Showing any interest in the schoolgirls?"

"He's got to love the attention."

"What kind of attention are *you* giving him?"

Katie finished up her dessert and set the empty plate on the step beside her. "I'm..." She paused and then sighed. "Being careful."

Emily reached for Katie's glass, poured her some more tea, and handed it back. "Don't be so careful he forgets you're around," she advised.

Katie sputtered on her drink. "Subtlety really is not your gift, you know that, Em?"

She sniffed. "And what kind of attention is *he* giving *you*?"

Keep it light, Katie, she told herself.

"Well, he denies it, but I'm pretty sure it's Keith who's leaving anonymous gifts in my campus mailbox." The first week it had been the inevitable apple, buffed to shiny perfection; the next week a tiny bouquet of dried wildflowers and a little red-haired doll dressed in Irish folk costume. She smiled. "Last week it was half a maple bar wrapped in a napkin. A dead giveaway."

Emily made a face. "Sounds messy. Why a dead giveaway?"

"It's a thing he did when we were kids."

"And he says it's not him?"

Katie nodded. "Shook his head when I ventured the subject and told me, 'What some of these kids won't do for a grade!'" *There now*, she told herself. *That wasn't so bad.*

Emily was silent for a moment. Then she took a deep breath and said, "Girlfriend, you're not being straight with me. What's *really* going on in your head about Keith?"

A frown appeared between Katie's brows. "What do you mean?" she evaded.

Emily didn't answer; she just looked at Katie.

"He's fun," Katie said. "Like he always was. I see him on campus. We have lunch in the cafeteria once in a while."

"And?" Emily prompted again.

"Em, you are so nosy!"

"I know. So?"

Katie sighed. She should have known she couldn't hide from Emily, who saw through her easily. Usually, eventually, she did tell her friend most of what she was thinking about. She just didn't know *what* she was thinking right now. When it came to Keith everything seemed so confusing...

"*Okay*, I *like* him!" she answered irritably. "That's no news to you."

Emily was silent for a moment, then said in a hurt voice, "I'm sorry for prying, Katie. I thought you'd want to talk about him."

"Oh, Em, I didn't mean to hurt your feelings." She put an arm around her friend and squeezed her shoulder. "You're right, I have been holding back, but it's only because I'm so confused. It probably would do me good to talk about Keith. Maybe you can help me figure out what's going on."

She dropped her arm from Emily's shoulder and sipped at her iced tea. "It's awkward that he's a student where I teach," she finally said. "I shouldn't even think about dating a student."

"He's not *your* student, is he?"

"No. At least not now."

"Does the college have a policy?"

"Only about students enrolled in a professor's class. But I'm still not sure it's a good idea to go out with Keith." She lifted her glass to her lips and drained it. "Not that he's asked."

"Really? What about your downtown date? And your Gorge hike?"

"Those weren't really *date* dates —"

"Oh, right, just a couple of those *non*-date dates," Emily interrupted, nodding sagely. "And what about these lunches in the college cafeteria?"

"Collegial."

"Mm-hm." Emily sounded skeptical.

"It is interesting how easily we've seemed to slip back into our old friendship," Katie admitted. "It's comfortable. The relationship fits, like an old pair of jeans. It's almost as if those five years never happened. But…" She paused.

"But?"

Katie raised her shoulders and let them drop again. "I don't know. Sometimes he's my old friend Keith, the boy I grew up with, my oldest friend. And sometimes he's — a man, for one thing, not a boy anymore. A man I don't know at all."

"Because those five years *did* happen, Katie. Whatever happened when his mother died, everything since, the way he's responded to all those things — that's part of who he is now."

"Yes. The part he won't tell me." She set her glass on the plate next to her. "It's almost as if — he wants me in his life again, but only on the old terms. Only if things can be the same as they were before he left. No, even before then. He wants us to be fifteen and sixteen again. Best buds. He wants uncomplicated friendship."

"Katie — uncomplicated is something you are *not!*"

"Thanks — I think!"

"Believe me, it's a compliment. Katie, you were a wonderful friend when we were in junior high and high school, as good a friend as anyone can be at that age. It's just that you have so much more to give now. How can he not see that?"

"Truthfully?" Katie pulled her hair up off her neck, holding it on top of her head for a moment before letting it fall again. "I don't think it has anything to do with me. I think he wants to convince himself I haven't changed so he can pretend he hasn't changed, either. But he has, Em. He has secrets he isn't willing to tell. At least not to me."

"Secrets?"

"He won't talk about…certain things."

"Such as?"

"Anything to do with his mother's death. Anything to do with God."

"God?"

"I invited him to come to church with me. To *our* church, *his* church. He told me he doesn't go to church anymore." Katie wrapped her arms around her legs and rested her chin on her knees. "He sounded bitter. There's something cynical about him that wasn't there before his mother died. I think…." She paused for a moment, then continued, "I get the impression he feels God abandoned him."

Emily looked puzzled. "I can understand him feeling that way when his mother first died. I mean, she was young, and she adored Keith, and her death was tragic. I can't imagine how it would feel to lose Mom or Dad. But after all this time it seems a little extreme to still be blaming God. Keith's faith seemed stronger than that."

"I know. I can't help but think it was something more than his mother's death that made him run away. Something more than grief. Maybe it's wishful thinking, but I honestly don't think he'd have left me and Doc the way he did without a reason. He's got secrets, Em, and it's clear they don't sit easy."

Emily was silent for a moment. "Katie — it's not up to you to 'fix' him, you know," she said gently.

Katie felt her shoulders tense. "I'm not trying to fix him!" she protested. "I *care* about him."

"I know you do," Emily said, her tone soothing. "I just meant — oh, never mind what I meant! I care about him, too. He was my friend, too."

Katie straightened her back and stretched her arms to relax the tight muscles in her shoulders. "Anyway — there's stuff he has to deal with before we could be any more than friends," she said.

She didn't want to reflect on why she'd reacted with such immediate resistance to Emily's comment. It just sounded too much like criticism, she told herself. Criticism wasn't Em's style.

"Thanks for the snack," she said, picking up her plate and glass and getting to her feet. "I've really got to get going."

Emily pushed herself up from the stairs. "Thanks again for helping me hang the wallpaper, girlfriend. It looks great."

"Yeah."

They stood looking awkwardly at each other.

"I'd give you a hug, but it's getting harder and harder," Emily finally said, her hands resting on her belly.

"Oh, Em." Katie put an arm around Emily's waist and laid her head on her shoulder for a brief moment. "Thank you for being my friend."

CHAPTER

Eight

❧

Katie blinked as she emerged from the dim light of the music building into the brilliance of an absolutely perfect October day, color-drenched and dazzling. A kaleidoscope of gold, burnt umber, scarlet, and burgundy shifted around her as a cool wind stirred the leaves against the sapphire sky.

Without thinking, she ran down the stairs and across the sidewalk, straight into the middle of a neat pile of crispy leaves. Closing her eyes, she whirled around, her briefcase bouncing against the pumpkin-colored sleeve of her turtleneck as she stretched out her arms. She would have kicked her way across campus to the gym, sending leaves crackling into the air, had she not heard Doc's shout across the lawn.

"Irish! I just raked them leaves!"

She turned sheepishly, swiping at the leaves that clung to her orange tights. "Sorry, Doc — I just couldn't help myself," she said as he approached. "Besides, what are you doing raking leaves? I figured you'd save the menial tasks for your underlings."

"You figgered wrong. Rakin' leaves happens to be one of my fav'rite parts o' the job," he said crossly. "I wouldn't be givin' it away every time."

"Then I've done you a favor?"

He swished the rake at her. "Git, girl!"

Katie laughed. Dropping her briefcase on the grass, she grabbed the rake from his hand. "Here, let me do penance for my sins."

"You are an *imp*, you know that?"

"You sure it's not a *leprechaun* you're meanin'?"

Doc grabbed the rake back and tried to glare at her, but the twinkle in his eyes gave him away. He shook his finger at her. "Off with you now! Leave a poor man to his work!"

"But it's such a perfect day to play, Doc," Katie protested.

His eyes sparkled. "And it's fine to see you playin', Irish. You don't make the time for it enough any more."

"As if you do?"

He shooed her off with the rake. "Go on now!"

She didn't try to keep the bounce out of her step as she crossed campus, whistling a happy tune and swinging her briefcase. Rounding a corner, she sprinted up the steps of the old brick gymnasium. Moments later her briefcase lay open on a slatted wooden bench in the locker room. A pair of red nylon running shorts and a baggy white T-shirt lay beneath the stack of notebooks and musical scores.

Doc was right, she told herself as she changed into her running clothes. Since school had started, she hadn't taken much time for herself. It was a beautiful day for an easy run on the trail that circled the campus.

She brushed her auburn hair away from her face and secured it with a scrunchee. The curly ponytail made her

110

look like a schoolgirl, something she tried to avoid on campus, but she liked the feel of it swinging back and forth when she ran. Besides, she excused herself, she'd be off campus in a few minutes. And oh, did she mean to make the leaves fly!

At the top of the stairs, Katie paused for a moment, catching her breath at the beauty of the day. Then, closing her eyes, she lifted her face to the warm afternoon sun and the cool breeze blowing off the slough, breathing deeply of the crisp autumn air.

"Hey, Squirt!"

Her eyes flew open in surprise. "Keith!" Standing several steps below her, he was exactly at eye level and not two feet away, watching her with frank amusement.

She blinked, her surprise dissolving into pleasure. She'd forgotten the color of his eyes, a smoky green that made her think of the ocean after a storm. It had been a long time since they'd stood face to face like this. In fact, she wondered if they ever had — he'd always been tall for his age, and there was a justifiable reason he'd nicknamed her "Squirt."

She placed her hands on her hips and tilted her head to one side, her expression inscrutable. "What's got *you* in such a good humor?"

His dark brows rose on the inside corners — his trademark expression, it seemed. Somehow it gave him the look of a schoolboy hiding a frog in his back pocket. Or a donut. She grinned at the thought.

"You, Miss Katie-Bug, Lady-Bug, scuttling around campus like a beetle," Keith teased. "What are *you* grinning about?"

"Just thinking how much more fun school would have been if you hadn't gone off to kindergarten without me."

"You've never forgiven me, have you?" he asked mournfully.

"Don't be silly — you were my trailblazer! How would I ever have gotten through first grade without your tutoring? Or sixth grade without your hints on making Mrs. Gundlegrieg happy? Or high school French, except that you'd broken in Mademoiselle Auberge before I got there?" She hopped down a step and linked arms with him.

Dropping his backpack, he sat on the stairs and pulled her down next to him. He slipped her hand in the crook of his arm and cupped his own hand over it. Katie liked the comfortable intimacy of the unconscious gesture.

"Ah yes," he said, "the lovely Mademoiselle Auberge. *'Parlez-vous français, Mademoiselle Katie?'*"

"*'Oui, Monsieur Castle. Où est la bibliothèque?'*"

"You're going to the library in running shorts?"

She laughed. "No, that's all I can remember how to say. Except *'Tu n'aime pas la glace au chocolat.'*"

"*Au contraire*, I love chocolate ice cream," he answered. "As I recall, it's you who doesn't like chocolate. Positively un-American."

She sniffed. "At least I'm not a chocoholic, like some people I know."

"But…" He rustled around in his backpack with one hand and withdrew a small white bag. "I've never seen you turn down a donut." He handed her the bag. "I'm warning you, this is a bribe."

Katie raised her eyebrows, but took the sack without hesitation. "A bribe, huh? Just what is it you want?"

"Let me give you a little background first. Remember the carnivals we used to go to at Cully Center when we were kids?"

"You mean the Cully Community Fair? With the cake-walk and the clowns and the big stuffed-animal prizes? It was great fun! How come they don't have those anymore?"

"My boss in the city recreation department says some kids caused trouble a couple of years in a row — fighting and vandalism — so they canceled it. There hasn't been a Cully Community Fair for fifteen years."

"Don't tell me," Katie said. "You're bringing it back!"

Keith nodded. "Yep. Got permission last summer, as long as we came up with a good plan for crowd control. We're hiring security guards, but what I'm looking for now is a volunteer policeman or two." He grinned, rubbing the knuckles of the small freckled hand still nestled in the crook of his arm. "If anyone could keep order, it's you. How about it?"

"A policeman?" Katie poked him in the ribs with her elbow and looked at him indignantly. "You need a *policeman* and you think of *me?*"

"Not a *policeman* policeman," he hastened to assure her. "A member of the Clown Patrol. We decided to have clowns infiltrate the fair."

"Clowns," she said dubiously. "As in Bozo."

"Whatever. You'd come up with your own identity."

Katie pulled her arm away from his to look into the bag he'd given her. "Hmm. An old-fashioned with lemon icing."

She considered him for a moment, then grinned. "Just one thing." Jumping up, she struck an affected pose, her expression haughty. "If I take your bribe," she said pretentiously, "there won't be any of this Bozo business." She fluttered her eyelashes. "I'll be the most cultured, elegant clown you ever set eyes on."

He waggled his eyebrows. "I'm sure you will. Oh, hello,

Dr. Gillette," he added casually, rising from his position on the steps and extending his hand.

Katie spun around, her face growing hot as her hauteur dissolved in embarrassment.

"Excuse me for interrupting," Henry said coolly, briefly shaking Keith's hand. "Kate, I have an idea for the Christmas concert I wanted to go over with you. Are you free after your two o'clock tomorrow?"

She thought for a moment. "I think I have a student coming in after class. Is four o'clock too late? Or would you rather talk over lunch?"

Henry glanced at Keith. "You're sure you're free?"

Katie felt her face grow hotter. "I'm sure, Henry. I'll come by your office at noon, and we'll go from there."

He nodded shortly, wheeled around, and left as though a dog were nipping at his heels.

"I have the distinct impression Dr. Gillette doesn't care for me," Keith drawled.

"Nonsense," Katie snapped.

He arched a brow. "A little testy about the good professor, are we?"

Katie took a deep breath. "Sorry. It's just that — well, I don't know what's come over Henry lately."

Keith was silent for a moment. "It's none of my business, Katie, but what *is* Henry Gillette to you?"

Was it only curiosity, she wondered, or could he be a little jealous? She had to admit the idea pleased her. "What do you mean? He's a good friend and a valuable colleague. My mentor, in many ways."

"And?"

She turned her head, her eyes following Henry's retreating figure. "We dated for a couple of years," she finally admitted. "He asked me to marry him. I said no."

Keith whistled. "And you don't know what's come over him lately? Get a grip, Katie. He obviously still has feelings for you and sees me as a threat. Want me to explain our relationship to him?"

Katie turned her eyes back to Keith's, a tiny frown between her brows. "Explain our relationship? What would you say?"

"That I've known you forever. That we're just friends."

The sinking of her heart told her the very thing she didn't want to know: nothing had changed about her feelings for Keith. She dropped her eyes, afraid of what he might see. "I've told Henry what I need to tell him," she said tightly. "There's nothing else I have to explain to him. Or to you, either." With an effort, she forced a light note into her tone. "So tell me more about the Clown Patrol."

She listened with half an ear as Keith described the community fair his staff had planned. Profits would go to fund children's activities in the city. Most of the "carnies" would be high school volunteers. The Clown Patrol would include men and women who participated regularly in center activities and had a special concern for the Northeast neighborhoods served by Cully Center. Keith would be the Clown-in-Charge.

"All right," Katie said shortly. "It sounds fun."

Keith looked at her with a puzzled expression. "You don't sound overjoyed. Are you sure?"

"I said it sounds fun," she said brusquely. "I'll do it." Dropping to the ground, she stretched her bare legs out in front of her and reached for her toes. *Go away*, she telegraphed to him. *I need some space.*

He watched her for a moment in silence as she stretched out in preparation for her run. "Katie?"

She didn't look up. "Hm?"

"Forget Henry. He's not right for you."

Katie twisted her head to look up at Keith, who still stood over her. "Thank you so much," she said flatly.

"You're annoyed with me."

She sighed. "Castle — don't you need to be somewhere?"

He put up his hands and backed away. "I'm gone. See you around, Squirt."

Somehow the day had lost its bright edge for Katie. She started a trudging jog toward the path that ran for a mile along the Columbia Slough before it veered back north around the campus.

The brilliant leaves on the trees along the banks weren't beautiful at all, she thought pensively; they were dying. The flock of Canada geese flapping and honking overhead would have been a source of delight at any other time. Now their squawking seemed intolerable.

Why did she let Keith affect her this way? Not just now — always. Why had she wanted to crawl under a blanket and stay there for months when he'd discovered Toni? Why had she moped around for weeks after he'd gone away to college, cried for days when he'd left after his mother's funeral without saying goodbye, hurt for years when her mailbox remained empty? And why did she feel so glum at his off-hand comment that they were "just friends"? It wasn't news. He'd never given her a reason to believe they were anything more.

She rounded a bend, squinting from the bright reflection

of the late afternoon sun on the water. Twenty minutes ago she would have seen diamonds; now the reflection hurt her eyes. The real question, she thought, was why she couldn't let go of an old dream that had run its course.

Why, why, why, why, why? The word pounded rhythmically through her head as she picked up her pace along the path, the wood chips beneath the fallen leaves absorbing the impact of her feet against the ground. Running had long been her method of slowing down her brain, a way to clear and focus her mind when her thoughts were scattered or the details of her life seemed overwhelming.

Today was no exception. Slowly, as she fell into a steady rhythm, the tension drained from her body and the questions cleared from her mind.

A song played through her head, one of the first songs she'd written after learning to play the guitar as a teenager. A love song to the God who wanted her, that summer ten years ago when the world had seemed perfect:

> *Father, I lift my heart to you*
> *to let you shine forth*
> *your gentle love —*
> *Love that can build up bridges*
> *and tear down walls —*
> > *I lift my love.*

God, if it's loving and not just wanting that I feel for Keith, she prayed, *then teach me how to give it unselfishly.*

> *Father, I lift my mind to you*
> *to let you pour in*
> *your perfect wisdom —*
> *Thoughts that can reach to heaven*

and out to others —
    I lift my mind.

Teach me how to think your thoughts, she prayed.

Father, I lift my voice to you
to let you sing out
your perfect song —
The song that through endless ages
will still go on —
    I lift my song.

And teach me what to say.

Father, I lift my soul to you
to let you use me
within your plan —
The plan that before the earth was
became my meaning —
    I lift my soul.

I lift my soul, God, Katie prayed. *If you've brought Keith back into my life for some reason, make me open to it. Make me sensitive to you and to him.*

Then the words in her mind stopped altogether. She breathed and ran and breathed and ran, and the day become bright and dazzling once again.

Keith felt restless and distracted as he pushed his cart around the market later that afternoon. He'd been down the cereal aisle twice without remembering cereal was on his grocery list. Now he had to wait for a traffic jam to clear at the end of the aisle before he could get back to it.

He couldn't believe Katie had been so dismissive with him. It wasn't like any behavior he'd ever experienced with her. She was the one person he counted on to be there when he needed someone, to hear whatever he had to say, to listen not only with her ears but with her heart. He'd always felt free to be completely honest with Katie; they knew each other too well to pretend.

An impatient voice interrupted his musings. "Excuse me —"

He looked up to see that the aisle had finally cleared, but traffic was stacking up behind him. Mumbling an apology, he maneuvered his cart around a display of pumpkins and between the shelves stacked high with cans and boxes.

Maybe he should have kept his mouth shut about Henry Gillette, he thought. He really didn't know the whole story. Maybe she was still considering saying yes to the professor's marriage proposal. Maybe he'd been presumptuous, telling her that Henry wasn't right for her.

But darn it, it was true! He *knew* Katie, and Dr. Gillette was far too serious and…well, *pompous* was the word. Katie needed someone *playful*.

He pulled a box of Cheerios off the shelf and dropped it in his cart. *Come on, Castle,* he told himself. *You're not going to like* anyone *Katie gets involved with. No matter who it is, he's going to take her away from you.*

The thought brought him up short. Maybe it wasn't Henry who considered Keith a threat after all. Maybe it was the other way around.

Nine

꧁ ꧂

Keith pulled into the driveway of his neat, slate-blue bungalow on Northeast Alameda Street at dusk, just after six. The house was modest compared to most of the other large, stately homes along the Alameda Ridge, but the dark roof was new, the trim freshly painted, and the crisp white and brick-red around the windows and eaves called attention to the clean lines of the Arts-and-Craft architecture.

The yard was tidier than it had been that morning before he'd left for classes. The landscape service must have come by the house earlier in the day, cleaning out the spent annuals, cutting back the rhododendrons, weeding grasses from the rockery and flower beds. A good amount of color still remained, even this late in the season: yellow, rust, and burgundy chrysanthemums, the tiny bunched flowers of white and indigo alyssum, violet cosmos, a few pansies in deep purple and orange, the lavender-blue hydrangea against the house.

He slammed his door and walked around to the passenger seat to gather up the bags of groceries. The well-kept yard pleased him. Someday when he had more time, he'd like to do the yard work himself. One of the legacies Doc had passed on to him was a love for gardening. Every spring until Keith entered junior high and had "more important" things to do, Doc had set aside a patch of garden for him and one for Katie. He'd loved digging in the dirt, planting seeds and burying bulbs, watering, watching eagerly for the first green shoots to push through the soil.

Katie planted onions and tomatoes and salad greens, corn and beans and zucchini squash, but Keith planted flowers. Doc helped him choose varieties that would bloom in stages all the way through spring and summer to early autumn. Nothing had made him more proud than bringing his mother a bouquet of flowers he had grown himself, fresh every week all through the growing season.

He'd bought this house as much for his mother's memory as he had for himself, knowing she would have loved the flower beds and the succulents splayed across the rock garden, the friendly front porch, the back deck overlooking the city below. It was the kind of house in the kind of neighborhood she would have loved for herself but had never been able to afford, not even working two jobs.

It still angered Keith that life had been so hard for her, so much harder than he'd ever guessed — that she'd never really had a fair shake. How was it that people like Doc and his mother, whose lives had been so difficult, whose losses so great, were able to hold so strongly to their faith? How did they continue to see God as loving and giving? What made them believe, in the face of all evidence to the contrary, that somehow things would work out?

He slammed the door of the Montero as though he could

slam the door on his thoughts as well, but the questions persisted as he carried his two bags of groceries through the narrow walkway between the garage and the house and fumbled with the key at the side door into the kitchen pantry. The beep of the answering machine greeted him as he set the bags on the kitchen counter. He ignored it while he put the groceries away and retrieved the mail from the front hall, then punched the button as he leafed through the ads and bills.

"Kee, it's Doc." Keith was instantly alert. An undercurrent of anxiety shaded Doc's tone. "Ruggles didn't come in after dinner last night and he been missin' since. Danny's beside hisself. Could you come?"

He was out the door before the answering machine had rewound, grabbing his leather jacket off its hook on the way.

By the time he arrived on Dearborn Street it was dark. Katie's car was parked in the driveway behind Doc's pickup, and the porch light was on, but no one answered when Keith rang the doorbell. *They must be out looking for Ruggles,* Keith concluded, though it seemed ridiculous to think they'd find him in the dark. He went back to his truck and reached under the seat for the heavy-duty lantern he kept there for emergencies.

A moving light appeared around the corner as he shut the door, and then Doc, Katie, and Danny appeared in the halo of a streetlight, their faces drained and ghostlike. Doc's shoulders were slumped, and Danny walked with his head down, dragging his feet. Katie's face was creased with worry.

Keith hurried across the street to join them. "Doc, I'm sorry. I came as soon as I got your message."

Doc turned out his flashlight. "Thank you, Kee. Don't

know what more we can do, anyways. We been out callin' his name two hour now without any luck."

"Doc," Katie placed a hand lightly on his shoulder. "Why don't you take Danny inside and see if you can get him to eat? I'll fill Keith in and we'll come up with a plan."

"Don't want nothin' to eat," Danny muttered.

"He hasn't eaten since last night," she murmured to Keith.

Keith squatted down to the boy's level. "Danny, if something's happened to Ruggles you're going to need all your strength to help him. Eating is your job right now. Can you do that? For Ruggles?"

Turning away without answering, Danny trudged slowly up the sidewalk to the house, still looking at the ground. Doc shrugged helplessly at Keith and Katie, then followed his grandson.

"Did you call animal control?" Keith asked as the man and the boy disappeared into the house.

"Doc did. Before he called you and me."

"And your search — nothing?"

Katie leaned against her car in the driveway, her arms crossed tightly over her chest. She was still wearing the jumper and turtleneck she'd worn to school, with a nondescript corduroy jacket thrown over it. Apparently she too had come as soon as she'd received Doc's call.

"Nothing. But Doc told me out of Danny's hearing that Ruggles has been getting weaker. Yesterday after he disappeared, Doc discovered he'd had an accident on the rug." She rubbed one hand up and down her bulky sleeve as though to warm herself from a chill far deeper than the autumn air. "There was blood. Doc suspects he's crawled off somewhere to die."

Keith's heart sank. "Oh, no."

They were silent for a moment, preoccupied with their own memories. Keith's mother, because of her work schedule, had pets that needed very little care, but also didn't have much to offer a young boy: a very independent Siamese cat and a pair of angelfish. The Brannigans didn't have pets at all; Katie's mother was allergic to everything.

So Ruggles was something special. From their first encounter with the little long-haired dachshund, they had been enthralled. The puppy Doc had rescued from the pound had droopy ears and soulful, dark brown eyes, and a slow, sad, Eeyore kind of personality. When Katie first saw him flopped in front of the fireplace, unmoving, with his long body stretched out and his short legs tucked under him and his silky red coat shining in the firelight, she'd exclaimed, "He looks like a rug!" And Ruggles he had been ever since.

Keith leaned heavily against the car next to Katie. "If you were a sick old dog, where would you go?"

"I don't know. It rained last night. Somewhere warm and dry."

They looked at each other, then ran at the same time for Doc's front porch. Keith turned on the lantern and shined the bright beam across the latticework at its base. At one end, the boards had loosened and a gaping hole led beneath the veranda. Keith knelt down and swept the light from side to side as Katie peered through the lattice.

"There!" she said. "That pile of rags against the foundation."

Keith brought the light around again. The pile of rags whimpered weakly.

124

Instantly Keith was on his stomach wriggling through the hole. "There's a blanket under the backseat of my truck," he called over his shoulder. "Get Doc and Danny. We're going to the vet."

Twenty minutes later they were racing through the door of the emergency veterinary clinic in northwest Portland with Ruggles slung between Doc and Keith in a wool army blanket. Keith's nose twitched at the pungent hospital smell of antiseptic and medicine.

Doc insisted his grandson wait in the reception area with Keith and Katie while he accompanied the veterinarian to the examining room. He stood next to the metal table, answering the vet's questions while she gently poked and prodded. When she finished her examination, she stroked the dog's fur softly and shook her head.

"I'm sorry. His kidneys have failed. He has a few days at most, maybe only a few hours."

"Is he in pain?"

"Some."

"What can we do?"

"I can give him an injection," she said gently.

"Put him to sleep?"

She nodded. Doc just looked at her, his eyes wet. She handed him a Kleenex and suggested, "Or you can take him home and make him as comfortable as possible. I can give him something to make him rest easier."

Katie knew as soon as she saw Doc's face that it was the end. He sat down next to her and pulled his grandson into his lap. "We're takin' 'im home," he told the boy quietly. "There's nothin' the vet can do to give 'im more time."

Danny turned his face into Doc's shirt and cried as if his

heart would break. Keith ran his fingers nervously through his hair, feeling suddenly claustrophobic in the small waiting room. Once again, as they had the day of their first meeting, Danny's tears were drawing his own tears to the surface, tapping into his own sorrow. The anguish that swept through his heart was far more than grief for Ruggles's dying. Keith had so much to grieve for. So much had been taken away.

With a tremendous effort, he closed the door in his mind against the wave of emotion that threatened to engulf him. "I'll get Ruggles," he said gruffly, rising from his chair without looking at anyone. "Katie, take Doc and Danny home. I'll call you for a ride later."

"Excuse me?"

Keith kept on walking.

"Keith!" She followed him into the examining room, angry. "Danny needs to be with him. What if Ruggles dies on the way home?"

When he finally looked at her, the heartbreak in his eyes stopped her short. "That dog is about the only friend Danny has," she said quietly. "At least take him with you."

He acknowledged her plea with a brief nod, then carefully picked up Ruggles. Katie held the door and followed him through. As they reentered the waiting room, Doc looked up and released his hold on Danny.

"Let's go home, Danny Boy," he said gently. Then, hesitantly, he added, "Kee and Irish, will you stay with us awhile?"

Katie carried the tray of mugs into Doc's living room and set it on the coffee table in front of the sofa, where Ruggles lay quietly across Danny's lap. "Hot cocoa for you, Danny," she said, picking up a mug with a cloud of whipped cream on top and setting it on the end table where the boy could more easily reach it. He didn't look up, but continued stroking Ruggles's fur in a steady rhythm, almost as if in a hypnotic trance.

"Strong coffee for the rest of us," she added, handing full mugs to Doc, who shared the couch with his grandson, and Keith, slumped in a chair across the room.

The aroma of the coffee seemed to pull Keith together. He moved the overstuffed chair closer to the sofa and patted the chair's wide upholstered arm, silently inviting Katie to sit next to him. She complied, slipping out of her loafers and curling one leg beneath her as she balanced on the arm.

Keith tugged once at the toe of her pumpkin-colored tights. "Remember how Ruggles used to love to take off our socks?" he asked, smiling a little.

Katie nodded. "I'm surprised he never took off our toes!"

"Your grandpa taught him that trick so well he tried it on everyone, Danny," Keith said, trying to bring the boy into the conversation. "My mom was sitting on the steps out in front of our house one time in her stocking feet, scratching Ruggles's head while she talked to me and Katie. All of a sudden that dog grabbed hold of the toe of her nylon in his teeth and pulled so hard he jerked her foot off the step. He lost his balance and went tumbling down the stairs!"

Danny looked up anxiously. "Did he get hurt?"

"Nah, just bruised his pride a little. Ruined Mama's nylons. She wasn't very happy!"

"I might of taught 'im to take off my socks, but I never taught 'im how to fold 'em," Doc said, reaching a hand over to run it along Ruggles's furry tail. "He learned that all on his own. He's a smart 'un, Ruggles is."

The little dachshund seemed to know they were talking about him. He didn't move his head from Danny's lap, but his tail waved weakly and his brown eyes shifted from one person to another as they talked.

Katie wrapped her fingers around the warm coffee mug. "Did you ever see him fold a sock, Danny?" she asked. He shrugged and looked down, as though uninterested.

"Well," she continued, "the first time I ever saw him do it...."

For the next hour Katie, Keith, and Doc told story after story of their adventures with Ruggles. Keith had just reminded Katie of a fishing trip they'd taken together when Danny suddenly interrupted, his voice frightened.

"Grumpy! Is he just sleepin'?"

Doc reached over and laid his hand on Ruggles's side. "You see that risin' and fallin', Danny Boy? That's his breathin'. When he stops that, he'll be gone. But don't you worry, it'll be an easy goin' for 'im. The vet's made sure of it. And I wants you to know, before he goes, that he's lived a long life, an' a good 'un. Wouldn't you say, Kee? Irish?"

"He was well-loved," Keith agreed.

"And he knew how to give love back," Katie added. "That's the best you could say about anyone's life."

"I think it's proper we be tellin' stories 'bout Ruggles bringin' good things to us," Doc added. "Like fun, an' laughin'." He gently stroked the dog's fur.

After a moment he said to Keith and Katie, "Danny and Ruggles has had their adventures, too. That dog never did get to likin' the water, but Danny loved it — mud puddles 'specially. An' you knows we got plenty o' them around! Well, Danny was leanin' over a big ol' puddle too far, droppin' rocks in — he was four, mebbe — an' he falls headfirst right in! I seen it from the window an' come rushin' from the house, but by the time I gets there, Ruggles has 'im by the seat of the pants, haulin 'im out. Then he let 'im go and set to howlin' like a banshee!"

Danny finally looked up, his eyes round. "Did he save me, Grumpy?"

"He might of. I was there pretty quick, but what if I hadn't been lookin' out the window?"

Danny lifted Ruggles to his chest and held him close. "He's the best dog in the whole world," he said solemnly. "He's my best friend ever."

Ruggles let out a sigh and stopped breathing.

Ten

The sun was barely up when Katie pulled into the parking lot of Cully Center the Saturday of the community fair. Already the site was buzzing with activity as Keith's staff and a crew of volunteers set up for the day-long event. The sounds of hammering and good-natured banter reached Katie as she stepped from her car. A group of jean-clad men struggled with the poles and canopies of a series of striped pavilions laid out on the lawn, and a trio of teenagers stretched to hang a large banner across the front of the building.

Keith stood near the front entrance of the center, jotting something on a clipboard as he talked to a bronzed, muscular young man wearing a City Parks sweatshirt. The man glanced at Katie as she approached, then lifted a hand, smiling warmly. "Come to help set up?" he called.

When Keith turned and saw her, his face lit up. "Hi, Katie!"

"So *this* is Kate," the other man said, looking her over from head to toe as she approached. Katie looked at Keith, perplexed by the man's attention.

Keith's face reddened as their gaze held for an instant. Clearing his throat as he shifted his eyes away, he made the introductions: "Katie, Rito Martinez, my right-hand man. Rito, Kate Brannigan."

"Exactly what I had pictured," Rito said, grinning. Seeing Katie's puzzled frown, he added, "Don't worry, Kate." He held out his hand. "The boss-man has only good things to say about you."

Katie's eyes widened. So Keith talked about her at work. "What has he told you?" she asked curiously.

Keith grabbed her elbow and steered her toward the front door. "No time for chitchat," he said brusquely. "I need you inside."

In the gymnasium several groups of volunteers, both adults and teenagers, were setting up carnival booths: bottles for a ring toss, balloons for throwing darts, beanbags to throw into the large cutout mouth of a wooden clown face, and other tests of coordination. A tiny Asian girl dressed in jeans and a flannel shirt trotted from booth to booth, gesturing wildly, her shiny black hair bobbing around her shoulders as she moved.

"One of my part-timers, Debi Chang," Keith told Katie. "She's involved in theater production at her college and jumped at the chance to stage the carnival. She'll be doing the face painting for the Clown Patrol as well." Placing a hand at the small of Katie's back, he guided her across the gym. "Debi's a real firecracker — reminds me of you," he teased.

The girl glanced up, waved, and hurried toward them, bouncing with enthusiasm. Katie shook her head, smiling.

"A nice thought," she said to Keith, "but I'm afraid I haven't had that kind of energy since I was in grade school."

"Hey, Chief!" The girl gave him a high five, then pushed her wire-rim glasses higher on her nose. "How's it goin'?"

Without waiting for an answer she thrust a hand at Katie. "Hi, I'm Debi. You must be Kate. We've heard a lot about you. Can't wait to find out if it's true."

"Keith!" Katie wailed. "What have you been telling these people?"

Debi laughed. "You *are* Kate, right? Don't want to get him into trouble. But we have to *drag* this kind of stuff out of him. You'd think he was embarrassed." She grinned at Keith. "No need, Chief, we approve. You've got the green light from me and Rito." She gave him the thumbs-up sign.

"Can it, Debi," Keith said between his teeth, his face red. "I should know better than to tell you *anything* about my personal life."

"Hey — I'm just happy you've got one! We've been sort of worried about him," she added to Katie. Then her attention was back on Keith. "When's Fast Eddie setting up the barbecue grills?"

"Don't you worry about Fast Eddie. When it's time for ribs, I'll let you know."

She raised her eyebrows at his irritated tone, then shrugged. "All right then. Catch you later!" She was off like a whirlwind.

"Whew!" Katie said, both hands on her head as if to keep it from flying after Debi. "I see what you mean!" She looked at Keith from the corner of an eye. "So just what have you been saying about me?"

He snorted and waved a hand dismissively. "It wouldn't

matter what I'd said — Debi would make it whatever she wanted! Just so you know, between her and Rito, they've got us married off."

Katie sputtered.

"I know," he agreed, rolling his eyes. "But they won't listen to me."

He led her to the largest of the center's meeting rooms, where a pair of volunteers was setting up tables for the craft fair. "This area could be a bottleneck," he told the three of them, his manner suddenly brisk and businesslike. "We need the tables arranged somehow to keep traffic flowing as efficiently as possible."

Struggling to adjust to his sudden change of mood, Katie glanced around the room, noticing where the two exits were located. "I think we can do that."

"Good." He leafed through the papers on his clipboard and pulled one out, explaining what else needed to be done before the fair opened at noon. "I'll be back to check on you before lunch."

Katie's mouth watered at the mention of lunch. Fast Eddie's Famous Ribs was closing its doors for the day, and Eddie was setting up his barbecue grills outside Cully Center. Eddie and Willie Mae Cornelius's hole-in-the-wall restaurant had been a Northeast Portland fixture for thirty years, and they'd catered the Cully Community Fair as far back as Katie could remember. In addition to pledging a percentage of today's profits to help fund children's programs in the city, the two had promised to serve lunch to Keith's volunteers and staff before the fair officially opened at noon. Eddie's Blue Mountain smokey spareribs would sell as fast as he could cook them, with Willie Mae's corn on the cob, buttermilk biscuits, and sweet potato pie equal draws.

By the time Keith returned, the crafters' room had been transformed. Quilts, wall hangings, and vine wreaths decorated the walls, and the tables were laden with handmade articles of every imaginable sort, much of it ethnic in flavor: dolls, toys, candles, ceramics, wearable art, jewelry. The artists who had finished setting up their displays were wandering about the room, admiring each other's craftsmanship.

Katie followed Keith to the gym while he gave his stamp of approval to the work there and released the volunteers for lunch. A local radio station had set up a large stage with karaoke equipment at one end of the gym. The basket at the opposite end remained open for a free-throw challenge, and a dozen colorful booths formed a square in the center of the remaining space. The tables inside the square were crowded with prizes, from plastic rings and chocolate coins to stuffed animals and T-shirts, donated by retail businesses from all over the city. Debi had disappeared — doing faces for the first shift of clowns, Keith told Katie.

The lawn outside the center had been transformed as well. Several red-and-white-striped pavilions protected the picnic tables beneath them from the sporadic rain forecast for the day. Strings of white twinkle-lights bordered the poles and awnings.

Katie's nose twitched at the sweet, smoky aroma rising from the row of barrel-topped barbecues lining the sidewalk. Within a few minutes, she and Keith were sitting at a table beneath a canopy, and the delicious smell was rising from their loaded plates.

Katie gingerly picked up a sparerib slathered in sauce. "Everything ready to go?" she asked.

"Can't think of anything else that needs to be done," he said, rolling his corn in a slab of butter. "That doesn't necessarily mean everything's ready."

She laughed. "Knowing you, it does! The center looks great, Keith. You should be proud."

"I'm proud of my staff and volunteers."

They settled into some serious eating, not talking much for the next few minutes. The down-home cooking was delicious.

Keith crowned the heap of bones piled on his plate with one last sparerib. "D'you know if Doc's bringing Danny by today?" he asked.

Katie shook her head. "I meant to call Doc last night, but the time got away from me. Want me to try him before I leave?"

"Would you? I'm afraid I won't have an extra minute. And see how Debi's doing with the clowns while you're in the office."

A quartet of clowns was filing out of the office as Katie entered the building. A slight figure dressed in a Harlequin-patterned peasant's shirt and trousers peered at her through a black half-mask. Another figure, made up like a classic Bozo, including a tufted ring of bright orange hair around a bare white skull, pumped her hand. Rito, she guessed. He grabbed her around the waist, swung her around, and deposited her, laughing, in front of the office door.

Debi was straightening her collection of wigs, noses, and face paints when Katie walked in. "Hi, Kate! Sorry, you'll have to wait. There's a plate of ribs out there with my name on it —"

"It's okay," Katie interrupted. "I just came in to use the

phone, Deb. I'll be back this afternoon for you to do my face." She reached for the telephone and dialed. "By the way — you're really good!"

Debi flashed a smile and tossed her hair back from her face. "Thanks! See you!" Then she was gone.

Doc sounded resigned when Katie asked if he was planning to bring Danny to the fair. "Don't think so," he said. "I've tried to talk 'im into it, but he says he just don't care about goin'."

Katie commiserated. "That's too bad. It would probably be a good distraction — the carnival especially."

"He's awful sad these days," Doc said, his voice heavy.

"Do you think he'd like to see Keith and me in our costumes?" Katie asked. "Maybe we could come by later this afternoon."

"He hasn't much wanted to see folks lately, but..." He hesitated. "Mebbe if I told 'im you two was comin' by all dressed up like clowns for the carnival. Mebbe you'd have an easier time talkin' 'im into goin' than I've had. Nothin' seems to be workin'."

"I'm sorry, Doc. I wish there was more I could do."

"Lovin' 'im is the best any of us can do, Irish." He was silent for a moment, as though considering. "Well, the two of you might come on by an' try your luck with 'im. Can't hurt," he finally said.

When she tracked down Keith to tell him the plan, he hesitated, then shook his head regretfully. "I just can't spare the time, Katie."

"Can too," a voice behind her said. She turned to find Bozo shaking his finger at Keith. "In the middle of an eighteen-hour day, you can take an hour," Rito insisted behind his large painted grin. "You'd think he didn't trust us," he added to Katie, pretending injury.

Keith laughed. "Okay, okay! You can tell how much authority *I* have around here!"

Katie stepped to the office window at the center early that evening, tuning out the lighthearted banter between Keith and Debi behind her. She caught her breath. In the blue-violet twilight outside, the moon was a huge golden globe rising like a ball on a string. A few wispy clouds, all that was left of the earlier overcast, chased across its luminous surface. The lights on the pavilions twinkled like a thousand fireflies. A young couple held hands as they strolled across the court-yard, and Katie didn't look away when they stopped to share a kiss. She sighed. It was a night made for romance.

Then she caught sight of her reflection in the glass and grinned. A bright red cupid's bow grinned back. *And don't you look the part, Lady Katie,* she said to herself.

"Katie-Bug!" Keith had said with delight when he'd seen her.

"That's *Lady* Katie," she'd told him coquettishly, striking a pose and batting her eyelashes.

Lady Katie, Queen of Clowns. Debi had painted her face white, heavily rouged her cheeks, exaggerated her lips, arched her brows in an expression of permanent surprise, added false eyelashes preposterous in their thickness and length. Her curly ponytail, sprayed with gold glitter, spouted like a fountain of flame from the top of her head.

The pieces of her costume had been garnered from garage sales and thrift stores the previous weekend: an oversized,

137

shapeless dress in pink chiffon worn with black fingerless gloves, black-and-white striped stockings, and a pair of very large black hightop canvas shoes. Unmatched rhinestone earrings dangled from her ears, and half a dozen strands of paste "jewels" and plastic "pearls" hung around her neck.

Katie batted her long lashes at the image in the window, then turned around to see how Keith's transformation was progressing.

"Hey, Chief, you've *got* to sit still," Debi was complaining. "Now let me see…." She took his chin in her hand and moved his head from side to side, nodding in satisfaction. "Perfect!"

Keith stood and looked at Katie for confirmation. She grinned and nodded at the large, disheveled hobo. He wore tails and black tie, very worn and wrinkled. His face, like hers, was painted white, but he sported a bulbous red nose, and a tear descended from the corner of one black-rimmed eye. Although his wide red mouth was turned down in a sad expression, when he saw her approving nod his eyes squinted into a smile that belied his melancholy air. He bowed deeply, then took her arm.

"A stunning pair," Debi said, reaching to pat herself on the back. "Now get out of here, would you?" She waved them away.

Ten minutes later they were pulling into Doc's driveway on Dearborn Street. "Danny hasn't been to Cully Center since the scrap he had with that bully at day camp," Keith commented as he helped Katie out of the Montero. "I wonder if he might be afraid to come to the fair."

Katie looked at him in surprise. She wouldn't have made the connection. "That was a long time ago," she said doubtfully.

"True." He took her elbow as they climbed the stairs. "I know he's still feeling sad about Ruggles, too."

"Danny!" Doc called as he let them in a moment later. "Come see who's here! My, but don't you look like a couple o' Joeys," he added. "Set yourselves in that chair there, like you was settin' t'other night, and I'll find my camera. This deserves commemoratin'."

Keith settled into the overstuffed chair and Katie perched on the arm. "I like being taller than you," she announced, looking down her nose at him.

"Forget that!" Before she knew what he was doing, he'd grabbed her around the waist and pulled her into his lap. She screeched and flailed her arms and legs. "There," he said smugly. "Right at eye level."

She stopped flinging her arms around and turned her head toward him. The breath caught in her throat as she grew still. He seemed to be holding his breath as well. Their faces were only inches apart, too close to notice the face paint and the exaggerated expressions, too close to notice anything but each other's eyes. Keith tightened his hold at her waist. His gaze flickered to her lips, then back to her warm brown eyes.

"You guys look funny."

"Danny," Keith said, his breath rushing out in a sigh that tickled her ear.

Katie twisted in Keith's lap, embarrassed, just as a flash went off. Danny stood in the doorway, barefoot, dressed in his jeans and a white sweatshirt, and Doc stood behind him with his camera to his eye.

"We're *supposed* to look funny," Keith said to Danny in a matter-of-fact voice, lifting Katie easily from his lap back to the arm of the chair. "We're clowns." He didn't seem a bit flustered. Katie, on the other hand, felt completely discomposed. "You ready for a night of fun at the carnival?" he added.

"I'm not goin'," Danny said.

"Why not?"

"Don't wanna."

"Well, would you 'wanna' have your picture taken with the glamorous Lady Katie and her lackey?"

"What's *lackey?*" Danny asked, curious in spite of himself.

"That means he's my servant, Danny," Katie told him. "Here to do my every bidding."

"You got *that* right," Keith muttered. "Since I was three years old!" Katie couldn't tell if he was serious or not behind his face paint.

"Go on, Danny," Doc urged his grandson. "Let me get your picture with Kee an' Irish."

The boy considered them for a moment, his blue eyes serious, then nodded and walked over to the chair. Keith lifted him onto his lap and settled him in the crook of his arm.

"Come here, Katie-Bug." He reached his other arm around her shoulders and pulled her toward him.

"Just right!" Doc said, snapping the picture. "One more, for good measure…"

Danny scrambled off Keith's lap after the second flash, as Katie pulled away from Keith. The boy climbed up on the sofa across from them, his expression solemn, and sat on the edge of the cushion with his legs dangling, his ankles crossed, and his hands folded in his lap. "Grumpy says you're gonna be clowns at the carnival."

"That's right, Danny," Katie said brightly.

"Are there gonna be big kids there?"

"Some," Keith acknowledged. He hesitated, then added, "Are you scared of the big kids, Danny?"

Silence.

"There won't be any problems like you had with Jason," Keith told him gently. "That's why we have the Clown Patrol."

Danny looked at his lap. "Some big kids are mean."

So Keith had been right, Katie thought.

"That's true, Danny." Keith cocked his head to one side, not taking his eyes from the boy's pale face. "But *I'm* the clown in charge today. I'm taking special care of the little kids."

The boy regarded him silently.

"If you decide to come, I'll take special care of you."

Doc cleared his throat. "We'll talk about it, Kee. Meantime, would you like a cup o' hot cider before you go? I've got a pot steamin'."

Keith shook his head. "Thanks, Doc, but we need to get back. A couple of clowns are waiting for us to take over. Talk to you later, okay? Danny..." He reached down and tousled the boy's hair. "Take care, Sport. You don't have to be scared of anything."

They were both quiet on the short drive back to Cully Center. Katie was still discomfited by the brief, unexpected moments in Keith's arms. Only a couple weeks ago he'd made a point of telling her they were just friends, but the look in his eyes in those few moments tonight had said something else, hadn't it?

When he helped her down from the Montero, his hands seemed to linger at her waist for a moment before he grabbed her hand and led her through the crowd to the front door of the center. His hand grasping hers felt slightly dangerous, as if things had changed between them in some subtle, inexplicable way. She pulled her hand away and tugged at the sheer sleeves of her costume with the fingerless gloves. He glanced over his shoulder and then away again. Was it just the light, or was he having trouble meeting her eyes?

She tried to shake off her discomposure as she settled into the job of policing the crowd in the gymnasium, but Keith had stationed himself in the gym as well, and she was acutely aware of his presence.

Early in the evening the crowd was mostly young parents with children. More than once Katie saw Keith pick up a child to help him throw a pebble in a dish or knock over a pyramid of wooden blocks with a softball. The little ones never seemed to shy away from him. She wondered if it was the clown they trusted or if they sensed something intrinsically trustworthy in Keith himself.

As the evening wore on, the carnival attracted more and more teenagers, the boys cocky as they demonstrated their prowess and the girls ready to squeal and cheer on cue. Keith's interactions with them, as well as with his teenaged volunteers and his employees, were cheerful and positive; he was obviously well liked and well respected.

The gym was noisy and crowded, but people were in good spirits, and Katie had little to do in the way of policing. Still, by the time the doors finally closed and the last person had gone, she was exhausted. Slumping in a chair along the wall, she closed her eyes and rolled her head in a circle, trying to relax the tight muscles in her neck. *Too bad Doc and Danny hadn't made it to the carnival,* she thought.

She jumped as a pair of hands touched her shoulders and began a gentle massage. "Did I wear you out, Lady Katie?"

She twisted in the chair, shrugging away from his touch. "I am a little tired....."

"Me, too. Thanks for your help tonight, Katie." Keith took her hands in his and pulled her up from the chair. "This morning, too. I really appreciate it."

She pulled her hands away. "You know me — I'll do anything for a slab of spareribs and a slice of sweet potato pie," she said lightly.

He walked her to her car a few minutes later. She leaned against the door of the Civic and looked up at him in the spectral light of the full moon, but the moment her eyes found his, she glanced away again, aware once more of the sense of imminent danger in his gaze.

"You're great with kids," she said after a moment's silence.

"Kids are great," he answered simply, leaning next to her against the car. "I didn't know how great till I started working at Cully Center. I only took the job because I didn't know what to do with myself when I got back from Japan, and Chappie knew someone who knew someone.... You know how that goes."

She rubbed her hands up and down her arms. The sheer sleeves of her costume weren't nearly warm enough for a late October night, but she was reluctant to say goodbye just yet. "Will you stay there for a while?"

"Only till I'm through with school. I decided last week I want to be a teacher. Grade school. What d'you think?"

"Keith, that's wonderful!" A memory flashed through her mind: five-year-old Keith standing in front of the chalkboard her mom had set up in the front porch, spelling out her name. "I think we need more male elementary teachers — so many kids don't have dads around these days."

Keith stood away from the car. "Yeah. I know." His voice was ineffably sad.

"Oh, Keith…" Katie reached out and gave him a spontaneous hug. "I had fun today," she said. "Thanks for sharing your life with me."

"How could I not? We've been sharing our lives so long." He pulled away, holding her at arm's length. His eyes met hers for an instant before they both glanced away. "Thanks again for your help with the fair."

He pulled her close once more and kissed the top of her head. "You're very dear to me, Katie," she heard him say.

Just for an instant she relaxed in his embrace, smiling into his tattered costume.

You're very dear to me. Katie dipped her fingers in the jar of cold cream Debi had loaned her to remove the heavy theatrical makeup. She closed her eyes and rubbed the cream in circular motions over her cheeks, her slow movements almost hypnotic.

It doesn't mean anything, she told herself. *It's the same thing you told Henry.* Still, that look in his eyes…

When she crawled into bed, a sheet of paper lay on her desk, the ink fresh:

Crazy eyes,

Eyes that dare stand still
only a moment
(mine or yours, I cannot tell —
perhaps both)

Not knowing apart
  if I want
  you want
    eyes to stand still together…

Too much said
  might prove embarrassing
  unless alone in the night
    and even then —

If only your eyes (or mine)
  would stand still
  more than a moment
    to know.

Eleven

᭯᭯

The loud electronic buzz of Keith's alarm woke him from a fitful sleep the morning of November 3. He must have set the alarm out of habit; he'd scheduled himself a day off and had intended to sleep in.

Groaning, he fumbled to hit the button on the clock and succeeded only in knocking it off the nightstand. It kept droning. He groaned again and pulled the pillow over his head, but he couldn't block out the buzz. Finally he flung the pillow aside and struggled against the snarled bedclothes to pull himself upright.

The sheets and blankets seemed to tighten around him like a snare, and for a brief moment he felt unaccountably panicked, and then simply angry. When he got himself untangled, he leaned over the edge of the bed, savagely punched off the alarm, and banged the clock down on the nightstand.

He sat for a moment on the edge of the mattress, slumped over with his head in his hands. He was so exhausted he might as well not have slept. His head felt too heavy for his neck to hold up; his whole body felt heavy, as if a giant, invisible weight were pressing him down.

Why did it feel so unimportant to get up this morning? He gathered the blankets and crawled beneath them again, covering his head. *No reason at all to get out of bed,* he thought glumly.

Curled on his side, he wrapped his arms around his pillow and closed his eyes, but now every little sound seemed magnified a hundred times: a car door slamming and an engine turning over as one of his neighbors left for work; the firing of the gas heater in the hallway when the thermostat kicked on, and then the whir of the fan; the rain against the roof and the water draining in a steady stream from the eaves outside his window.

There was something about rain that reminded Keith of his mother. During his childhood, on rainy days when she was home, she set aside her chores and made him feel like the most important person in the world. They were the best of companions — finger painting, reading story books, baking cookies...

He remembered abruptly why he'd given himself the day off. Today would have been Christine Castle's forty-fifth birthday.

A year ago, he would have scheduled himself for a double shift so he'd have been too busy to think about his mother or feel the emotions those thoughts brought up. But he'd returned to Portland precisely because keeping himself busy hadn't worked. After more than five years of running away from his grief, of pouring his energies into what he thought was his dream career, he didn't feel any closer to resolution or happiness than he had the night his mother died — the night he'd discovered her horrible secret.

Chappie had been there that night, at Christine's request, solid and comforting for both of them as Keith kept vigil by her hospital bed. Comforting until Keith realized his mother had called the minister to her bedside for one purpose: to get ready to die. More specifically, to confess the lie she'd lived for over twenty years.

It was Chappie's knowledge of his mother's secret, not his position as a minister in the church, that made him the one Keith sought out for counsel on his return. In fact, in Keith's mind Chappie's connection with the church had been a strike against him. No, that wasn't quite right — his connection with *God* had been a strike against him. If there was anything Keith knew about his feelings, he knew how angry he was at God.

Still, Chappie had been there the night his mother spilled her secret. He was the only other person on earth who knew. The thought of having to recount his story to someone else in order to help him figure out how to be happy again seemed unbearable. Answering Chappie's gentle, perceptive questions was hard enough.

Surprisingly, Chappie hadn't censured him for his anger at God, only quietly asked him to talk about it. "What is it you believe about God that makes you hold *him* responsible for your pain?" he asked after Keith had expressed his feelings quite volubly. "And for your mother's pain as well? How is it that God has disappointed you?"

He'd looked at Chappie incredulously. *"How has he disappointed me? He's God! He's all-powerful — he can do anything — and he chose not to!"*

The minister considered him silently for a moment.

"Have you told him how angry you are?" he finally asked.

Keith looked at Chappie as if he were crazy. "You can't talk to God that way!"

"Who says?"

"You just can't!"

Then the minister had posed a seemingly unrelated question: "Why do you think God created humankind, Keith?"

"I don't know," he answered impatiently. "Because he was lonely, you used to tell us."

Chappie nodded. "Here's what I believe: God took great pleasure in creating the universe. When he'd finished with it, he saw what he'd created, and it was very good. But something was missing: someone to share it with. Someone who, like him, could take pleasure in his creation. Someone capable of thinking and feeling. And someone willing to be involved in an ongoing relationship with him. God created us in his image so he could experience communion with beings like himself."

Keith had found he was listening in spite of himself. "Hasn't worked out so well for him, has it?" he said cynically.

"You could make a case for that. Certainly there are times he must be infuriated with us, and times he weeps over us as well. But the fact is, sorrow and anger don't happen outside of relationship. The reason God gets angry at us or feels sad for us is because he loves us."

Keith shook his head. "You're losing me."

Chappie leaned forward, his expression intent. "If we choose to be engaged in the process of knowing and being known — the real stuff of true relationship — sorrow and anger will be part of our experience. Just as it's part of God's experience. God knew when he made us it wouldn't always be easy. He —"

"So what's the point, Chappie?" Keith interrupted. "Why did he bother?"

"What do you think?"

"I'm asking you."

"Don't you think," the minister said slowly, "there might be times God truly delights in us?"

"I can't imagine."

"I can," Chappie countered. "What I can't imagine is God giving *me* the capacity to delight in people without having the same capacity himself. I think God finds incredible joy in his relationships with us. In our creativity and our capacity for love, in our response to him."

Keith had looked at him without answering.

"God thought it was worth the risk, Keith. He took the same risk we take in all our relationships: we don't experience the richness without the risk of pain. You've spent five years running away. Maybe it's time to engage again." He paused, then added, "My best advice is to tell God what you think of him."

It was worth a try, Keith had decided. At first he'd been ill at ease expressing his anger directly to God, but the uneasiness faded over the weeks. God hadn't struck him with a bolt of lightning.

Besides, it seemed to be working. He was still angry — he couldn't see how he'd ever be able to give that up — but at least the feelings had lost some of their power. He'd continued to see Chappie once a month, and often found his insights clear and helpful.

Not yesterday, however. Keith felt the blood rush to his face as he remembered. This time Chappie was way off. What did he really know, anyway? How could he possibly understand?

Keith's indignation gave him enough energy to drag himself out of bed. He pulled on an old pair of sweatpants, a ragged T-shirt, and a white sweatshirt with the Cully Center logo on the front. Moving around the kitchen like an automaton, he fixed himself a couple of slices of toast and a mug of black coffee, then stood at the kitchen sink staring out the window over downtown. Clouds sat over the city like a gray wolf on its haunches. The weather suited his mood.

Pulling a hooded raincoat over his sweats, he took a pair of scissors into the yard to see if any late season flowers were still blooming. Not much color was left, but he found a trio of autumn chrysanthemums and one small, faded blue hydrangea still fresh.

The cemetery where his mother's ashes were interred was less than a mile away. With the flowers tucked in a plastic grocery bag along with several sprays of colored leaves, he set out on foot, his hood pulled over his head. It was still drizzling, but he hoped the exercise might help revive his energy. He walked briskly, his back hunched against the rain as he splashed through the puddles on the uneven sidewalk.

The cemetery was hidden from the city street behind a tall hedge. He remembered how overwhelmed he'd felt the first time he'd walked through the front entrance and seen tombstones stretching into the distance. It had been springtime then, early spring, not long after his birthday. The trees had been bursting with a brilliant translucent green that fairly shouted new life and new beginnings, in strange contrast to the cold marble grave markers below.

Today a few splotches of orange and burnt umber from the scattered oak and maple trees stood out against the somber gray-green of cedar, pine, and fir. The birches, white trunks peeling, had already lost most of their yellow leaves. Their gray branches reached into the sky like arms raised in supplication. *An altogether more suitable setting for the dead,* Keith thought grimly.

He followed a winding road between two rows of holly trees, trimmed appropriately like umbrellas, and kept to the right when the road forked, shuffling through the wet, matted leaves on the pavement.

On one side of the road were a few ornate family crypts and endless rows of marble gravestones. Flowers and potted plants stood here and there, testimonies to the love someone still felt for the dead. He stopped to read a marker over a double grave: "Beloved Husband," "Beloved Wife." Buried at each other's side. His mother had never had the chance to be beloved by a husband, Keith mused, never had a man to adore her during life and grieve over her death.

On the other side of the road was a field so overgrown he almost missed the flat gravestones hiding in the grass. No beautiful trees shaded the graves here; no flowers symbolized the continued memory of those who were buried beneath the soil. Keith stepped off the road to wander between the markers and saw that many of them dated to the late nineteenth century. In another fifty years would the entire cemetery look like this? Would everyone who remembered the dead be gone as well?

He continued to follow the road past a series of large mausoleums, his footsteps getting slower as he approached the structure in the farthest corner of the cemetery. Here were the more recent graves, many of them decorated with elaborate floral arrangements and some of them with cards and notes taped to the plaques: "Rosalie, I miss you every day. Your loving husband, Frank." "Daddy, you'll always live in my heart. Jeannie."

His mother's ashes rested in a crypt in a protected corner of the mausoleum, roofed over but open to the outdoors. It was marked by a simple plaque engraved with her name and the dates of her birth and death. Keith removed the vase from the bracket secured to the wall and filled it with water. Placing it back in its support, he arranged the flowers and sprays of leaves he'd brought with him and then sat restlessly on the edge of the sheltered bench in the open vestibule. His leg shimmied with agitation.

He thought again of his appointment with Chappie the day before. He'd been so upset when he left, he wasn't sure he wanted to go back. Sitting here in front of his mother's grave on a rainy morning, the anniversary of her arrival in the world, he finally understood why.

"Keith," the minister had asked near the end of their meeting, "have you ever considered that some of your anger at God might be displaced?"

"Displaced? What do you mean?"

"You've talked a lot about your anger at God and some about your anger at the people who hurt your mother. But you've never talked about being angry at your mother."

Keith had exploded. "Angry at my *mother?* My mother was a *victim!* How could I be angry at *Mama?*"

Chappie was silent for a long time. It was a silence of expectancy, as if he thought someone else might pop in with an answer if he waited long enough. Finally he'd said quietly, "It's all right, Keith. Give yourself permission."

Chappie's right, Mama, Keith said silently, his heart in his stomach. *I've been angry at God, I've been angry at the people who hurt you, but what he says is true: I'm so angry at you!*

His body felt even heavier than it had when he'd first awakened that morning, but the weight seemed to be building up inside rather than pressing down from above. He dropped his head into his hands. *How could you lie to me all those years, Mama? And then when it couldn't do anything but hurt me — why did you have to tell the truth?*

He rose from the bench with an effort and stood silently for several moments in front of her grave. "I love you, Mama. I wish I could forgive you," he said quietly. "But I don't know how."

For the first time since she and Keith had reentered each other's lives, Katie was lonely. Their renewed friendship in the last couple of months had begun to fill a void she hadn't even realized existed until now — when the friendship felt suddenly threatened.

She'd been increasingly uneasy since the day of the community fair — more and more aware both of her attraction to Keith and of his subtle withdrawal. He'd joined her for lunch in the school cafeteria yesterday, as had become their habit, but he'd seemed distracted, had hardly talked to her. When she'd asked him if anything was wrong, he'd said no — but he'd also avoided her eyes. Was that really how things were going to be from now on? she wondered. She and Keith avoiding each other's eyes because they were both afraid of what they might find there?

As much as she'd dreamed about it over the years, she didn't even want to entertain the idea of Keith as a romantic partner right now. For one thing, he was keeping secrets from her. That hurt enough as a friend; if they were involved romantically and he kept large parts of himself hidden from her, she wouldn't be able to bear it. In addition, there were parts of herself he wouldn't allow her to share with him.

What was the point of romance without intimacy? she asked herself. Without the mutual desire and effort to know and to be known? Her spirituality was more than an important element of her life: it was her reason for existence. How could she be involved romantically with someone with whom she couldn't even bring up matters of faith?

She was back on the roller coaster, and she didn't like the ride. If this romantic attraction thing was going to make them so uncomfortable with each other they couldn't even carry on a normal conversation, she didn't want it. Their friendship was too important to her.

Her detour down Alameda Street on her way home from work was an impulsive decision. She had to talk to him, and a phone call wouldn't do. Besides, though she'd driven by Keith's house and admired it from outside, she hadn't yet seen the interior. He lived barely two miles from her; it was downright unneighborly she hadn't dropped by with a housewarming gift.

Once again she detoured. Yesterday she'd seen some lovely fruit baskets at Nature's, a few blocks back. The perfect thing.

Ten minutes later, Katie was standing on Keith's doorstep, basket in hand. She pressed the doorbell a second time. The Montero was in the driveway. He must be home. Opening the storm door, she rapped impatiently on the brick-red door behind it.

"Keith, it's me," she called. "Answer the door! It's freezing out here!"

"What do you want?" Keith asked from the other side of the door.

His tone of voice raised the hackles on the back of her neck. "What do you mean, what do I want? It's *Katie!*"

The front door opened just a crack, and Keith peered out. "Katie, it's really not a good time."

"What's wrong with you?" She narrowed her eyes. "Have you got a woman in there?"

"Wh — of course I don't! Who put the bee in *your* bonnet?"

"Well, *excuse* me! *You* did, if you must know! I came by to bring you a housewarming gift, and what do I get? Yelled at through the door!"

"I wasn't yelling."

He sounded so forlorn she forgot her indignation. "Are you sick?"

"No, I just —" He stopped. "Yeah, I'm not feeling too good. Maybe you'd better come back some other time…"

"Nonsense. I've got just the thing for you." She nudged the door with her hip. He really didn't look well — his face pale behind the dark stubble of a day's growth, and purple shadows under eyes without any sparkle. "Come on, Keith. I know it's a man thing to take care of yourself when you're sick, but —"

"I'm not sick, Katie!" She took a step back at the frustration in his voice. He must have seen the hurt on her face, because his voice softened as he dragged his fingers through his dark hair. "I'm just…sad."

"Oh, Keith. I'm sorry." They stood looking at each other awkwardly. "It really is cold out here," she finally said. "Can I come in for just a few minutes? Please?"

"You wear me out, woman," he muttered under his breath as he let her in.

Pretending not to hear, she brushed past him. "Fruit," she said unnecessarily, lifting the basket. She glanced around for a place to set it down. A fire burned behind glass in the stone fireplace in the living room to the left of the foyer. The floor in front of it was littered with dusty books and scattered papers. *No*, she corrected herself, *photo albums*. Along with a few loose photographs and yellowed news clippings. It looked as if someone had dumped the contents of a bookshelf in the middle of the room.

"You need a maid," she teased.

He didn't look amused.

"May I cut you some pineapple?" she tried again. "Fix some coffee or tea?"

"You don't have to play hostess to me in my own house."

She looked away quickly to hide the hurt in her eyes. Spotting the table in the dining room, she crossed the front room and set the basket down. Taking a deep breath, she turned around to face him. "Isn't there something you'll let me do for you?" she asked miserably. "You make me feel so… *left out* sometimes. Like I'm not important to you."

His arms were crossed over his chest in a self-protective gesture. "You *are* important to me," he protested.

"Then please — don't shut me out. You don't have to tell me anything you don't want to tell me, but let me *do* something."

He regarded her silently for a moment, then sighed. "All right, Katie. Cut some fruit. Make some coffee. Make dinner if you want. I'll be in the living room."

Twelve

❧

When Katie brought him his coffee several minutes later, Keith was sitting on the floor, leaning against the sofa amid the pile of albums and papers. The light from the fire flickered across his face as he stared into it. She kneeled to set the mug next to him and rose to go, but Keith grabbed her hand and held it. She looked down at him.

"I'm sorry I hurt you, Katie. I don't mean to."

"I know."

He glanced at the mess on the floor. "Would you like to help me look through these albums? I pulled out the box Chappie threw together before the estate sale — all the personal stuff he thought I'd want to keep. This is the first time I've looked at it." He paused. "It…would be easier with you here."

Knowing how much the confession had cost him, she squeezed his hand and nodded. She wondered what had motivated his sudden change of heart.

"It's my mother's birthday today," he added. "I've been thinking about…lots of stuff."

Katie knelt again and took his hand between both of hers. "I'm sorry, Keith," she said gently. "I didn't know." She paused. "Sometimes I'm like the proverbial bull in the china shop, aren't I? How in the world do you put up with me?"

He smiled for the first time that afternoon. Weakly, but it was still a smile. "Dangerous kind of question." His voice was almost teasing.

She jumped up. "You're right. Don't think I'll wait around for an answer!" Heading back to the kitchen, she added over her shoulder, "I'd love to look at pictures. Hang on just a couple more minutes."

A few minutes later she was back with a tray of sliced fruit and cheese and crackers, which she set down on the floor between them. "Thanks for letting me do my nurturing woman thing," she said, settling back against the sofa and reaching for a stack of news clippings.

He nodded and smiled again, without commenting. An album lay open on his lap.

The yellowed clipping in Katie's hand was a news photo of Keith at sixteen or seventeen, dressed in his high school basketball uniform. He was several inches off the floor, with his long arm stretching for the basket. A basketball floated at the tips of his fingers. "Wow! Great shot! My folks have news clippings about my musical competitions, but I never got my picture in the paper."

"Face it, standing around with your mouth open doesn't have nearly the same visual impact," he teased, looking over her shoulder. "We can't all be poetry in motion."

She rolled her eyes. "Give me a break, Castle!"

"I think I remember taking pictures of Ruggles when he was a puppy," he said, ignoring her mock disdain. "I'm trying to find them for Doc and Danny."

"What a good idea! Anything else you're looking for?"

"No. Yes. Pictures of my mother. I don't know how many we'll find, since she was usually the one with the camera. Pictures of me when I was little, too."

The tension between them dissipated completely as the photos and news clippings brought back memory after warm memory of their shared childhood. They'd started out with individual stacks, but had interrupted each other so often Katie finally scooted over next to Keith and they leafed through the same album, the front cover propped on his knee and the back cover on hers. Katie forgot she'd dropped by the house mainly to confront Keith about their relationship; the conversation they might have had seemed moot now. As for Keith, the images and the telling of tales from the past lightened his spirits more and more.

They found a number of snapshots of Ruggles for Danny. In one, Keith held Ruggles in his arms as the puppy struggled to lick his face, which was screwed into a wonderfully comic expression as he tried to avoid the wet tongue. In another, he tumbled in the grass with Katie. "I can't believe I was still such a tomboy in junior high!" she groaned.

"You're telling me you're not anymore?" Keith teased.

There were almost as many pictures of Keith and Katie together as there were of Keith alone: Keith pushing Katie on the swing; the two of them straddling their bicycles; Katie climbing the apple tree to the treehouse above where Keith waited, his head poking out a window and a large crooked grin on his face. Doc appeared in some of the photos, too, and there were a few snapshots of Katie's parents, arms around each other at a neighborhood backyard barbecue.

Katie finally spotted a photo of Keith's mom, standing guard at the front door of their little brown house, looking like a tired angel.

"Do you have pictures of your mom when she was a girl?" Katie asked, running her hand across the plastic page of an album to smooth a wrinkle.

"No."

"Really? My mom and dad both have shoeboxes full of fuzzy black-and-whites from their childhood. I never saw them till we were packing up for their move to Arizona. It was so much fun hearing my parents reminisce about the 'olden days'!"

Keith closed the album, their last, and reached for the final pile of loose prints, shuffling quickly through them without finding anything of interest. "I wonder if Mama would have had more stories to tell if she'd lived to be older," he said, passing the photos over to Katie. "Sometimes people don't tell stories about their childhood till they're in their second one."

"Except for you and me, I guess." She finished riffling through the stack and handed it back, smiling. "We're getting a head start. Either that, or we're already *in* our second childhood."

"Of course the other possibility is we haven't graduated from our first," Keith reminded her.

Katie laughed. "Well, there's something to be said for that, too. Childlike wonder, childlike innocence, childlike faith: isn't that what everyone longs to get back to?"

"Yeah." Keith's voice was flat. When she glanced at him curiously, he quickly changed the subject. "Should we call out for pizza? I know it's past *my* suppertime."

Katie pulled the phone from the Stickley end table next to her and dialed a number, then handed it to him.

"You have the number memorized?"

"American Dream. My favorite. You choose what kind."

When he'd finished placing the order, he passed the phone back to her. "Forty minutes. Can you survive?"

"We did have an appetizer."

"Hours ago."

"Will *you* survive?"

He grinned. "I'll survive. Want to see the house while we're waiting?"

The little bungalow was classic Arts-and-Crafts style, clean, simple, natural. Large casement windows let in the gray light of dusk. The stone fireplace had cabinets built in on either side, and the dining room featured a built-in sideboard with beveled glass doors. The oak wainscoting had the warm, dark patina of age, contrasting nicely with the rose-colored walls. In the living room and dining room, two oriental rugs in rich tones lay across the hardwood floors.

Keith had had the bathroom remodeled, adding a whirlpool tub big enough, Katie told him, to use as a swimming pool. The larger of the two bedrooms, on either side of the bath, was painted a smoky green, and the smaller, set up as a study, in a lighter shade of the rose from the living areas of the house. The furniture throughout was Mission style, its clean, square lines in harmony with the architecture.

They finished the tour in the newly modernized kitchen, where they joined forces to make a salad, Katie washing lettuce while Keith cut up tomatoes, zucchini, and green pepper. When the pizza arrived, they ate in the breakfast nook off the kitchen, admiring the watercolor lights of the city below through the rain. After supper, the fireplace in the living room drew them back to finish their drinks.

Katie resettled on the oriental rug, leaning against the sofa as Keith dumped the albums and papers on a chair and dimmed the lamp. He pulled an afghan from the back of the sofa as he sat down next to her. "Chilly?"

"A little."

He threw it loosely over both of them and settled against the sofa. Without thinking, Katie relaxed against his shoulder and snuggled into the soft warmth of the mohair afghan. They sat in companionable silence for a few minutes, watching the steady flicker of flames in the gas fireplace. Looking at the fire and listening to the drum of rain against the rooftop made her eyelids heavy.

"Katie…"

"Hm?" Yawning, she arched her back and stretched her shoulder blades.

He hesitated. "I keep forgetting how easy you are to be with. Can't believe I almost drove you off earlier today."

"Mmm. Some people are just slow learners, Castle."

They sat in silence for another languid moment before Keith said, "I want to tell you a story. At least, I think I do."

"You think you do?" she murmured drowsily.

"It might be a hard story to tell." He glanced at her from the corners of his eyes. "It might be a hard story to listen to."

She sat up. There was a quality to his voice she'd never heard before. "Keith —" she stopped, then started again. "I don't know how to say this, so I'll just say it. Whatever you have to tell me, it won't be as hard for me as your silence has been these last five years."

"I know. I'm sorry. I just couldn't do it."

"If you're ready to talk, I'm ready to listen," she said gently, her languor gone. "I'll try my best to understand."

"I *want* you to understand." He stared straight ahead at the fire for a full two minutes while Katie waited. Finally he nodded toward the albums on the chair. "Did you notice anything missing in all those pictures we looked through earlier?"

"Missing...."

"Yeah. You asked if I had any pictures of my mom as a child, but you didn't take it any further. Don't you wonder why there aren't any pictures of — the wedding? My mother's husband? No pictures of them together or of him in uniform? No newspaper clippings about his heroic death?"

Katie shook her head, puzzled at his questions. "Maybe your mom destroyed them. Maybe she didn't want to be reminded. It must have been a terrible shock, finding out about his death when she was pregnant with you."

"Oh, it was a shock all right." His voice sounded dead. He squeezed his eyes shut for a moment, then opened them to stare into the fire. "There aren't any wedding pictures because there wasn't a wedding."

"There wasn't a wedding," Katie repeated slowly. "You mean — they hadn't actually married when your father left for Vietnam? She didn't find out she was pregnant till after he was gone?"

"Vietnam was a lie."

Katie was feeling more and more confused. "He didn't *go* to Vietnam? What are you saying, Keith? Your mother lied about your father dying in the war?"

"My mother told me a fairy tale for twenty-two years."

"Wait. If your father —" She tried to gather her thoughts.

"If he wasn't who she said he was, who *was* he?"

"My *father* was nowhere close to a hero. He was *scum*."

Katie sucked in her breath at the loathing in his voice.

He looked at her with bleak eyes. "Mama was raped, Katie. I have a *rapist* for a father!"

Katie was so staggered she couldn't speak. Keith wrenched his arm away from her. "I'm sorry, I can't do this, I thought I'd be okay. I...I just *hate* him!" The anguish in his voice drove straight to her heart.

"Keith, please —" She knelt beside him and put her arms around his neck, gently rocking as he leaned his head against hers. The tension in his body released in a sudden flood of shivers. "It's okay. It's okay," she soothed.

"I can't stop shaking." His voice was muffled against her neck. "I can't stop shaking, Katie."

It took half an hour for him to get the rest of the story out. Katie listened in stunned silence as he told her the story he'd heard for the first time as his mother lay on her deathbed.

The man to whom Keith owed his existence had been a dishwasher at the restaurant in Seattle where Christine had waited tables part-time. One stormy night just a few months after her high school graduation, she'd missed her bus home and accepted a ride from her co-worker — a ride that had ended with the rape.

Her terror hadn't ended with the physical violation. Her mother shamed her instead of offering love and support, suggesting her daughter had somehow invited the assault. The police convinced her even if they found the guy, which was unlikely since he'd cleared out of town, the trial process would be a living hell. Six weeks later when she discovered she was pregnant, her father kicked her out of the house.

Her savings dwindled quickly, and when she started to show, she'd been let go from her job. Finally she'd arrived on the doorstep of a crisis pregnancy center, where she was well taken care of but encouraged to give up her baby for adoption when he was born. Instead, barely eighteen, with a five-week-old baby strapped to her front, she'd boarded a Greyhound bus with forty-five dollars and a paper bag holding one extra set of clothes for herself and two extra diapers for Keith.

By the time she'd arrived in Portland, her story was set, created from overheard conversations on the bus and her own imagination. She was a grieving young widow whose husband had died a hero in Vietnam, not knowing he had left behind a son. A mixup with the State Department was holding up her death benefits. Her parents had disliked her husband and refused to help her out.

She was smart enough, in those first few years, not to appear too desperate; she'd learned people were more comfortable helping her out if she told them she was doing fine, thank you, but oh — there *was* one little thing.... Life unfolded, and somehow she survived it and even learned to enjoy it again.

"She died telling us her life had been a gift from God," Keith said angrily. "The only thing she regretted was lying all those years, because she knew God hated liars!"

Keith dug his hands into his hair and pressed the palms against his temples. "I...just couldn't deal with it. So I ran away."

Words seemed inadequate. Katie gently pushed him down on the floor in front of the fire, laid his head in her lap, and massaged his scalp until he fell asleep. Her heart felt heavy with grief for the magnitude of his losses. When his mother had died, it wasn't only her presence in his life he'd lost. He'd lost the fairy tale, everything he'd ever believed about his parents and his place in the world. Everything he'd believed about God.

Before she let herself out the front door, she tucked a blanket around him and touched her lips to his forehead.

Keith woke with a start in the middle of the night, stiff and disoriented. The gas fire cast unfamiliar shadows in the dark room. What was he doing lying on the floor with the wool blanket from his bed wrapped around him?

He remembered when he sat up, rubbing the sleep from his eyes, and saw the photo albums stacked in the Morris chair across the room. "Katie?" he called softly. With the blanket draped over his shoulders, he wandered through the dark house. "Katie?"

The last thing he remembered was lying on the floor, eyes closed, with his head in Katie's lap. As she'd rubbed the tension from his temples, he'd imagined her face in his mind, gazing down at him with tenderness, light rippling like fire through her hair as she bent over him. He'd imagined lifting his hand to stroke her cheek, hearing her sudden intake of breath, watching her close her eyes and turn her face into his palm. He'd imagined reaching behind her neck and pulling her beautiful face toward him, her eyes open now and brimming with emotion. Katie, his love…

No! he told himself savagely. What was he *thinking?* He clutched the ends of the blanket together under his chin. He knew better than to do this to himself!

Katie was his *friend*, the best friend he could ever imagine. His awareness of her as a lovely woman to whom he was attracted, an awareness that had been growing over the last few weeks, sent a tremor of fear through his body.

He would have to watch himself with her. He would have to be careful. A romance that might last a few months or even a few years wasn't worth the risk of losing her. She meant too much.

Thirteen

❧

Y ou're not yourself today, girlfriend," Emily observed through a mouthful of pins. "What's wrong?"

Katie sighed. "Nothing, really." She lifted her arms slightly, lapsing into silence again as Emily bent to pin the side seams of the fitted bodice. Though Katie had tried to talk Emily out of it, she'd insisted she wanted to make an evening gown for her friend to wear to emcee the Christmas concert. Today they were doing a preliminary fitting.

When she finished pinning the seams, Emily stepped back, eyeing her friend with concern. She waited as Katie slipped out of the emerald green silk bodice and into a borrowed robe.

"So how did the fair go?" she finally asked, deciding to try another tack. "Did Doc and Danny show up?"

"We stopped by Doc's to see if we could talk Danny into coming to the carnival. He adores Keith, but he didn't bite."

"That's too bad. D'you think he would have enjoyed it if he'd gone?"

Katie perked up. "He couldn't have helped it! It's incredible what a professional job those kids did!" She launched into a colorful description of the carnival. "Keith gave most of the credit to his staff, but I think he's being modest. Motivating kids to work that hard takes a special gift. I think Keith's got it."

Raising her eyebrows, Emily murmured, "Well, he's certainly got *something*."

"What's that supposed to mean?"

"Katie, can't you just admit you're in love with the guy?"

She sputtered. "Come on, Em. You know Keith and I've been friends practically since time began!"

Emily sat down to the portable sewing machine set up on the kitchen table, slid the silk jacquard under the presser foot, and reached for the pedal control. "Look, Katie, you read me the poems. You sang me the songs. You can't believe I'm going to fall for that 'just friends' stuff."

"Em, I was a teenager! Give me a break! You know everything that's happened since then."

Snipping the threads and moving the fabric to sew up the other side seam, Emily asked, "So how do you explain your excitement the day Doc told you Keith was back in town? And your disappointment when I told you he'd been back for months?"

Katie was silent.

"What I do know, girlfriend," Emily continued, "is what's happened since Keith came back to Portland. I know how *alive* you are when you talk about him. And I know you *never* felt this way about Henry." Pulling the bodice from the machine, she handed it to Katie. "Here, put this on and see how it fits."

Silently shrugging out of the robe, Katie slipped into the

stitched bodice. Emily pulled at the fabric in several places, nodded in satisfaction, and stepped back, leaning against the counter with her arms crossed.

Sitting on the edge of a chair, Katie slid out of the bodice, letting it drop into her lap. "It's hard to know where friendship ends and love begins," she said slowly.

Emily lifted the bodice from Katie's lap and draped it over the sewing machine. "I think you need to talk this through," she said firmly. "Get dressed while I make us some hot tea."

"And you call *me* bossy?"

"I've had a good teacher," Emily returned.

Katie sighed in contentment a few minutes later as she lay stretched out on her friend's bed. "This feels like old times, Em. You and me figuring out life together. Me on the bed staring at the ceiling with a mug of hot tea balanced on my stomach, you curled up in the chair by the window."

"*Spread out* in the chair by the window, I'm afraid," Emily corrected, patting her rounded belly. "This child won't allow me to curl anymore. Okay, what gives?"

Katie didn't answer right away, as if she were taking time to collect her thoughts. "Yesterday was Christine Castle's birthday," she finally said.

"Did you see Keith?

"Not by his choice, but yes, I did."

"And?"

"Em, do you feel sometimes like you've lived a charmed existence?"

Emily frowned in confusion at the sudden turn in the conversation. Katie didn't usually wander. "What do you mean?"

"I mean," Katie said slowly, "what have you and I ever

had to face in life that was really too big to handle on our own? How do you know if something really terrible happened to you or someone you loved that you'd still believe the world was a pretty good place and God was on your side?"

"'God's in his heaven, all's right with the world.'"

"Exactly. Who could say that except someone who's always pretty much gotten their own way in life, who's never had to struggle over losing anything?"

"How about Doc?"

"Hmm. Good point." *And Christine Castle herself,* Katie added to herself. Knowing Keith's mother, whoever would have guessed the hell she'd lived through?

"My parents, too, for that matter," Emily continued. "The miscarriage Mom had before I was born, and then the one between Olivia and the twins. Dad getting laid off at Boeing with a wife and three kids to take care of. Struggling through seminary, having more kids, raising them on a minister's salary. Those must have been horribly difficult things to deal with. But I'll bet if you asked them, they'd both say they've led charmed lives."

Katie nodded. Chappie and Mary Lewis had dedicated their lives to Christian ministry. Doc wore his faith on his sleeve. Keith's mother had seen her life as a gift from God. All four of them had joyful spirits and generous hearts. Where did that kind of faith come from? After the crushing losses they'd suffered, how was it possible that they, of all people, should be able to delight in their lives the way they did?

"I think it's all a matter of perspective," Emily said thoughtfully. "We tend to hyperfocus when things seem bad. But time and distance let you see the whole picture."

"Maybe you're right."

Emily grinned. "Remind me of this conversation when I need it, will you?"

Katie set her mug on the nightstand and rolled on her side, propping her head up with her hand, and grinned back. "Don't worry, I will!"

"So…"

Katie looked at her friend with an inquiring expression.

"Keith finally talked to you about what happened when his mother died."

"Yeah. He still has a lot of unresolved feelings. I don't think I should tell you what —"

"You shouldn't," Emily interrupted. "Keith needs to decide that. It's okay, girlfriend. I'm just happy he told someone, for his sake, and that the someone was you — for your sake. Just remember, it's not your job to 'fix' him."

"Why do you keep bringing that up?" Katie asked irritably.

"Because I know you."

Katie woke sleepily Thanksgiving morning to the sounds of Tchaikovsky's first piano concerto and the smell of fresh baked bread. She stretched slowly, enjoying the expressive music and the yeasty fragrance tickling her nose. Clock radios and bread machines — what decadent luxuries!

Suddenly realizing what day it was, she leaped out of bed, propelled as much by anticipation as by the tasks that lay ahead. Even the gray drizzle outside her window didn't dampen her spirits. Keith had accepted her invitation to Thanksgiving dinner eagerly, especially when he'd heard that

Doc and Danny would be there. Three of the people she cared about most were coming to share the day.

Humming, she bustled around her bright kitchen, the room in her small apartment she liked best. French doors opened to a flagstone patio in the private backyard she shared with her co-tenants in the fourplex, all young single women like herself. Several fruit and nut trees, their branches bare this late in the season, shared space in the yard with tree-like rhododendrons and one tall spruce.

Emily had helped her make the simple gathered curtains and matching valance at the window over the sink, in an Oriental print of warm-toned camellias, lilies, and dahlias against a pale yellow background. Katie had papered the wall adjacent to the french doors with an unusual collage of art reproductions from cards and calendars, selected contemporary works mixed in with her favorite Postimpressionist prints. Just because she'd never be able to afford an original Van Gogh or Gauguin didn't mean she couldn't enjoy their genius over breakfast.

After her parents had moved to Arizona and sold the house on Dearborn Street, she'd dreaded the thought of living in an apartment complex. In a Northeast neighborhood of single-family homes, she'd been thrilled to discover the downstairs apartment in an old Portland house that had been subdivided into four units.

"It's got character," she'd told her mother enthusiastically. "You'd really like it." Not only was the house rife with architectural features like gables, french windows, built-in shelves and cabinets, and graceful arches between the rooms — all of which lent it a special charm — but it had also been lovingly cared for over the years by tenants and landlord alike.

A huge maple tree with only a few shriveled leaves still hanging on stood guard in the parking strip out front, and carefully tended rock gardens bordered the twin stairways leading to the apartment entrances on either side of the drive in the middle. The front door opened into the living room. A hallway led to her bedroom on the right and a tiny bathroom on the left. Farther down the hall was a dining room, open to the kitchen at the back of the house where she now stood at the counter.

The sweet, spicy smell of sausage frying with onions, celery, and chunks of apple filled the apartment. Katie added the mixture to the crumbly cornbread she'd made the night before, moistened it with chicken broth, and stuffed the hollow of the turkey. It felt odd to be making the family recipe for cornbread dressing in her own kitchen instead of her parents', where she'd made it every year for longer than she could remember.

Midmorning she called long distance to Phoenix to wish her family a happy holiday. Her father answered the phone.

"Happy Thanksgiving, honey! How's my girl?"

"Great! Got my turkey in the oven and my potatoes peeled. Doc and Danny and Keith are coming over about one. Think we'll all fit in my little apartment?"

Thomas Brannigan chuckled. "From your description, before the meal, just barely. Afterwards, if you're cooking up the kind of meal your mother is, I'd recommend moving out on the patio."

"Mom's cooking Thanksgiving dinner?" Katie was shocked. Her mother hadn't had the energy, let alone the desire, to cook a big holiday meal in years.

"She is. Your mom's doing great, honey. I'm glad you

called while she's out walking —"

"Mom's taking a walk?" Shock again.

"Believe it or not, she walks every day! I'm telling you, she's a new woman. She's made friends in the church — goes to services even when I'm out of town." He paused. "Your mother is not just making dinner today, honey, she's having people *over* for dinner."

"You're kidding! But the asthma and her arthritis," Katie protested. "And the…the female problems." *The ones that started when she was pregnant with me,* she added to herself, feeling the twinge of guilt that always accompanied the thought.

"All I can tell you is she seems healthier than she has in years."

"Dad, when did all this *happen*?"

"It's been gradual. The climate change helped, but that's only part of it." Katie heard him take a deep breath. "You know, I wasn't sure we'd done the right thing at first, moving down here. Your mom was so depressed after you went back to Portland."

"I had to be here for work," Katie said, the guilty twinge increasing.

"Of course you did. To tell the truth, I'm convinced it was best all the way around."

Katie was feeling increasingly confused. What was her father saying? "This is all just so…*sudden,*" she said in a bewildered voice.

"I've been meaning to write." Her father sounded embarrassed. "But you know how it is…."

"It's okay, Dad. I'm just glad to hear — I mean, I've seen mom as an *invalid* for so long…."

"I know." He paused. "I think that was the problem. We both saw her as an invalid. We took care of her."

Katie felt suddenly defensive. "So what's wrong with that? Aren't you *supposed* to take care of the people you love?"

"Maybe she didn't need to be taken care of. Maybe we kept her from taking care of herself."

Katie was silent for a moment. "Are you saying Mom's better off without me?"

"You sound hurt. Don't be, honey. Mom misses you. She just realizes she depended on you for a lot of things she could have done herself."

"I'm looking into the doctoral program at Arizona State," she said irrelevantly.

Her father understood. "Of course it would be nice to have you closer, honey. But don't move to Arizona if we're your only reason. We're fine. And you have your own life to live."

Emily called a few minutes after Katie had said goodbye to her father and immediately picked up on her agitation. "What's up, girlfriend? Everything okay?"

"Yeah, I think so." Katie gave her friend an edited version of the conversation with her father. "I'm just feeling a bit dazed. Of course I'm thrilled that Mom's doing so well, but I feel so...I don't know. Left out. Unimportant."

"Oh, Katie! Of course you're important! Your parents adore you. Your mom's just at a new stage, and you're having a hard time letting go."

"I thought it was *parents* who had a hard time letting go of their *children*."

"Depends," Emily answered cryptically. "Listen, I've got to go. I just wanted to wish you a happy Thanksgiving and see if you could come over in the morning — we need to do another fitting. Ten o'clock okay?"

"Sure. See you then."

Katie's disquiet vanished when she heard the doorbell just after noon and opened the door to Keith, carrying a large cardboard box with a wicker basket balanced on top. Wearing khaki slacks and a sweater the same smoky green as his eyes, he looked as delicious as her kitchen smelled. She smiled at the thought.

"You're early." She held the door open as he walked in sideways with his burden.

He shrugged and grinned his lopsided grin. "Couldn't wait. Okay with you?" Without waiting for an answer, he sniffed and headed unerringly for the kitchen. "Nice digs, Katie," he said approvingly as he walked through the apartment. "Can't believe you haven't invited me over till now." He smiled at her over his shoulder.

Setting the box on the kitchen table, he gently lifted the large wicker basket and carried it to a spot on the hardwood floor near the stove. Katie watched from the doorway, her curiosity piqued.

Looking up over his shoulder, Keith beckoned with a nod. "Come see." His eyes were shining like a child's at Christmas. Katie bent down next to him as he pulled back the blanket covering the basket and reached inside. When he lifted his hands, they were full to overflowing with fat, fuzzy, russet-haired puppy.

CHAPTER

Fourteen

❧

O h, Keith, he's adorable! Let me hold him," Katie begged.

"*She's* adorable," he corrected. The pup barked joyously and set her fluffy tail wagging as Keith lifted her out of the basket. Katie reached for the joyful ball of fur, getting several wet puppy kisses as she tried to settle the squirming body against her chest. After a moment the puppy snuggled against her.

"Irish setter?" she asked. They were both still kneeling by the basket.

He nodded, reaching over to scratch the pup's silky head. She burrowed into his hand. "Look, she's exactly the color of your hair, Katie." Keith's hand left the puppy, gently pulling Katie's hair over her shoulder and running his fingers the length of it. Katie held her breath and gazed at him, her eyes wide.

Keith looked startled. "Your eyes, too!" He dropped his hand from her hair and took the puppy, holding it up to her face and glancing back and forth between them. "The same warm, brown eyes." He searched her face as if seeing it for the first time. "No. Amber. You have beautiful eyes, Katie."

She laughed shakily. "You realize you're comparing me to a dog," she said. "How should I be taking this?"

Keith grinned. "Believe me, with *this* dog it's a compliment. She's a beauty, isn't she?" He picked up an oversized foot hanging over his arm and added with bemusement, "I'm afraid she's got feet like mine, though."

"Poor thing," Katie sympathized, scratching under the puppy's chin.

"You got something against my feet, Squirt?"

Katie raised her hands. "Hey, you're the one who brought it up!" Thank goodness he was back in his teasing mode, she thought with relief. If he'd looked at her one more moment the way he'd been looking — the way she'd dreamed he might look at her someday — she didn't think she could be held responsible for her actions. "Let's hope she grows into them," she added.

"She will," Keith promised. "Like it or not! Come on, girl," he coaxed, placing her back in the basket. "Go back to sleep."

Kneeling together in the warm kitchen, they watched the puppy make a complete turn on the cushion before settling into it, then stood at the same time, as if their bodies were synchronized.

"She's perfect, Keith. For Danny?" Katie asked softly.

He nodded.

"She looks an awful lot like Ruggles, with that red coat and those floppy ears. Is that why you got her?"

"To tell the truth, I hesitated for that very reason." Unexpectedly he reached over and ruffled her hair. "Guess I've just got a thing about redheads," he said. "Saw her in the window at the pet store and I couldn't resist."

Katie dodged away. "Quit it, Castle," she told him crossly, only because she wanted to hug him and was afraid to. Immediately contrite for her tone of voice, she smiled and said quietly, "You're a very nice man, you know that?"

Their eyes locked for a brief moment. "You bring it out in me." Then he looked away, breaking the shimmering spell of tenderness between them with a mundane question about where to put the pies.

Doc and Danny arrived just as Keith was pulling the golden turkey from the oven. The older man sniffed appreciatively as he coaxed his grandson into the house. "Smell that bird, Danny Boy! We'll eat like kings today, eh?"

Danny mumbled an unintelligible reply, stuffed his hands in his pockets, and stared at the floor.

"Where's your manners, boy?" Doc chided. "Say hello to Kee an' Irish, or they'll be askin' us to leave."

"Not a chance," Katie said firmly, pulling Danny to her side and giving him a quick squeeze. "We could never eat all this food. We're counting on you guys!" Danny didn't return her hug, but he didn't resist it, either.

Doc sniffed the tantalizing aroma and rubbed his hands together in satisfaction. "Well then! *We* won't disappoint, will we, Danny Boy?"

The boy shrugged, his eyes still on the floor. Doc shot them a helpless glance over his head.

"Come here, Danny," Katie said, crossing the dining room to open the cupboard door in the antique sideboard. "Dishes," she pointed. She pulled out one of the drawers. "Flatware. As your grandpa once told me, 'Them what works, eats!'" Bending close to his ear, she whispered loud enough for the men to hear, "If you set the table, you won't have to do dishes. Keith and Doc —"

"What?" Keith interrupted in mock indignation. "No fair! Come on, Doc, let's beat him to it!" He lunged for the place-mats and napkins Katie had set on top of the sideboard and waved them over his head.

Doc laughed with glee and reached around Danny with one hand, grabbing the dinner plates, which clattered dangerously.

"Doc, you'd better not break those dishes!" Katie shouted, shaking her fist.

Danny's mouth dropped open at the sudden pandemonium. Then he grinned and scooped up a handful of flatware from the open drawer.

"Stop!" Katie commanded, her hands on her hips. Keith and Doc stopped in mid-action and Danny followed suit. "You gentlemen break one dish," she threatened, "and I'll...I'll give the *dog* your dinners!" At which opportune moment the puppy, awakened by all the noise, draped her big paws over the edge of the basket in the kitchen and barked sharply, her tail wagging her entire hind end.

Katie clapped her hand over her mouth and stared at Keith. Doc followed the sound of the bark with a blank look on his face. Keith watched Danny anxiously. Danny stood for a long moment as if frozen, then slowly turned his head in the direction of the barking.

"A puppy." His voice held hurt and happiness in heart-rending confusion. He looked up at Katie, his blue eyes solemn, and said, "Ruggles died."

"I know, honey. It was really sad, wasn't it?"

Danny nodded and looked back toward the basket where

the setter pup still stood on her hind legs, panting, her liquid amber eyes bright with excitement. Katie saw the tension in the boy's slight body. Part of him wanted to rush across the room to the puppy, but something stronger than his curiosity and desire held him back.

The three adults remained silent. Danny pointed to the puppy and, looking at Katie again, asked, "What's his name?"

Keith cleared his throat. "*Her* name. She's mine, Danny. I haven't named her yet." He deliberately began to lay the multicolored placemats and napkins at intervals around the table. "Maybe you can help me think of a good name later on. I'm afraid if we don't get the table set, this woman really *will* feed our dinner to that dog! Come on, help me out here."

When they sat down to the table a few minutes later, Doc prayed simply, "Lord God, we thank you for the blessin' of good friends and good food. Be with Katie's ma and pa down there in the desert lands, and Toni up on the ranch in Montana. Thank you for Kee's mama lookin' down on us from heaven. Amen."

Katie darted a quick glance at Keith, but the mention of his mother seemed not to have affected him.

The meal was delicious, the turkey moist and succulent, the cornbread dressing perfectly spiced, the herb bread warm and crusty. Doc's contributions of homemade cranberry-orange relish and a baked corn casserole added just the right touch. Although Danny kept craning his neck to keep his eye on the puppy throughout dinner, he managed to down a little bit of everything and even seconds of mashed potatoes and gravy. He was in much better spirits than Katie had seen him since before Ruggles's death.

Keith helped her stack the dishes on the drainboard after the meal and then herded everybody into the living room and switched Katie's television on to the football game. He insisted Katie join them. "I'll do the dishes," he assured her. "But first things first." In a low murmur he added, "Let's leave the kitchen empty for a while and see what happens."

One end of her living room was taken up by the baby grand piano her parents had bought her as a graduation gift when she finished her master's, leaving little room for any other furniture. Katie insisted Keith and Doc take the two upholstered chairs as she settled into a stack of bright floor cushions that added seating space to the room. "You can sit with me, Danny," she said, patting the floor beside her.

"Some guys have all the luck," Keith grumbled, dropping into the chair nearest Katie. He looked very large in it; his feet, stretching out in front of him, reached almost to the television. Katie stifled a giggle.

Although watching a football game wouldn't have been her first choice of entertainment, she found herself enjoying it. As patterns emerged, she began to appreciate the careful orchestration of the players on the field. She even figured out a few of the frantic signals the referees directed to the announcer's box every time a flag was thrown for a penalty. Her father would have been proud, she thought with amusement. Stunned, but proud.

Doc, Keith, and Katie pretended not to notice when Danny disappeared into the kitchen, although it was all Katie could do to keep from getting up and tiptoeing to the door to watch. Keith reached over to touch her lightly on the arm. *Wait,* he seemed to be saying. *Let him take his own time.*

Danny came back through the dining room to the living

room a little later and demanded of Katie, "'Irish' isn't your real name, is it?"

She blinked. "No. It's your grandpa's pet name for me. Can you believe he's called me that since I was younger than you are?"

"He has?" Danny looked doubtful that Katie had ever been younger than he was. "What's your real name?"

"Katie. Well, Kathryn. Kathryn Leigh Brannigan, to be exact. Why?"

"Just wonderin'," he said and disappeared again.

Doc looked at her as if to say, *Now I wonder what that was all about?* Katie shrugged.

A few minutes later, Danny was back. This time he hung on the arm of Keith's chair and announced, "I think the puppy's hungry. Could we give him some turkey?"

"Give *her* some turkey," Keith corrected once again. "Good idea. She probably *is* hungry." He unfolded his body from the chair as if he didn't care that his team was down six points and in position for a touchdown. Even Katie knew what a sacrifice he was making. "Let's slice some meat, okay?"

"Okay." Danny grinned up at him, then calmly reached up and slipped his small hand into Keith's large one.

They were in the kitchen for a long time. When they came back, Danny was hugging the puppy to his chest, his eyes shining. The dog squirmed in his arms and licked the boy's face with fervor. Obviously a love match, Katie thought, smiling. How had Keith known?

"I named him!" Danny said excitedly. "Keith said it's a good name, too."

"He did, did he?" Doc said, his face lit with pleasure at his grandson's excitement. "And what's the name, Danny Boy?"

"Brannigan!"

Katie jumped. "Brannigan!" she protested. "But that's *my* name!"

"I know," he said proudly. "Keith says he's a Irish setter, and Grumpy calls *you* Irish, and Brannigan and you have 'zactly the same color hair! So Keith said it's a good name."

"He did, did he?" she said darkly, unconsciously parroting Doc's words. She glared at Keith. Naming a *dog* after her, of all things!

He looked as if he could barely contain his lopsided grin. Lifting his shoulders in a helpless gesture, he said, "It was all his idea, Katie, I swear it. I should think you'd be honored."

"But a *dog!*" she wailed. Then she looked at Danny's eager face and relented. "Brannigan," she said faintly, reaching out to scratch behind the puppy's ears. She sighed. "Well, I suppose it'll do, considering she's such a beauty. But don't expect me to call her anything more than Bran," she grumbled.

Keith sank back into his chair. "I don't know what to do about Brannigan," he said, his voice grave. He avoided looking at Danny, directing his words to Doc and Katie instead. "I can't keep her. With work and school I'm not home enough to take good care of her. It just wouldn't be fair."

"Oh, Keith, that's too bad," Katie sympathized.

Keith shook his head sadly. "I'd like to find a good home for her, but I'm not willing to give her up to just anyone."

Doc nodded, his expression thoughtful. "That's a tough one! Good dog people ain't easy to find."

"What kind of person are you looking for, Keith?" Katie asked with the same seriousness.

"Well, I can tell already this dog is going to need a lot of attention. She needs someone to be her *friend*, not just someone to feed her. Know what I mean?"

Katie nodded sagely.

Danny was practically dancing with excitement. "I could be his friend! I'd be a *real* good friend, Kee." He shifted the dog in his arms. His expression was a confusion of hope and fear.

"Hmm…" Keith pretended to deliberate. Katie wondered how on earth Danny could miss the twitch at the corners of his mouth. "You're a bit young, but you do have some experience.…"

Danny nodded vigorously.

Keith looked at Doc. "It's your house, Doc. Would you have room for a big dog like this one's going to be?"

All eyes turned to Doc as he cocked his head to one side and pretended to consider the idea.

"Oh, *please*, Grumpy!" Danny finally burst out. "He can sleep in my bed!"

Doc nodded, his blue eyes twinkling. "Our house has been mighty empty with Ruggles gone. Brannigan might be just the thing to fill it up again, Kee. What d'you think, Danny Boy?"

"I think I love him," he said solemnly. He buried his face in the silk of Brannigan's fur.

"*Her*," Keith told him.

"Hmm?" Danny mumbled without looking up.

"I think I love *her*."

This time Keith was looking straight at Katie, a tender smile lighting his face.

When Katie served Keith's pies later on — both pumpkin and apple, which Keith claimed to have made himself — Danny ate his on the kitchen floor next to the wicker basket where Brannigan was sleeping. When he left with Doc, the boy struggled with the large basket alone, unwilling for anyone to help him. He couldn't keep his eyes off the puppy for one minute.

"Well, you certainly read that one right, Mr. Castle." Katie smiled as she dug an apron out of a drawer and tossed it across the room to him. "You sure you don't want to be a child psychologist?"

"When are you going to figure out that I am just one perfectly nice guy, Miss Brannigan?"

"You think I don't know?"

Keith shook out the apron. "Hey, don't you have anything less frilly?"

"Nope." She leaned back against the drainboard and watched him slip the apron over his head and reach awkwardly behind his back to tie the strings. It was entirely too small to cover his chest, and the strings were tied closer to his armpits than his waist. She stifled a giggle. "You wash, I dry?"

"In a minute," he said, ignoring her sputter and disappearing into the living room. "I need music to wash dishes by."

A few moments later she heard the opening strains of Gershwin's *Rhapsody in Blue*, the clarinet trilling and then wailing up to the high note. One of her favorites, alive with rhythm and energy.

She eyed him approvingly when he came back through

the door. "Perfect music to wash dishes by. We should finish in record time!"

"*CD* time you mean," he said. She rolled her eyes.

When the last pot was washed and dried, Keith arranged his allotted portion of leftovers in the cardboard box he'd brought with him, while Katie went for his coat, thrown carelessly across the foot of her bed. She picked up the soft leather jacket, stared at it, then suddenly buried her face in the warm lining. It smelled like Keith, clean and masculine.

A lump formed in her throat for no reason at all.

Keith slipped into the jacket a few moments later, smiling at her with infinite gentleness. "Thank you, Katie. It's been so long since I really felt part of a family."

He opened his arms and she moved into them as if it were the most natural thing in the world, laying her head on his chest and feeling the strong beat of his heart as he held her.

She pushed away slightly and looked up into his face. His green eyes caught her golden ones. In the background a piano riffled lightly. Katie's mouth went dry as Keith slowly lowered his head.

The meeting of their lips was tentative, exquisitely gentle. Katie gave herself wholly to the sensation. So many years she'd waited for this kiss!

The music continued in the background. Keith tightened his hold around her and his kiss suddenly roughened. For an instant she drew back, startled.

He abruptly lifted his face and dropped his hands from her arms. She caught a fleeting glimpse of his flushed face and smoky eyes before he turned away. *No*, she protested silently. *Don't leave me*. But she didn't have the courage to say the words aloud.

When Keith turned back he was smiling sheepishly. "Sorry, Katie," he said lightly. "I didn't mean to get carried away. Forgive me?"

Forgive you? For something I've wanted since I was sixteen?

She looked at the floor and nodded slowly, not saying a word.

He lifted her chin and leaned forward, placing a chaste kiss on her forehead. "You're very special to me, Katie. As true a friend as I'll ever have. Thank you again."

She stood in the doorway and watched him leave, rubbing her hands up and down her arms against the cold. But she couldn't get warm. A winter wind had swept through her, leaving her cold and empty.

When he was gone, she stretched out on her bed, staring at the ceiling as if she might find instructions for her life written across it. Nothing was there.

Fifteen

※

Keith cursed himself as he pulled away from Katie's apartment. Over the last few months they'd slipped into such a comfortable relationship it almost felt as if they'd never been apart. When had this other thing crept in — this romantic gravitation that threatened to ruin their friendship? Even before tonight it had influenced his responses to Katie. He'd been less affectionate lately, in the easy way he'd always been with her, afraid that somehow he might betray the unwanted feelings she stirred in him.

But today had been so *warm*. So *family*. He hadn't planned to kiss her, but when she'd looked up at him with those big brown eyes, her face flushed with happiness, he hadn't been able to resist. And when her lips had been so soft and receptive — who could blame him for getting carried away?

Stopping at a red light, he flipped on his blinker and waited for the signal to change. Obviously, Katie had been as carried away as he'd been. She'd just realized it sooner. When she'd pulled away from him with that look in her eyes, like a scared rabbit, he'd been mortified. What was he thinking? A kiss like that was totally out of place between two friends.

So why can't the relationship change? another part of him argued. *Who says things have to stay the same? What's wrong with falling in love?*

Falling in love! He shook his head to rid himself of the dangerous thought. First of all, he'd already decided Katie meant too much to him to screw up their friendship with an attempt at romance that might or might not work out. Secondly —

He heard a honk behind him and realized the light had turned green. *You're losing it, Castle,* he told himself as he crossed the intersection onto Alameda. "It's not the right time to fall in love," he said out loud. "With Katie or anyone."

Why not?

"Look at my life! I'm just starting to figure it out. I'll be in school another year and a half. When I do my student teaching, I'll have to cut back at work. What am I supposed to do — have someone support me while I get my life together?"

Is that really what's bugging you?

He knew the answer, as soon as he posed the question in his mind. It wasn't uncertainty about the outward trappings of his life that made him feel unready for love. It was something inside. It was the uncertainty he felt about himself.

Pulling into his driveway, he turned off the engine and sat slumped over the steering wheel in the dark. Did he have the capacity to love Katie — or any other woman, for that matter — the way she deserved to be loved?

Keith had always believed that love was a function of the soul. And the state of his soul, in his own mind, was suspect.

Was his spirit too wounded to be able to give what love demanded?

Katie deserved to be adored. He didn't know if he had it in him. Too many ghosts stood in the way.

Katie stood on the Bradleys' front stoop the next morning, hands thrust into the deep pockets of her quilted jacket, waiting for Emily to answer the doorbell. She had such a bad case of the blues, she'd almost called to cancel the fitting. After yesterday, she was so thoroughly confused about her relationship with Keith she didn't know which end was up. Maybe Emily could help her sort through her feelings.

Her friend opened the door with a smile. Before she could say anything Katie blurted, "He kissed me."

"He did? Then why do you look so glum?"

Katie shrugged out of her jacket as she stepped into the house. "Afterwards he apologized."

"No! It was so lame he had to apologize?" Emily closed the door and followed Katie into the warm kitchen, where the sewing machine was once again set up on the table.

"Hardly." Katie slumped into a chair, draping her jacket over its back. "It was *wonderful.*" She sighed. "He apologized for, quote, getting carried away. Which means he hadn't *meant* to kiss me at all."

"Maybe he thought *you* didn't want to be kissed, and he was just being polite."

"Right." Katie rolled her eyes.

"Think about it, girlfriend. You've been careful not to do anything to make him think you might feel about him how you actually *do* feel about him." Emily stopped, a confused

193

look on her face, and bobbed her head as she replayed the sentence in her mind. "I never thought it made much sense, but what do I know? And more to the point," she added, "*how* would *he* know?"

"I did kiss him back."

"Hmm."

"But you do have a point."

"Of course I do! Here, try on the dress and tell me about your day while I pin up the hem." She slipped the freshly pressed gown from its hanger. "The whole thing. From the beginning."

"D'you think we could have a cup of tea first?" Katie asked forlornly.

Em nodded in sympathy. "Sounds to me like we'd better." She rehung the dress as Katie got up to fill the teakettle with water and turn the burner on. "Thanks, Katie. So — you interested in hearing about *my* Thanksgiving?"

"Oh, Em, I'm sorry. Sometimes I get so self-absorbed," Katie said as she took her seat again. "Of course I want to hear."

"Hey, I'm only teasing! I thought I'd take you off the hot seat for a minute or two." Emily pulled a box of tea from a cupboard and placed two bags in the ceramic teapot on the counter. "We did have a very nice Thanksgiving. You know Gram and Zack flew up from San Diego — somehow Zack arranged to take a whole week off from school — and of course Gram took over in the kitchen. Actually, I think Mom was happy to let her. Gave her time to visit with Abby, who drove down from Seattle just for the day."

"How's Abby doing? I haven't seen her for an age."

"Not bad. She's still waiting tables part-time, but sales are up at the gallery and a few small commissions are trickling in." Emily removed the whistling kettle from the burner and poured hot water over the tea bags in the pot. "She had to be at the gallery this morning, said she couldn't afford to miss the busiest retail day of the year."

"Your sister's incredibly gifted, Em. I hope she'll be able to make her living as an artist someday." Katie paused. "How are you two getting along, by the way?"

Emily sighed. "We're not close. I still don't get it — we have a lot in common, but Abby acts so uncomfortable around me, we can't even seem to keep a conversation going."

Katie nodded. "If it's any consolation, she's quiet around me, too."

"I expect it'll all work out one day," Emily said philosophically. "Sooner than later, I hope. What else? Oh — Owen brought his new girlfriend to dinner, and Izzy totally embarrassed her by saying in front of everyone she'd seen them kissing on the back porch."

"Owen's old enough to be kissing girls?"

"A senior in high school," Emily answered as she poured two mugs of tea and dropped a dollop of honey in each. "And Isabel's almost seven. Where've you been?" She handed a mug to Katie.

"Where *have* I been! I remember changing Owen's diapers! Okay, that leaves the twins. What's up with Eddie and Alex?"

"Still the family athletes. Finished soccer season and moved straight into basketball. They're both still taking karate, too. They gave us a demonstration yesterday. Pretty impressive — at least they've got the yell down!"

Katie sipped at her tea. "Your mom and dad are amazing," she said. "I can't imagine raising seven kids."

Emily held her mug between both hands and blew across the top to cool the steaming beverage. "What can I say? They love kids. They're going to be fabulous grandparents for Skippy."

"Skippy." Katie shook her head. "No matter what you decide to name that baby, I'm afraid it's always going to be Skippy."

Emily grinned. "Nah. We'll make the transition." She joined Katie at the table. "Okay, your turn. Shoot."

"From the beginning?"

"From the moment you opened the door to find Keith on your doorstep."

Katie smiled, remembering her thought that Keith had looked delicious. "It was a wonderful day, Em! We felt like family, Keith and Doc and Danny and I." She filled Emily in on the events of the day, enthusiastically recounting the part Keith had played in Danny's love affair with Brannigan. "Brannigan! Can you believe he named her *Brannigan?*"

"You did say she was a beautiful little thing."

"True. At least. Anyway, Keith pretended it was all Danny's idea to take the puppy home. The kid didn't stand a chance against Keith and that Irish setter."

Emily grinned. *"You're* the one who didn't stand a chance. No wonder you kissed him back!"

"Yeah. Well."

"Be straight with me, girlfriend — what are you feeling?"

Katie didn't hesitate. "I'm in love with him. I think you're right, that I've been in love with him for a long time."

"Well, hallelujah! She admits it at last!"

"You notice *I'm* not singing hallelujah," Katie said wryly. "What's so great about unrequited love?"

"You really don't think he's attracted to you?"

"I don't know." She tugged at her lower lip, remembering the gentle kiss, the way it had changed before he abruptly broke it off, the look in his smoky eyes as he'd turned away. "Yeah, I think he's attracted. That doesn't mean he's in love."

"No, it doesn't. But open your eyes, girlfriend — you've got to know how special you are to him!"

Katie stared down at the mug in her hand, unconsciously rubbing her finger around and around the rim. "You think?"

"I *know*." Emily banged her mug down on the table in front of her. "Why are you so unhappy about this, Katie? I don't get it."

"It's just —" Katie paused. "It's hard being in love with someone who's been my friend for so long."

"How so? Sounds perfect to me!"

Katie got up and poured herself another cup of tea. "A romance would change our friendship forever," she finally said.

"You're right about that. But change doesn't have to be bad, you know."

Sitting down again, Katie pulled her chair up to the table and sat over her mug of tea, her elbows supporting her chin. The smell of honey rose with the steam and tickled her nostrils. "Okay. I know. *But...*" She looked directly at her friend. "What if it *didn't* work out? I couldn't bear to lose Keith's friendship."

Emily shook her head. "You really think that would happen? Look at you and Henry — you're still friends."

"True. But I was never in love with Henry. And even

though Henry asked me to marry him, I really don't think he was in love with me either. Maybe we're still friends because the end of our romance wasn't a horrible blow to either of us." She picked up her mug and added, "If something like that happened with Keith — I can guarantee you, it *would* be a horrible blow. I'd be devastated." She looked at Emily across the table, her expression bleak. "I just can't lose him again."

"Ahh. That's what it's all about, isn't it? You're afraid of losing him again. No — more — you're afraid he'll leave you again."

Katie could hardly swallow around the huge lump in her throat. She nodded without saying anything.

"All I can tell you," Emily said quietly, "is that love isn't love without risk. It's part of the package, girlfriend." She lapsed into silence, leaving her friend to her own thoughts.

Scooting her chair back from the table, Katie pulled her feet up on the seat and wrapped her arms around her legs. She knew Emily was right, that choosing to love meant taking risks. In her mind she saw the expression on Danny's face when he'd first discovered the puppy in her kitchen — the mixture of hope, fear, and confusion. She knew how he felt.

The image shifted. She saw Danny's face again, after Doc agreed he could take Brannigan home with him. Pure joy. Ecstasy.

While Katie drank tea and talked to Emily, Keith worked out his frustrations on the basketball court.

The first thing he'd wanted to do when he got up this

morning was run to Katie's house in the rain and kiss her again — never mind the consequences. The impulsive thought scared him so badly he made up his mind not to be alone with her for a while. He was sure all he needed was a little space to regain his equilibrium.

Because no aerobics classes had been scheduled for the holiday weekend at Cully Center, the gym was open for free play. He got there by eight o'clock, shot a few baskets and played some one-on-one with Rito until enough weekend athletes showed up for a pickup game.

The court felt familiar, like an old friend he hadn't seen for too long. *Like that day in the city with Katie*, he thought fleetingly before blocking her image from his mind.

Often when he played at Cully Center, Keith held himself back; not many of the center's clients could match him for size or skill, so he handicapped himself to keep the game fair. Today he held back nothing. He jumped and whirled, scattering the sweat that flowed from every pore. He stuffed the ball and plucked his opponents' shots off the backboard and threw three-pointers that whisked through the net without touching the rim. His play seemed to inspire rather than intimidate the other players. The competition was fierce; the court became a battlefield and a testing ground.

The physical exertion drew off some of his nervous energy, but he still felt wired as he showered and changed into jeans and a striped rugby shirt. When he looked in the mirror to comb his hair, he found himself studying his image and wondering how Katie saw him. Was he still a skinny school-boy in her eyes? Did she know he was a man?

When he realized what he was thinking, he bared his teeth at the image in the mirror and threw his comb across the locker room. Getting back into his sweaty shorts and tee shirt, he played another hour, till he was almost too exhausted to think.

Now what? he asked himself as the hot water beat down on his shoulders once again. An afternoon to kill, and then he'd promised Katie he'd be at the coffeehouse to hear her sing. How would it be if he didn't show up? No — she'd think something was wrong. She'd call, and he'd have to make up some excuse. Besides, he wanted to be there. Just not alone.

Doc and Danny! A Thanksgiving reprise, only this time he'd make sure he came and went with the others. Maybe he could pick them up and take them home. Protection in numbers.

His mouth twisted in a wry grin as he realized he was setting up a six-year-old boy and his grandfather to protect him from a little redhead who barely topped five and a half feet. *You really are losing it, Castle,* he told himself.

Nevertheless, it would be fun to stop by and see how Danny was faring with Brannigan. They weren't far away.

Keith pulled into Doc's house on Dearborn Street just before noon, half-expecting to find the boy and the puppy tumbling together on the lawn, even in the rain. Then again, he reminded himself as he took the porch steps two at a time to get out of the weather, Doc was pretty protective of his grandson. It was the season for colds and flu. He rang the doorbell and waited, looking at the floor.

When the door swung open and Keith glanced up with a greeting on the tip of his tongue, he quite literally forgot what he'd planned to say. In fact, he almost forgot to breathe.

A beautiful woman, her dark, wavy hair brushed away

from a face that might have been the pattern for an exquisite porcelain doll, stood before him. She carried Brannigan in her arms and wore a look which was changing rapidly from curiosity to surprise to delight.

"Keith Castle! It is so good to see you!" Her smile lit her face, animating her perfect features and brightening the deep blue-violet of her exotic, almond-shaped eyes. "Danny," she called, not taking her eyes from Keith's, "come see who's here!"

Danny came running across the room, so excited his feet barely touched the floor. "Kee! Mama's home!"

Keith struggled to shift his gaze from the woman to the boy dancing at her side. "So I see! Toni…" He looked at her again. The delicate flush across her cheekbones matched the pale rose of the oversized angora turtleneck she wore with black leggings and ankle boots. "You look incredible," he said.

He watched in fascination as she kneeled to place Brannigan in Danny's arms. When she rose with a graceful flourish a moment later, she threw her arms around Keith, laughing. Then she pulled him into the house and, placing one hand on his left shoulder and the other in his right hand, danced him around the living room.

A door slammed down the hallway and Doc called out, "What's all the ruckus?" When he came through the door and saw Keith and Toni dancing around the room, breathless with laughter, and Danny watching them with bright eyes as he hugged the Irish setter puppy to his chest, he smiled as if the world had finally come out right.

Sixteen

❧

Toni pirouetted away from Keith and fell laughing onto the sofa. Danny stood nearby, watching her with adoring eyes. "Haven't had such a fine partner since the junior-senior prom, Mr. Castle," she drawled. "All that leaping around the basketball court gave you the *moves*."

"Not the kind of moves you were looking for, as I recall," Keith reminded her dryly. "You broke up with me the next morning."

Toni sighed. "Ah, foolish youth!" She pulled Danny, still holding Brannigan, down on the sofa next to her and wrapped one arm around him while she scratched the puppy's tummy with the other hand. Brannigan stretched and waved a paw in the air.

"I don't know if I should thank you for this dog or not," she complained to Keith. "She's pretty tough competition for an old woman!"

Yeah, right, Keith thought to himself.

Without warning she began to tickle Danny, who collapsed giggling on the sofa. The puppy licked his face, then wriggled from his grasp. Toni pinned her son with both arms and pelted him with kisses as Brannigan pranced on the sofa next to them, her tail wagging, barking joyously at the excitement. Danny pretended to struggle against his mother, but his mouth quirked in a big, foolish grin. He was loving every minute of the affectionate attention.

She gave him one last hug and let him go. Giggling, he grabbed Brannigan and raced around the room, holding the puppy out in front of him. Keith had never seen him so wound up.

"Have you had lunch?" Toni asked Keith.

"No." He dropped onto the arm of the upholstered chair across from her as Doc joined her on the sofa. "I swore after yesterday I wouldn't have to eat for a week, but suddenly I'm starving."

"Good! I was about to fix something for the three of us. You'll stay?"

"I'd love to."

Over a simple lunch Toni made because Danny said it was his favorite — celery sticks with peanut butter, tomato soup, and grilled cheese sandwiches — Keith learned that Toni was on a holiday pass from her drug rehab program and had landed at the airport only minutes after Doc and Danny had left for Katie's house the day before.

"Oh, no! You sat here alone while the rest of us were enjoying a big turkey dinner at Katie's?" Keith asked.

"Poor me," Toni pouted. "Pop says you had a great time, too. I should have called ahead, but I really wanted to surprise Pop and Danny."

"You su'prised us, sure enough," Doc said, raising his bushy eyebrows.

"You sure did, Mama!"

"All the lights was on when we got home," Doc explained to Keith, "an' —"

"Let me tell it, Grumpy!" Danny interrupted.

The little boy continued to be more lively than Keith had ever seen him. Was he showing off for his mother, or did her presence simply energize him? *The way Katie energizes me,* he mused before he could stop the thought from forming.

"Go on, then, Danny Boy."

"Grumpy thought maybe we had burglars!" Danny told Keith, his eyes wide. "Me an' him sneaked up to the window on the porch, an' at first we didn't see nothin', but then Mama comes walkin' down the hallway, an' I yelled 'Mama!' right through the window, an' she looked up an' we both went runnin' for the front door, an' Brannigan woke up an' started barkin' like crazy —"

Toni smiled at her son. "It was the very nicest homecoming I could have imagined," she said. She scooted her chair away from the table. "C'mere and sit on my lap for a while, Danny."

He eagerly complied, and Toni sat with her chin resting on his head, her arms wrapped around him as they continued talking. She was the picture of devoted motherhood, Keith thought, a far cry from the angry druggie Doc had described a few months earlier, the day Danny had swung at another boy to defend her honor.

He remembered he'd had a huge crush on Toni in high school, and that she'd nearly broken his heart. It was odd how little else he remembered, except that he'd thought her the most beautiful girl he'd ever seen. Beautiful, a little wild, a little dangerous. Maybe that was her strongest appeal for a seventeen-year-old straight-arrow who'd always played by the rules.

Toni hadn't taken long to figure out Keith was too tame for her. Keith was a slower learner. He hadn't even known until she'd broken up with him that she'd been seeing other guys all along. Guys who *weren't* such straight-arrows. Thank goodness he'd had Em to hear his righteous anger and Katie's shoulder to cry on — the fearsome threesome once again, at least for a few short months before he went off to college. What different paths their lives had taken, his and Katie's and Em's and Toni's, and how odd those paths should be converging once again....

"How much longer is your rehabilitation, Toni?" Keith asked.

"I'll be out the end of January," she replied. She rubbed her chin across Danny's hair and smiled across the table at Doc. "Then I'm coming home to stay." She went on to explain that her Thanksgiving pass and another four-day pass at Christmas were the only off-campus allowances of the structured, six-month residential program that she credited with returning her to sanity. "It's the hardest thing I've ever done in my life, and the hardest part is yet to come."

Keith questioned her with his eyes.

"I have a lot of amends to make," she explained. "I'm going to make them. I've set my mind."

Later when she stepped out on the porch to smoke a cigarette, Doc entreated Keith to do an old man a favor and introduce Toni back into their group of friends. "She's doin' good now, in the program," he said quietly. "But I'm scared for 'er, Kee. She'll be needin' to see some friendly faces when she gets back home. You an' Irish would be just the thing, and mebbe that girl o' Chappie's you used to hang 'round with. Mebbe she'd even go to church if it was you who asked 'er."

"I'd be happy to show her around again, Doc," Keith assured his old friend. "In fact, Katie's singing at the Lighthouse tonight. Maybe I'll call Emily and her husband to meet us there. Shall we all go?"

"It's a bit late for Danny. Besides, I don't think he'll be wantin' to leave Brannigan so soon," Doc told him. "We'll stay home. You young people go on out. Then Sunday, mebbe you can drop on by an' we'll all of us go to church conjointly."

Keith nodded. As long as he was going to church for Toni's sake, he expected he could manage it one time. He smiled to himself, thinking how happy Katie would be to see him in church again.

And wouldn't she be surprised to see Toni at the coffee-house tonight!

A beautifully painted seashore mural covered every inch of wall at the Lighthouse, the coffee shop near Columbia River College where Tomahawk Community Church ran a week-end ministry. The painting, the live music, the smell of fresh-brewed coffee, and most of all Chappie Lewis's compelling presence combined to create an ambiance that made the coffeehouse a favorite student haunt on Friday and Saturday nights.

The ministry had been Chappie's brainstorm and had become a favorite part of his job as college minister at Tomahawk. A good night, according to him, had nothing to do with receipts; a good night was a night when the air was thick with arguments — or "discussions," as he preferred to call them. Politics, religion, sex, philosophy, popular culture — no subject was taboo.

On the small stage tucked into a corner of the room, Katie looked up from an electronic keyboard as she sang the last lines of Amy Grant's "House of Love." Because many students had left campus for the four-day Thanksgiving weekend, the crowd at the Lighthouse was unusually sparse tonight. On a normal Friday evening during the school year there was hardly room to move.

Katie glanced toward the table where Beau and Emily had settled when they'd first come in. She noted with pleasure that Keith was sitting with them now, as was Chappie, who was deep in conversation with an indistinguishable figure in the shadows. Refocusing on the binder of sheet music in front of her, she leafed through it with one hand, absently running the fingers of her other hand up and down the keyboard. She needed one last song to finish her set: something suitable for the Thanksgiving season, something to express her gratitude to God for the warmth and love that had filled her house yesterday....

Securing her hair behind one ear, she cleared her throat quietly and turned on the microphone. Her fingers moved into an introduction of the song she'd chosen as she leaned into the mike. "I'd like to dedicate this piece to my very good friends, Beau and Emily, and to three special men who shared Thanksgiving with me yesterday."

Flashing a smile toward the table where her friends sat, she spoke the first two lines of the song in her rich contralto:

God has given life and God has given love
So let us give him thanks together....

She'd written the tune for Beau and Emily's wedding two years before. They'd chosen a verse from the Psalms as a theme for their marriage and asked Katie to write a song based on it, something they could carry with them as their relationship grew and deepened. She began singing:

O magnify the Lord with me
and let us exalt his name together!

Giving himself, he teaches to give;
living his life, he lets us live
to touch him together.

O magnify the Lord with me
and let us exalt his name together!

The unexpected swing from major to minor key between the chorus and the verses punctuated the swings in mood, from exultation to contemplation and back again.

Looking inside us, he makes us see;
filling our spirits, he makes us free
to know him together.

Katie looked up from her music when she reached the chorus again and glanced around the room. Keith was winding through the tables, balancing two large ceramic mugs. He looked up, as if he knew she'd spotted him, and smiled his wonderful crooked smile. Her heart jumped. She looked quickly back to the music in front of her, afraid she'd lose her place if she spent even a moment more watching him walk across the room.

List'ning in silence, we understand —
uniting our spirits with his tender hand
to love him together.

O magnify the Lord with me
and let us exalt his name together!

At the end of the song, amid scattered applause, she announced a fifteen-minute break, slipped a tape into the player next to the keyboard, and threaded her way through the closely set tables to the back of the darkened room where her friends sat.

"Hi, guys!" she called.

Keith was sitting next to Chappie and across from Emily, who was pulling out a chair. The figure Katie had noticed earlier still sat in the shadows on the other side of the table, leaning away from the dim hanging light. "Hey, girlfriend! Good singin'!" Emily said. "Have a seat — Beau's gone to get some coffee for you."

"What a nice surprise, having everyone show up tonight," Katie commented as she dropped into the chair Emily had pulled out for her. "What is it, old home week?"

Suddenly she felt an elbow in her side. "Ow!" She jerked away from Emily, looking at her in bewilderment. Her friend's eyes seemed to be trying to telegraph some urgent message, though what it might be Katie didn't have a clue.

"More than you know, Katie." She swung her head around to Keith. He was grinning and looking at the figure in the shadows. "Remember Toni Ferrier?"

209

Katie stared as an invisible hand seemed to reach around her heart and squeeze it like a bellows. The woman on the other side of Keith leaned forward into the light, smiling, and stretched a graceful arm across the table. Her hand was cool and soft.

"Hi, Kate. It's nice to see you again — and *hear* you again. You really sound great."

"Toni!" She wondered if her voice expressed even a fraction of her shock. "Wh…what a surprise!"

Beau saved the moment by returning with Katie's coffee and setting it down a little too hard in front of her. The brown liquid, cream still swirling at the top, sloshed over the edge of the mug. Toni withdrew her hand from Katie's to grab for a napkin.

"Sorry, Red. Kind of a klutz tonight," Beau apologized. He wasn't looking at her. He was looking at Toni cleaning up the spilled coffee.

Not that Katie could blame him. For purely aesthetic reasons, it was hard *not* to look at Toni. She'd been beautiful as a teenager; as a woman, she was stunning. Her wavy, blue-black hair set off a face so exquisite Katie wanted to cry. Flawless ivory skin, in startling contrast to her dark hair, stretched over well-defined cheekbones and an aquiline nose. Beautifully shaped brows and thick black lashes framed a pair of exotic almond eyes the deep purple blue of dusk.

Pushing the wet napkin out of the way, Toni looked up, her lips curving into a perfect smile, a smile that belonged on a magazine cover, not here, illuminating a dim corner of the Lighthouse. Her enigmatic eyes glittered silver in the soft light. Was it just Katie's imagination that her gaze seemed to linger on Keith? And that he looked a bit dazed?

Toni lifted her mug. "To old friends."

They were all in a daze, Katie thought. Keith, Beau, even Emily. Lifting their mugs to clink against each other's, they each added their own toast.

Beau: "To good times."

Emily: "To laughter!"

And Keith: "To starting over…"

Katie's throat tightened. She couldn't have said a word if she'd tried, couldn't have lifted her mug off the table. No matter. No one even noticed.

She saw the group at the table as if from a long way off, jerking like puppets on strings. She listened to their conversation without hearing the words, only the sounds lurching up and down, too bright, accompanied by tinny laughter.

Her memory carried her to the high school cafeteria the first day of her junior year, Keith's final year. Keith and Emily and herself together as usual, sharing lunch and discussing first impressions. She looked up in surprise when someone sat down next to Keith, jostling him in a too-familiar way.

"Hey, Keith, Pop said you'd watch out for me. You watching?" Katie looked on in dismay as the girl, too old for her age, smiled seductively and let her denim jacket slip off her shoulders to reveal a bare halter top. Keith's face had reddened, but he hadn't looked away. Neither had Emily, for that matter.

For the rest of that miserable school year, Keith hadn't taken his eyes off Toni — or his mind. He talked about her constantly, completely infatuated; in the throes of his own adolescent agony and ecstasy, he was oblivious to Katie's pain.

For the first half of the year, while Keith struggled over Toni's constant push and pull, Katie might as well have been invisible to him. For the second half, when he'd finally convinced Toni to "be his girl," Katie *had* been invisible to him. She'd felt as if, in his mind, she simply no longer existed.

It was happening again, she thought wretchedly as she glanced around the table at the Lighthouse. *No one sees me. I'm invisible again.* She believed it so thoroughly she decided she could slip away to the rest room without anyone noticing.

Leaning against the counter in the ladies' room, she closed her eyes, let her head drop forward, breathed deeply. *One, two, three, four…*

"Kate? Are you okay?"

She whirled around and found herself staring into Toni's inquiring eyes. They searched her face, as if looking for something in particular. She was not invisible to Toni, Katie realized with a start.

"Fine. Thanks, Toni." Katie rolled her head and reached to massage the back of her neck. "I get stiff after a couple hours performing."

"Here, let me do that." Toni moved behind her and began to expertly knead the tight muscles across her shoulders. Katie winced. "Stress ties me up in knots the same way," Toni said from behind her.

Shrugging away from the other woman's touch, Katie turned to face her. "Thanks. I'm fine, really." She smiled weakly. "How are you, Toni?"

"Good." She hesitated. "You know I'm in drug rehab?"

Katie nodded. "Doc says your treatment is going well."

Toni leaned back against the counter, her arms supporting her weight. "Yes, well… It's been tough. It's my second time. I feel different about it, though — I chose it this time. Last time the courts forced me into it. After I lost Danny."

She nervously pulled a pack of cigarettes out of her purse and offered one to Katie. Katie shook her head. "No, of course, you wouldn't smoke." She fished around in her purse for a lighter. Katie was silent as Toni lit up and took a couple of drags.

"Kate, Pop told me how much you've done for Danny. I know my...problems...have been tough for him. I just wanted to say thanks."

"He's a great kid, Toni. I have lots of fun with him and Doc." *And Keith*, she added silently.

Toni nodded. "You know," she said after a moment, "I really hated Pop for taking him away from me." She took another puff. "I think that's why the treatment didn't work the first time. I was too full of hate."

She stubbed the cigarette out in the sink and dropped it in the trash. "I'm getting better." She nodded at the trash can. "Three or four drags and I throw it out. No sense trading one addiction for another."

Not knowing what to say, Katie remained silent.

"I finally figured out Pop did what was best for Danny," Toni went on. "And for me, too. It might have been years before I'd have gotten help on my own." She stopped, and Katie saw that her dusky eyes were glistening with tears. "This time I'm doing it for all of us — for Pop and Danny, and for me. Because I don't want to lose them again."

This was a side of Toni that Katie had never seen, never even imagined existed: soft, unguarded, hopeful. Katie felt herself drawn to the woman, felt empathy for her struggles and her hopes.

"That's great, Toni. I'm really happy for you." *I really am!* Katie thought with amazement.

Toni shook her head. "I can't believe how badly I've screwed up my life! I'm glad I have Danny, of course, but I wish I'd done it differently. A wedding first. A daddy for my son." She crossed her arms, hugging herself, a faraway look in her eyes. "I had *Keith,* Kate! For a whole year, I had Keith in the palm of my hand. Since him, I haven't had anyone worth cooking a nice meal for."

Katie felt fingers of panic clutching at her throat. She didn't want to hear any more. "Maybe we'd better get back before everybody wonders what's happened to us, huh, Toni?" Her voice sounded falsely bright in her ears.

Toni stepped back from the counter. "I threw it away once, Kate. With God's help, I'm not going to throw it away again," she vowed. "Keith and Danny get along great, and Pop loves him like a son. It's not fair Pop should have to take care of us when he should be getting ready to retire." She opened the door, holding it for Katie. "I couldn't do better than Keith, and I know I can make things good for us."

Beau and Keith both stood as the two women approached the table, each pulling out a chair. Toni smiled brilliantly at Keith. "Thanks. Always a gentleman."

"Wondered if you two had flown away," he said. "Everything okay?"

He wasn't asking Katie. She looked around the table. Even Emily's attention was riveted on Toni. "Got to get to my last set," she mumbled.

She couldn't think of singing. Pulling out the score for a Chopin nocturne, she poured her feelings out on the keyboard, unaware of the hush that fell over her audience as she played. When she'd finished, she gathered up her music, slipped into her coat, and stole away, oblivious to the rousing applause that followed her.

CHAPTER

Seventeen

❧

Katie lay awake till the early morning hours, her mind a swirling eddy of thoughts and emotions. Wishing fervently she could dislike Toni, she found herself instead feeling compassion, even admiration, for her.

She couldn't guess what Toni's life must have been like growing up with a mother as selfish and unstable as hers had been. Mina had not only led Toni to believe she'd been abandoned by her father, she herself had abandoned her when her daughter had become an inconvenience.

Neither could Katie fathom what it must have been like to be pregnant and alone at seventeen or to be enslaved by drugs and alcohol the way Toni had been — to have reached a point where every choice she made was dictated by the need for a fix.

Mostly, she couldn't imagine the courage it must take for Toni to face every day: to endure the memories of the hurt inflicted on her by others and to acknowledge the pain she'd left in the wake of her own choices. To know that one slip could send her plunging back into the hell of addiction.

Whatever Toni had been in the past, today, by the grace of God, she was a new woman — clear-headed, courageous, determined to make a success of her life. She knew what she wanted. She'd set her mind to go after it. Katie had to admire that, even though what Toni wanted was what Katie wanted herself.

Thanksgiving with Keith and Doc and Danny had felt so *right*, she thought. So warm and wonderful and filled with love. So *family*. Now she questioned whether she'd made it all up. Was she trying to fit where she didn't belong, like an odd piece forced into a jigsaw puzzle? *Toni* was the piece that fit; Katie wasn't Doc's daughter or Danny's mother — Toni was. And it wasn't Katie Keith had meant to kiss. After hearing his apology and after feeling how invisible she was to him when Toni was around, it seemed clear: Toni was the one.

Try as she might, Katie couldn't find a flaw in the other woman's plan. What Toni said was true: Danny adored Keith, and Doc loved him like his own son. Keith could provide everything Doc and Danny and Toni were missing; what better man to be the son, the father, the husband they'd never had? In a practical sense he was already Doc's son and Danny's father. And Toni had been his first love. How many times had she heard that a man never forgets his first love? It seemed to Katie that a marriage between Toni and Keith would simply acknowledge the relationships that already existed.

In the morning, afraid she might get awkward questions about her abrupt departure the night before, Katie decided to spend the day hiding out. She got up early, not bothering with makeup or even a shower, and dressed hurriedly in jeans and a bulky ivory wool sweater pulled over a flannel shirt. Before she left the house, her briefcase laden with more than enough work to fill her day, she turned off her answering machine. She didn't want to know who tried to call today — or who didn't.

Rather than risk running into someone she knew on the campus of Columbia River College, she drove downtown to the Portland State University library to work. Unfortunately, it opened later than she remembered. She tramped back to the car, frustrated, and threw her briefcase on the front seat. Then, huddling into her bulky sweater, she walked the South Park Blocks all the way to the Performing Arts Center and back, stopping for a donut and a cup of coffee along the way.

The brisk exercise helped clear her mind and energized her for the paperwork ahead. Back at the library, she found a quiet table tucked into a corner on the fourth floor and spread out her papers. She had plenty to do: writing an update for Henry on her music ed class, reviewing student self-evaluations on the progress of their curriculum projects, rewriting the final exam for her general music class, posting quiz grades. When her stomach started to growl around two, she took three sets of papers and her gradebook with her to lunch to make sure no one would bother her.

The library closed at seven. Too early to go home. Checking the movie listings in the *Oregonian* on the first floor, she found a Chinese film that sounded interesting playing at the KOIN. Good. Concentrating on subtitles would keep her mind occupied. To pass the time before the late movie started and get herself in the mood for it, Katie treated herself to Chinese at a restaurant near the cinema, sitting in a dark

217

corner and feeling as invisible in her nondescript clothes as she'd felt at the Lighthouse sitting next to Toni.

By the time she got home, after eleven, Katie was exhausted from trying so hard not to think about the way she was feeling. But for the second night in a row, sleep eluded her till the early hours of morning. Lying in bed without any distractions, she couldn't disengage her mind.

Was she giving up too easily? Were Keith and Toni really a done deal? Was she dropping out of the race for Keith's attention because she didn't feel up to the competition? All's fair in love and war, she'd heard. She didn't have all of Toni's assets, but she did have some of her own. Maybe she could come up with a strategy to win him back....

Love isn't a competition, Katie. She didn't know where the thought had come from, but it continued to play in her mind like a mantra, finally hypnotizing her into sleep. *Love isn't a competition....*

The telephone jolted Katie awake. Morning light filtered through the sheer curtains of her bedroom window, though it seemed she'd only been asleep a few minutes. She reached for the phone, but hesitated before lifting the receiver. Who would be calling her before church on a Sunday morning? She still wasn't ready to talk to Emily, or Keith, or Toni, or Doc, and she couldn't screen the call; she'd forgotten to turn the answering machine on when she'd come home the night before. Burying her head beneath a pillow, she tried to ignore the insistent ring but found herself counting: *six, seven, eight....*

Finally the phone fell silent. Wide awake, Katie pulled her head out from under the pillow and looked at the clock. She had time for a leisurely bath and breakfast before church, if she wanted to go. Church was a customary part of her Sunday mornings, but she wasn't sure she was ready to come out of hiding. On the other hand, she found herself longing for the comfort and encouragement she always found when she attended a service at Tomahawk.

Feeling revived after a warm bubble bath and a breakfast of hot cereal with fruit and honey, she decided to take the chance. She lit a fragrant candle in the bathroom as she applied her makeup, breathing deeply of the vanilla-scented air and rubbing moisturizer into her skin in slow circles as if she were giving herself a facial. She'd forgotten what good therapy a little self-pampering could be.

By the time she was ready to go, she felt more herself than she had for a day and a half. The image in the full-length mirror pleased her. Her wool knit dress, a delicate periwinkle blue, swung softly around her knees when she walked, and the floral print sweater, white with lavender and royal, made her feel feminine and pretty. Her curly auburn hair was pulled back in a French roll with feathery bangs that framed her brown eyes — no, she reminded herself, *amber* eyes. She wasn't Toni, but there was nothing wrong with being Katie at her best, either. No matter how she'd felt Friday night, she didn't have to choose to be invisible.

She purposely arrived a few minutes late to church, picking up a bulletin in the foyer before stealing up the stairs to the balcony. The children's choir was singing as she slipped quietly into the last row, where the sun cast a golden glow through a stained glass window. Closing her eyes, she let the sounds of children's voices raised in a song of thanksgiving wash over her. She was glad she'd come.

Glancing through the bulletin as the song ended, Katie

saw that the service, in keeping with the season, had been set aside to honor God with thanksgiving: music and open worship instead of a sermon, a time for the members of the congregation to share the things for which they were especially grateful. It was the kind of service Katie liked best, and once again she felt happy to have made the choice to be there.

From the last row of the balcony, her view of the main floor was limited to the platform where the adult and children's choirs sat on either side and the ministerial team sat on the facing bench looking out over the congregation. But even without being able to see, she knew Doc's voice when he stood up to share in the middle of the service.

"Sometime happiness don't come easy," he said in his quiet voice. "But I found if you wait for the good Lord's timin', things has a way of workin' out. I'm right happy to have my daughter home, an' to see how the great God in his mercy be workin' in 'er life. An' I'm right thankful that my grandson be gettin' his mama back."

Keith shifted uncomfortably in his seat as Doc sat down. His first foray into a church service in over five years was not affecting him the way he'd supposed it would. Anger, he might have expected. Maybe impatience with the simple faith of simple people who didn't have enough experience in life to know the real score. Boredom, perhaps; he'd heard it all before.

But nostalgia? And worse, self-pity?

Tomahawk Community Church was a place where he had once without question belonged. Spiritual awareness was a part of his mother's legacy from early childhood on, passed down in the context of her love for him and her daily recognition of the miracles of everyday life. Although she worked on Sunday mornings until Keith was in his teens, she sent him off to Sunday school with Doc, and the church had come to feel as much like home as his own house did. A community built on the familiar awareness of everyday grace seemed normal to him. He didn't know for a long time that for many people, even people in the church, life was about acquiring and hoarding material things.

After so many years away, he felt like a stranger in the church today — like an outsider looking in. Not with contempt or condescension, he realized, but with sorrow, with longing. Like a Dickens street urchin gazing in the window of a well-lit home at Christmas.

How could I give up my faith when it was such an essential part of me? The question formed in his mind as he listened to the old familiar tunes and heard one person after another give thanks to God, common themes of love and grace woven through their stories.

I didn't give up my faith; it was taken away from me! he argued with himself. Aware of a sudden ache in his gut that felt more like hunger than anger or pain, he pushed the thought aside. Maybe a church service was the obvious time and place to explore one's thoughts and feelings about faith, but he just wasn't ready. He wondered if he'd ever be.

Deliberately shutting out the rest of the service, he let his mind wander. He'd been having fun with Doc and Danny and Toni. Yesterday they'd gone to the Japanese Gardens, then back to Doc's house, where Toni made dinner and the four of them spent the evening playing Uno, Crazy Eights, and Yahtzee. He'd had a good time, but he missed Katie. She was so much a part of his relationship with Doc and Danny.

Where *was* Katie, anyway? He'd tried to call her several times yesterday to have her join them, but she hadn't been home and didn't have her answering machine turned on. Then this morning he'd phoned to invite her to sit with them in church, but again no answer. He'd even waited around the foyer till right before the service began, but apparently she hadn't come to church.

Maybe she wasn't feeling well. Come to think of it, she'd been awfully quiet at the Lighthouse Friday night. And then she'd disappeared so quickly after her last number he hadn't even been able to tell her how moved he was by her performance — some classical piano piece that pulled at his heart the same way Danny's tears did.

Forgetting the vow he'd made only two days earlier not to see her alone, Keith was determined to drop by her apartment that afternoon after Toni was gone to find out what was going on. If something was troubling Katie, he wanted to know.

He glanced at Danny, who was sitting quietly between him and Toni, drawing on the back of the church bulletin with the pencil from the pew. His picture looked like the typical family portrait for a child his age, stick figures with happy-face smiles. One curly-haired figure wearing a dress, standing next to a house with smoke rising from the chimney. One small figure next to her, and then two tall ones, all in pants and shirts.

Danny tugged at Keith's sleeve and grinned up at him. As he leaned down to admire the picture, the little boy handed him the pencil and whispered, "Write the names."

Keith nodded and pointed to the small figure, then to Danny, his eyebrows raised in question. Danny nodded. *D-A-N-N-Y*, Keith wrote. He pointed to the figure of the woman. "Mama," Danny whispered. *M-A-M-A*. "And Grumpy," Danny added, pointing to the figure next to the one labeled with his own name. *G-R-U-M-P-Y*.

"Who's this?" Keith whispered, pointing to the last figure. Danny pointed at him and giggled. Toni glanced over, frowning at her son and lifting a finger to her lips. Her frown dissolved into a smile as she saw the picture on Danny's lap and watched Keith label the last figure: *K-E-E*. When he finished, the little boy handed the drawing to his mother. "For you, Mama."

"Thank you, sweetheart!" she whispered. "I'll put it on the wall right over my bed and think about you every day, okay?"

Half an hour later Keith and Toni stood in a quiet corner of the foyer waiting for Doc, who'd taken Danny to the rest room. Toni reached up to straighten his tie. "Pop and Danny sure do think you're something special, Keith."

His mouth quirked in a half smile. "The feeling's mutual, Toni. Danny has me wrapped around his little finger, and he didn't need to do a thing! And Doc..." His voice turned serious. "I don't know if you know how important your dad was in my life when I was growing up. I never had a father. Doc was the closest thing I knew."

Toni nodded. "It's odd, isn't it — you having him as a father all those years I didn't? Seeing Pop with Danny... He's so good with kids. It must have been horrible when my mother took me away." She grinned wryly. "And worse when she sent me back, I'm afraid!"

"You were pretty wild, all right! A regular heartbreaker, Toni."

She grew quiet. "I know. I have so much to make up to him and to Danny, too. I just —" Her voice broke. She averted her face, but not before Keith saw that she was crying. "I'm sorry," she said helplessly.

He cursed himself silently. "Toni, I can be such a klutz! *I'm* the one who's sorry."

"No, it's not you —"

"Come here." Keith held out his arms and Toni turned into them, tears running down her cheeks. "It's okay," he murmured into her hair. "It's okay."

"I just worry about them," she said between sniffles. "Pop's getting older, and Danny..."

Keith pulled away, holding onto her arms above the elbows. "Look at me, Toni," he said quietly.

She raised her tear-streaked face, and Keith was reminded of his first meeting with Danny, of the way the boy had cried as though his heart would break.

"I owe Doc as much as you do," he said solemnly. "When he needs help, you're not alone. And as for Danny, I know what it's like to be without a father. I *promise* you — are you listening?"

She nodded, her blue violet eyes searching his smoky green ones.

"I promise you that I will be here for Danny. Always."

"Thank you," she whispered.

Keith pulled her close once again, rocking her gently, feeling as fatherly toward Toni as he did toward her son.

Katie lingered in the balcony till it emptied before getting into her navy wool coat, thinking the longer she waited the less likely she would be to run into Doc and Danny or Beau and Emily. She wondered if Toni had come to church with her father and son this morning.

Her question was answered as she rounded the corner of the stairs and saw Toni standing in profile below, wearing an elegant, cranberry-colored coat that looked as if it had come from a designer's showroom. Katie stopped short and quickly backed around the corner, shaken.

Keith. With Toni. Here, in church, where he'd told Katie he didn't go anymore. What Katie hadn't been able to do in three months of spending time with him, listening to him, praying for him, the other woman had done in three days.

She leaned against the wall, her legs weak and her heart thumping in her chest. Maybe she really *couldn't* understand what Keith had been through in the same way Toni could, she thought miserably — one wounded soul to another. Maybe Toni could be an instrument for Keith's healing in a way she couldn't be. In the grand scheme of things, Keith's healing was more important than her desire that he love her.

Part of Katie wanted to retreat to the balcony and curl up on a pew until she was sure they were gone, but she couldn't keep herself from peering around the corner again.

Keith was holding Toni by both arms, gazing raptly into her upturned face. His voice rose clearly up the stairwell. "I know what it's like to be without a father. I *promise* you — are you listening?"

Toni nodded.

"I promise you that I will be here for Danny. Always." He

pulled her close. They stood together at the bottom of the stairs in a long embrace, broken only when Danny came running across the foyer, followed by Doc.

Keith smiled down at the little boy, his arm still around Toni's shoulder. "Ready for some lunch?"

They looked like a family that belonged together, Katie thought, heavy with grief as she watched them leave. She slumped down on the stairs, holding her head in her hands.

They *did* belong together. Toni and Keith obviously agreed.

For everyone's good, it was time for Katie to let go.

Eighteen

❧

Keith wasn't making it easy to say goodbye. On Sunday afternoon, Katie had answered her doorbell without thinking, to find him standing on her front stoop with a single yellow rose wrapped in florist's tissue with fern and baby's breath. Her expression must have betrayed her surprise. He looked embarrassed as he thrust the bouquet toward her.

"I've been worried, thought you might be sick," he explained, nervously running his fingers through his hair. "I tried to call yesterday and again this morning. You don't have your answering machine on."

"Oh?" She reached automatically for the flowers and stood aside to let him in. "I'll have to make sure it's working." *Yellow,* she reflected, fingering the soft petals. *A yellow rose, for friendship.* She wondered if he meant it as a palliative.

"*Are* you all right?" Keith asked hesitantly. "You sound low."

"I'm feeling a bit under the weather," she replied, leading him through the apartment to the kitchen to find a vase. It certainly was true, if not in the way she was implying. "Better not get too close."

Though she hadn't gone out of her way to make him feel welcome, he stayed for an hour, talking mostly about the weekend he'd spent with Doc, Danny, and Toni. "Doc is anxious for Toni to have some contacts when she gets out of rehab in January. That's why I kept trying to call — so you could spend some time with her, too. We had a good time, but we missed you, Squirt."

"I'll bet."

He glanced at her, a frown creasing his brow, but didn't comment on the cynical remark. "Toni looks great, doesn't she?" he asked instead.

"*Great* seems a little understated," Katie said dryly. "How about gorgeous? Dazzling? Stunning?"

He either ignored or didn't notice her sarcasm. "Yeah, she's almost too beautiful to be real, isn't she? What I really meant was how well she's doing — how she's getting her life together."

Katie was silent for a moment. *This is the woman Keith has chosen,* she told herself. *And he's right — she is doing great. Support his decision. Be his friend.* "She seems to be really serious about turning her life around, Keith. I'm really happy for her, and for Doc and Danny." She couldn't bring herself to add, *And for you.*

On Monday he called to see how she was. She didn't pick up the phone. On Tuesday, when they usually had lunch together in the school cafeteria, she asked Myra Heimbach to join them. On Wednesday he dropped by her apartment late, after he'd gotten off work at ten, to see if she wanted to go out for coffee. She told him through a cracked door she was ready for bed, but maybe some other time…

When their regular Thursday lunch rolled around and he found her sitting in the college cafeteria with Henry, he stood looking at her for a long moment, his expression puzzled. "Katie, are you avoiding me for some reason?"

She didn't answer the question directly. "I've been really busy, Keith. Term's over in a couple of weeks, Christmas concert's coming up. I have lots to do."

He turned on his heel and walked away.

Henry looked at her, his eyebrows raised. "What's going on with you and Castle?"

Avoiding his eyes, she answered, "Nothing." *I only wish something was going on,* she added silently.

Keith confronted her later in the day as she slipped the key into the door of her Honda in the school parking lot. She didn't notice him till he cleared his throat, and she whirled around, startled, to find him leaning against the trunk of a bare-branched tree. "Lying in wait?" she snapped.

He pushed away from the tree and walked toward her, his arms crossed and a frown between his brows. "Katie, would you mind telling me what's going on?" His voice was tight. "A week ago we had what *I* thought was a pretty special Thanksgiving together. Then all of a sudden — boom! I'm out on my ear. I don't get it. I thought we were friends."

He stopped not two feet away, close enough that she could have reached out to take his hand, tell him she was sorry, she didn't know what had come over her. Instead, she turned her head and gazed across the parking lot at nothing. *I can't do this,* she told herself. *I can't be around him, feeling the way I feel about him and knowing I'll never be more than a friend.*

Opening her car door and carefully placing her briefcase behind the driver's seat, she steeled herself to turn around and look at him straight on. "Look, Keith, I need some space, okay?"

"That's it? No explanation?"

"Oh, that's rich — *you* demanding explanations! How do you think *I* felt all those years you were gone? Never a word about where or why?"

"So you're paying me back? Is that it?"

"Don't be ridiculous!" She stepped behind the car door, holding it open between them. "Does everything have to be about *you*? I have my own life to live, Keith, just like you have yours."

His face was red with frustration. "You're *part* of my life!"

"Look, I just need some space." Her words were measured. "Go do your thing. And oh — invite me to the wedding. I wouldn't miss it."

"The *wedding*? What are you talking about?"

"Oh, for Pete's sake, Keith," she said irritably, "you think I'm blind?"

"You're jealous!"

"I'm not jealous. I just think it's time you made an honest woman out of Toni."

"Excuse me?"

Shaking her head, she got into the car and rolled down the window. "Look," she said, slamming the door shut and peering up at him, "Danny needs you. Marry his mother." She turned the key in the ignition and revved the engine. "Better late than never."

The look on his face was pure shock. "Are you suggesting that *I'm* Danny's father?"

"I don't care if you are or not!" Katie said through her teeth. "Just leave me alone!"

"*If* I were Danny's father," Keith said, his voice cold as ice, "I would *not* have abandoned him."

"You abandoned *me!*"

"You are *not* a *child!*" he shouted, clenched fists stabbing the air to punctuate his words. "Even if you *are* acting like it! What's *wrong* with you?"

"Nothing you can't fix by getting out of my life!"

"Fine! Good*bye!*"

Katie's hands shook on the steering wheel as she backed out of her parking space and screeched around a corner toward the street. She felt sick to her stomach.

Keith raised his fists to the sky and bellowed. He had never been so furious in his life. How could she even *think* — what had gotten *into* her? Katie, his best friend. Someone he'd believed understood and cared about him. The only person in the world he'd trusted with his secret —

Overwhelming fury. Betrayed again.

Katie had stopped shaking by the time she got across town to Bybee Elementary School. The buses were pulling out of the parking lot as she pulled in.

Unable to bear the thought of being alone, she'd driven to Emily's workplace on automatic pilot, with no plan except getting comfort however she could. She felt dead inside. The eyes staring back at her from the rearview mirror *looked* dead.

Emily, bent over a table sorting through magazines for pictures for her bulletin boards, glanced up when Katie walked through the door of her kindergarten classroom. "Katie!" she cried, pushing herself up from the table. "What's wrong? You're white as a ghost!"

"Em. He'll never forgive me." Katie's voice was bleak. Dropping into a pint-sized chair, she wrapped her arms around her knees and laid her head down. Emily carefully lowered herself onto the short table next to Katie and began to rub her back.

"I thought I was doing the right thing," Katie murmured.

"Don't try to talk yet," Emily soothed. "Relax. Take a deep breath. It's okay."

Katie uncurled her spine and rolled her head in a circle, her expression desolate. Emily moved her hands to her friend's upper arms and gently massaged.

"That's right. Relax those muscles. You're okay."

The human touch and the soothing words were slowly urging feeling back into Katie's body. She could almost sense the blood begin to flow again, warming her from the inside. Emily wrapped her arms around Katie from behind, holding her awkwardly against her large belly and rocking her side to side.

"Now tell me about it," she finally said, settling back on the table.

Katie glanced at her briefly, then stared at her lap. "I... insinuated Keith was Danny's father."

"You didn't! Where did *that* come from?"

"He just wouldn't leave me alone. I just wanted him *gone!*" Frustration colored her voice.

Emily shook her head in confusion. "What are you talking about?"

"Keith and I aren't meant to be, Em. I need to let go of him."

"By making up stories? By intimating Keith has character flaws big enough to fly a plane through?"

Katie looked at her friend forlornly. "I didn't mean for it to happen that way. It just did." She let her head drop forward and grabbed the back of her neck with one hand, squeezing the tight muscles. "Keith and Toni belong together, Em."

"When did you decide *this?*"

"Last weekend. When Toni was here." She related what Danny's mother had told her in the ladies' room at the Lighthouse and then what she'd overheard Keith telling Toni at church. "I know it's for the best — that's why I've been trying to bow out of the picture. Danny would have a father, Doc would have his retirement back, Keith and Toni would have each other...."

"Wait a minute. You heard Keith ask Toni to marry him?"

She thought back. "Well, no...I heard him promise to be there for Danny."

Emily shook her head. "Not the same thing."

"But he had his arms around her!"

"He's never had his arms around you?"

"But —"

"No buts. Katie, you know I love you dearly, but you've got a *blind* spot, girlfriend."

"What do you mean?"

"Has it occured to you how presumptuous it is to plan other people's lives for them?"

"Presump —"

Emily stopped her again. "What gives you the right to

decide what's best for Keith and Toni and Doc and Danny? Don't you think they ought to have some say?" She pushed herself off the table and began to pace back and forth in front of Katie. "Keith, for instance. He's a big boy now. Give him some credit for figuring out what he wants on his own."

"What is so wrong with wanting my friends to be happy?" Katie asked defensively.

"Nothing. Katie, you are a generous, loving woman." Stopping in front of her friend, Emily took a deep breath and looked Katie in the eyes. "But sometimes taking care of other people isn't about love or generosity. Sometimes it's about needing to be in control."

Emily started to pace again, her arms across her chest. "You're trying to take care of things that aren't any of your business to take care of, girlfriend. You're right when you say you need to let go — but not of Keith. What you need to let go of is your need to take care of things that aren't your responsibility." She hesitated, then added gently, "Look how good it's been for your mom."

Katie jumped up from her chair. "And you call *me* presumptuous! I can't believe you're saying this!"

Walking to the bank of windows, Emily gazed out on the playground for a moment before turning around to answer her friend. "I've kept my peace too long. Let go of it, Katie. You can't take care of everything. Let God do his work, and you do yours. Love Keith. Love Doc and Danny. Love me. That's what we need from you."

Katie stared across the room at her. "I don't want to hear this. I came to you for *comfort!*"

Emily sighed. "I love you, Katie. I wouldn't be saying these things if I didn't."

"I think I'd better go."

"All right. But think about it, girlfriend. There's so much at stake."

Keith's heart sank as he pulled into his driveway a little after ten. His headlights had picked up the small figure sitting on the steps to his front porch, her auburn hair curling around her face in the damp air as she huddled into her quilted jacket. He sat uneasily in the Montero for a moment before turning off the engine, wondering if he should back out of the driveway and find some other place to go. But he knew it wouldn't do any good. No matter how long he stayed away, Katie would be there when he got back. He knew her too well.

Slamming the door behind him, he thrust his hands into the pockets of his leather jacket and walked purposefully toward her. He stopped in front of her, looking down, not saying anything.

Her uplifted face, lit only by the silver glow of moonlight, was pale and beautiful. "Hello, Keith." Her voice was low, subdued.

He still said nothing. To open his mouth felt dangerous. Hurt, anger, desire, and fear struggled against each other in his heart like hoodlums in a gang war fighting over turf. If he opened his mouth, he didn't know what would come out; from moment to moment he wasn't sure which emotion had the upper hand.

Katie cleared her throat. "Remember that conversation we had a few months ago about saying you're sorry?"

Keith nodded.

"Love means saying you're sorry every single time you screw up."

He nodded again.

"I screwed up big-time, Keith. I didn't mean what I said. You can't know how sorry I am."

A long moment passed. "So why did you say it?" he finally asked.

He heard her inhale, as if gathering her courage from the autumn air. "I've been keeping a secret from you."

When he didn't respond, she took another deep breath. "I fell in love with you when I was fifteen years old. In ten years, I haven't fallen out. You were right about my being jealous of Toni. I was jealous then, and I'm jealous now."

He couldn't swallow, let alone respond. Desire and fear were at each other's throats inside him.

"When Toni came back, more beautiful than ever," Katie continued quietly, "happier, more together, filling the place in Doc's and Danny's lives I thought I filled — I lost all sense of perspective. I felt invisible. I knew I couldn't compete."

Keith felt a blow to his gut. Hurt and anger were throwing punches at each other. How could she think he'd want to give up the years of their friendship for Toni, who'd never even existed for him except as a fantasy?

He searched her face in the moonlight, feeling strangely tender. *You're not invisible to me,* he might have said. *You're the most beautiful woman I know.*

Katie hadn't taken her eyes from his face. "I don't know how you're feeling, Keith. About anything. But I want you to know I love you. I hope you can forgive me for the stupid, hurtful things I said. I believe in you, no matter how it sounded."

The silence stretched out between them like a fragile spiderweb. "Do yourself a favor, Katie," he finally answered, his voice low. "Forget the way you feel." *I can't love you the way you deserve to be loved,* he added silently. *I'm too afraid. You inspire things in me I don't know how to deal with.*

Katie looked away from him for the first time since he'd planted himself in front of her. Grabbing the wooden stair railing, she pulled herself up, stepped around him, and marched down the sidewalk, her back straight and her head high. He knew that gait and posture. She was pretending not to care.

As soon as she was out of sight of his house, Katie started to run, every breath a ragged sob. When she reached home, she collapsed on her bed fully dressed and wept until she was certain she'd cried every last tear. Finally she fell into an exhausted sleep.

In the morning, she sat for hours at the piano, unable to sing but letting her fingers work out her grief on the keyboard. After she'd played everything she could think of, she began to improvise. A series of chord progressions in a minor key led her to a haunting melody. As she played with the tune, words formed in her mind; she left the piano an hour later with the song complete, like a walnut in its shell. It lingered as she settled down to paperwork at her kitchen table — a song to say goodbye.

> *I dreamed that in our walk through life*
> *we'd never be apart.*
> *Now a lonely tune in minor key*
> *meanders through my heart.*

I understand that my desire
is not to be fulfilled.
I only wish the lonely tune
could be forever stilled.

Goodbye, my love, goodbye.
Goodbye, my love, goodbye…

Nineteen

Katie spent the following week in dread that she would accidentally run into Keith on campus. At first she responded to every heavy footstep and every deep voice with a quickened heartbeat and a sudden, involuntary tensing of her jaw, positive it was him and that she would have to turn and greet him, have to smile and make small talk and pretend her heart wasn't breaking.

One day she stood in line in the college cafeteria and, without turning, *knew* it was Keith who had moved silently into line behind her. Her hands shook as she slid her tray along the counter and ordered lunch. She splashed herself with hot coffee as she tried to pour a cup. And when she reached for her money to pay the cashier at the end of the line, her coins spilled across the floor.

Only when he bent to help her did she discover it wasn't Keith after all — just an anonymous stranger, solicitous and concerned. She turned down his offer of company for lunch and gulped her sandwich and coffee standing at the door. Then she hurried across campus, her eyes downcast, to meet

Henry for a practice session.

The professor had suggested they set the mood for the Christmas concert by performing a number together at the beginning, before the welcome or any other words were spoken. They'd chosen a folk carol that Katie remembered and loved from her childhood when she'd had Keith's mother play it over and over on her favorite Tennessee Ernie Ford Christmas album. "Some Children See Him" proposed that children in every country of the world saw the Christ child with faces like their own. It was perfect for the "Four Corners Christmas" theme of the concert. The melody was simple and beautiful, and Henry's arrangement was inspired.

As Katie opened the door to practice room 4-B and caught Henry's smile, she wondered once again if she'd been a complete fool to turn down his marriage proposal. Maybe the sweet affection of their relationship was what real love was all about. Maybe his steady calm was what she needed.

"Ready to go?" Henry asked, running his fingers over the keys in a series of arpeggios. She slipped off her coat and draped it over a metal folding chair, then sat on the edge of the seat, wishing she felt more like singing.

"Henry, do you really think this song is going to work?"

He lifted his fingers from the keys and looked at her, surprised. "Of course I do. It's perfect for your voice and for the story it tells. The beauty of simplicity. I could come up with another arrangement," he added doubtfully, "something showier, if that's what you want...."

Maybe it *was* the simplicity that didn't feel right anymore, Katie thought tiredly. The song seemed *too* simple now, too hopeful, too ingenuous. She wondered if she'd be able to carry it off.

"Why the doubts all of a sudden?" Henry pushed.

"Oh, I don't know...." She stood and took a series of deep breaths to relax her throat. "Holiday blues, I guess. Don't change the arrangement. You're right, it's a good match for the song and my voice."

Henry watched her for a moment, then turned back to the piano and hit a middle C. "Let's get going, then. Give me a few scales to warm up your voice."

"A few" turned into half an hour's worth, and then Henry wouldn't let her get through the song even once, making her repeat phrases over and over that sounded fine to her. She didn't ever remember being worked so hard, even when Henry had been "Dr. Gillette" and her undergraduate voice instructor.

"You're flat," he told her. "Think high!" "Try it again." "Too dark — bring it out to your teeth. Brighter, brighter!" "You're sliding up to the high note. Hit it exactly." "We'll do that phrase as many times as we have to." "Again." "Again!"

"Enough already!" Katie finally fumed. She spun around once, her arms crossed over the top of her head, and plopped down on the edge of her chair. "You're a slave driver, Henry!"

He grinned. "Now that's more like the Kate I know," he said. "You're downright morbid today, sweetheart. What's wrong?"

Her eyes shone bright with sudden, unshed tears. "Henry," she began. Then the tears were flowing silently down her cheeks. "Henry, I never told you — I just want to say how sorry I am — did I ever do anything to make you believe I felt something more...more than I do?" She shook her head and wiped her cheeks with the back of her hands.

"Oh, this isn't coming out right at all!"

Henry's expression told her he agreed wholeheartedly. He looked away, his fingers beating out an unconscious tattoo on the top of the piano.

"I'm sorry, Henry," she finally got out. "You are such a dear friend." After a moment's hesitation, she continued, "I know I must have hurt you when I said I didn't want to marry you. But here you are, still with me, still my friend. Why?"

Henry cleared his throat nervously. "Kate — what am I supposed to say? I'm here because we *are* friends." He got up and walked to the window, stuffing his hands deep in the pockets of his slacks. "Of course it hurt. It took some time to…adjust. But…" He turned to face her. "Well, Kate, you're not the only fish in the sea!"

She gave a startled laugh. The comment was so unlike Henry. Was that the secret, then? Time and continually reminding herself that Keith wasn't the only fish in the sea?

Henry's face was red with embarrassment. Jumping up from her chair, she hurried over and gently took his hands between hers. "You're absolutely right, Henry. I'm *not* the only fish in the sea. I love you dearly, but you deserve someone who *adores* you. I wish I did. You are such a good man."

"It's Castle, isn't it?"

She nodded.

"I've been afraid for you since the first time I met him, Kate."

She removed her hands from his and shook her head. "I don't want you to think badly of him, Henry. If Keith doesn't love me, he doesn't love me," she ended forlornly.

"His loss," Henry said gently. Then he sat down at the

piano and hit the opening note to her song, businesslike again. "All right. One time through, and we'll give it a rest till tomorrow. Take it from the top."

Katie was grateful for the myriad activities that occupied her mind as December marched on: grading term projects, conferencing with students, practicing with Henry, shopping for Christmas gifts for her family and friends. But in the dark, cold night, she couldn't keep Keith away. He was always there, just outside conscious thought, ready to intrude as soon as she let her guard down. She fell into bed exhausted every night, then lay awake for hours.

Why, God, why? her heart cried out. *Why would you give me so much love for Keith if nothing is to come of it? Please help me understand!*

At times her love felt more like hate, which added guilt and self-recrimination to her pain. But when she was most honest with herself, she knew her feelings meant that nothing had changed. She loved him and he didn't love her. It was as simple and agonizing as that.

She missed him horribly: missed his teasing and his half smile and his eyebrows raised in that carelessly deceptive look of boyish innocence. Missed his laughter, his quick intelligence, his enthusiasms, his easygoing manner.

Missed his touch...

Nothing had changed. And nothing would ever be the same again. *Help me, God,* she prayed. *Fill this emptiness....*

Doc and Danny saved seats for both Katie and Keith on Sundays, Danny keeping his eye on the door and waving excitedly when she entered, and always whispering,

"Where's Kee?" as she settled next to him. Each time she shook her head sadly.

The first Sunday after his mother had gone back to Montana, Danny had edged a little closer to Katie on the pew each time they sat down after a hymn or prayer. By the time the service was over, he was leaning comfortably against her, as he used to in the days before Ruggles had died.

The little boy's affection was the one bright spot in the seemingly endless days of December. *Seventeen more shopping days till Christmas....* Hadn't it been eighteen more shopping days weeks ago? Time seemed to have no relationship to the calendar.

Winter blew in with a vengeance one night in the middle of the month. Frigid winds blasted down the Gorge in the worst ice storm Keith could remember. By the time he woke in the morning, the bare branches of the birch tree in his front yard were encased in ice, and the icicles hanging from the eaves of his house flashed in the cold winter sun like brilliant electric stalactites. The deejays on his morning radio show warned that roads were slick with black ice, and even with chains on his tires and sand down on the major streets, the short drive to work was slow and slippery.

After his arrival he called the staff members who lived in outlying areas to tell them to stay home. Debi Chang, the last employee on his list, answered the phone on the first ring.

"Hey, Chief! You actually went into *work?*"

"I live close by. Rito couldn't get off Mount Tabor if he wanted to, and —"

He was interrupted by a shriek. "No! My car! I can't

believe it!" She was talking on a cordless phone and had walked into her living room to check out the scene through her front window just in time to see a large, ice-laden branch break off the maple in the parking strip. An instant later the roof of her car caved under its weight. "My new car!" she moaned.

Before Keith could respond, the phone went dead. He groaned. Last time a line had gone down, Cully Center had been without service for two days. Probably phones were out all over the city. Who knew how long it would take to get the lines working again in this weather?

He tuned the radio in the office to the local news station. Schools were closed all over the city. The weather might keep buses off the roads, but it wouldn't keep neighborhood kids away from the center. He hoped Doc and Danny wouldn't risk the walk. His stomach clenched as he made a round of the building, checking thermostats, vents, and windows. Unable to contact either Doc or Katie, he found himself imagining them in worst-case scenarios — caught without food in the house or having the heat go out; not being able to phone for help; braving the storm, but slipping and falling, breaking an ankle and lying helpless on the ice....

If something happened to Katie, he'd never forgive himself. He should be with her. He should be taking care of her...

No, he told himself fiercely, dropping into the office chair at his desk and tapping a blank tablet page with his pencil. He wasn't in a position to take care of Katie. He couldn't take her on right now.

Still, as soon as the phones were working again, he'd call Doc, he decided. Katie was sure to have been in contact.

He put the pencil down and pushed restlessly away from the desk. For a few days after his last encounter with Katie, it had been a relief not to see her, not to talk to her — even though he found it impossible not to think about her.

He wished she hadn't confessed she was in love with him; it complicated things. The intense feelings she stirred in him were more than he could deal with right now. He still had too much untangling of other emotions to do — feelings about his mother, about his own place in the world, about God.

He wasn't ready for Katie. He wasn't ready for love.

But he missed her incredibly.

Later in the day the electricity flickered several times and then went out for good. When the backup generator kicked in, the lights flickered again and then glowed steadily. Keith knew they would be like a beacon on the dark streets of the neighborhood, where not another shred of light penetrated the shadows of dusk. As the evening wore on and the streets remained dark, more and more people appeared, dressed in bulky layers against the biting wind, attracted by the lights and the promise of warmth at the center.

Keith's staff had been collecting canned food, blankets, and warm clothing for Christmas distribution to needy families in the area. Organizing a group of volunteers, he set up the gymnasium as a neighborhood emergency center to help out those most unprepared for the early cold spell, and resigned himself to making the center his home until the worst of the storm was over.

Katie tried for two days to reach Doc and Emily but couldn't get through. She knew from the radio that electricity and phones were out in pockets across the city and that for all practical purposes the tri-county area had come to a stand-still. Few people dared to drive on the treacherous roads; the buses were running hours late; and the light-rail system was closed down for almost forty-eight hours.

She finally got through to Doc, who said he and his grandson were doing fine — he'd done a grocery run before the storm hit, and Danny had helped him bring in enough wood from the garage that they'd kept a fire going continuously while the electricity was out. She couldn't help but smile when Danny got on the line to tell her Brannigan was keeping his feet warm at night.

Her phone rang as she set the receiver down. She grabbed it up again, breathing a prayer. *Please, God, let it be Keith....*

"Hello?"

"Hey, girlfriend!" It was Emily.

After a few days to think about her friend's intensely honest appraisal of her "blind spot" the week after Thanksgiving, Katie had managed to put aside her hurt. She couldn't disagree with Emily. She'd been in charge of things so long, it was difficult to know when she should hold on and when she should back off — and when she should let go entirely. Then, having made the judgment, it was even harder to follow through.

"You're right, Em," she'd told her friend. "I get this idea that if I don't take care of things, they'll never happen. And maybe they won't. Maybe God has other ideas. Anyway, my relationship with Keith is in God's hands now. There's nothing more I *could* do, even if I thought I should."

"Except keep loving him," Emily had reminded her.

"Yeah. Hard to do when he doesn't want me to."

"You know that isn't true. You loved him for a long time before this man-woman thing happened, and he'll never stop wanting that kind of love from you. I can't believe he's ready to give up on your friendship." She hadn't added that she also didn't believe he was ready to give up on a deeper relationship with Katie.

"He'll have to do without my friendship for a while," Katie had told her. "It's too hard being around him. I can't change my feelings at the snap of a finger."

Emily's voice broke Katie's reverie. "Sorry I haven't called sooner," she said. "The phone's been out. You doing okay?"

"In what way?"

There was a pause at the other end of the line, then, "That doesn't sound good. Let's start with the basics. Food? Fuel? Shelter?"

"Fine. I'm one of the lucky ones."

"Yeah, you sound ecstatic. What else is going on?"

"No word from Keith. I thought I meant enough to him he'd call to make sure I was okay."

"I'm sorry, Katie. Maybe his phone's been out, too."

"Maybe." She changed the subject. "Beau getting a lot of business in this weather?"

"Mm-hm. The tow truck at the garage has been on the road twenty-four hours a day. Beau's working day shift, six to six, and Dano and Billy are splitting graveyard. I begged him to take me out to the Gorge — supposedly Multnomah Falls is frozen in a spectacular ice cascade. But, as you can probably guess, he doesn't want me and Skippy out on the ice."

"Sensible."

Emily sighed. "I should have known you'd take his part!"

Classes at the college resumed when transportation was deemed safe by the highway patrol, although the cold wind continued to blow for several more days. The sky was electric blue above the naked trees, sharp and brittle, as though it might at any moment break apart in huge jagged pieces and pierce the earth below. Students scuttled like bright, hooded beetles from one building to the next, hands buried in pockets or pressed against their faces to try to keep warm.

Katie passed on her two pairs of complimentary tickets for the Christmas concert to Doc and Danny and Beau and Emily. "Don't you dare have that baby early," Katie told her friend. "I need you there!"

"What about you?" Emily countered, rubbing her rounded tummy. "Flying off to Arizona and not coming back till the actual due date! What if Skippy *is* early? You won't be here!"

"I'm sorry, Em. I wish I could stay. But Mom and Dad are expecting me for Christmas. And…" She grimaced. "I've got to get away from here." Away from *him*, her look added.

"I know you do," Emily reassured her. "I was only teasing. I want you to go home and have a wonderful time." She searched Katie's face. "But I'm worried you won't come back. You're not serious about that doctoral program in Phoenix, are you? Your life is here, Katie. Don't let Keith take it away from you. Promise."

Katie just nodded, afraid to speak around the lump in her throat.

The winds subsided and the weather warmed as Christmas approached. The days faded from brittle blue to gray. The sharp pain in Katie's heart dulled to a mild depression that was beginning to feel almost normal. She got out of bed each morning and did what she had to do, then went to bed at night, sleeping deeply and without dreams, to wake up the next morning and follow the same routine.

The days began to flow into each other.

Twenty

❧

"Good sermon this mornin', eh?" Doc commented to Katie on the Sunday before the last week of school.

"Hmm?" she answered distractedly. "Oh, yes — very nice." Then, because something in his direct gaze always inspired her to honesty, she confessed, "I'm afraid I wasn't paying much attention to the sermon, Doc. But I loved the service — the choir, the handbells, that wonderful spiritual the quartet sang. And the lighting of the Advent candle, of course."

Doc placed a hand lightly on her shoulder. "God be in the music and the light as much as in the words sometime," he said. "If it give you comfort, then it's good you come, Irish."

She smiled gratefully. "Thanks, Doc. Being with you and Danny gives me comfort, too."

"Well then! Danny and I was just goin' to Lloyd Center for a little lunch and a little Christmas shoppin' and maybe even a little ice skatin'. How 'bout comin' along?"

"Oh, I've got so much to do," she began automatically.

Danny tugged on her hand. "Please, Katie — I have to

buy Grumpy's present. I don't want him to see."

"Well, yes, then," she suddenly changed her mind. "Let's do it!"

For the next few hours Katie almost forgot her unhappiness. They had lunch at the food circus on the third floor of the mall under a towering glass ceiling and overlooking the ice rink two stories below. Danny ordered a burrito and politely offered her a bite, which she just as politely refused; Doc ordered an entire dinner plate of unpronounceable East Indian dishes; and Katie ate a fat turkey sandwich with cranberry and cream cheese — "comfort food," she told her companions. Then she took them downstairs to her favorite shop in the mall and bought each of them a sweet, sticky Cinnabon for dessert.

"That was too much for an old man," Doc sighed happily. "I'm stayin' put here for a bit. You go on an' buy your grandpa's Christmas present, Danny Boy." He winked at Katie. "Just make sure it ain't one of them frilly aprons Irish near made me wear at her house."

They were gone for half an hour, in which time Danny spent eight dollars, saved from his allowance over a period of four weeks, on six gifts for his grandfather: a pencil sharpener shaped like a nose, a pair of clown finger puppets, a blue Nerf softball, a California Raisin wearing sunglasses and high-top shoes, a Spiderman comic book, and a pack of playing cards with pictures of Irish setters on the back.

"I'm thinking of hiring this kid to do *my* Christmas shopping," Katie told Doc when they found him people-watching on the same bench where they'd left him. "He's got an eye for a bargain, and he doesn't mess around when he sees what he wants." She tousled his hair affectionately. "I was *astounded!*"

"I have two dollars left for a present for Brannigan, Grumpy." Danny was bouncing with excitement. "But I want Kee to help me pick it out. Can we call him?"

Doc caught Katie's pained expression over Danny's head. "Another day this week, Danny Boy. He'd like that, I know."

"Well!" Katie said a bit too brightly. "Are you up for trying your luck on some ice skates, Doc?"

"Yeah!" Danny tugged at his grandfather's arm. "Come on, Grumpy!"

"Skatin' don't take luck," Doc said. "Just balance."

Danny had never tried ice skating before, and Katie was rusty, but Doc surprised them both with his grace and agility. "Ain't no big deal," he said modestly. "Minnesotans learn to skate before they's walkin'."

At first Danny clung to the wall like a mussel to a rock, but with Katie and Doc's encouragement, he pulled himself around the edge of the rink once and then was willing to hang on between the two adults for another turn around the ice. By that time, Katie felt confident enough to show off a little bit, tried a pirouette, and fell promptly on her bottom. She brushed off her pants and Doc's concern with a sheepish laugh. "Serves me right," she said.

"Didn't it hurt?" Danny asked, his eyes wide.

"Only my pride. Ready to go again?" She held out her hand. Danny took it, hesitantly, then grabbed firmly as Katie pulled away. After a wobbly start, they set off around the rink once again. Doc followed for a short distance, then cut inside and in front of them, swinging around to skate backwards. He swayed from side to side with the music, grinning through his beard, his hands clasped behind his back. Danny's mouth dropped open.

"I swan, Danny Boy, you goin' to be catchin' flies if you don't clamp them jaws shut!" he shouted gleefully. Then he spun around and raced away.

At that point Danny lost all fear. If Katie could fall and get right back up again, without even *crying*, and if his grandfather could skate *backwards* all the way around the rink, nothing was going to keep him from skating on his own. He let go of Katie's hand and pulled away, wobbly at first but gaining confidence with each stroke of the skates against the ice. He made it halfway around the rink before he lost his balance and fell. Doc raced over, but the little boy was already up before he got there.

"I'm skating!" he cried. "Grumpy, I'm skating!"

"So you are, Danny Boy." The pride in Doc's voice was evident. "Take after your grandpa, you do!"

Katie skated off the rink to a seat and watched as the young boy and the older man played together on the ice. Neither Doc nor Danny had lived easy lives, she mused, but here they were, together now, helping each other in ways they didn't even realize.

Thank you, God, she breathed silently. *Thank you for sending us people to love.* Then Keith's image entered her mind.

Closing her eyes briefly, she breathed a prayer for him: *Be with Keith, God, wherever he is....*

Keith was, at that moment, lying on his bed with the shades drawn, nursing a massive headache.

He'd quietly slipped into the morning service at Tomahawk Community Church that morning, sliding into the last row of the balcony as the congregation sang an opening hymn: "God Rest Ye Merry, Gentlemen!" He sat half hidden behind a post, making sure he was out of Chappie's line of vision from the minister's position on the facing bench.

The discomfort Keith had felt on the day he'd attended church with Toni, Doc, and Danny hadn't been enough to offset his growing need to resolve his anger and his fears and to try to understand, if such a thing were possible, just who Keith Castle was and where he fit in the scheme of things.

Katie's confession that she was in love with him, even more than the near-catastrophe at Multnomah Falls, made him want desperately to be free to move forward in his life again. The past felt like a mire of quicksand from which he couldn't escape alone, no matter how hard he struggled. As much as he hated to admit it, his gut told him Tomahawk was where he needed to be. Unknown to Doc and Katie and even Chappie, Keith had been stealing into Sunday morning services since Thanksgiving.

He wasn't ready to participate in worship and his mind tended to wander during the sermons, but simply being present in the church he'd attended as a child, especially for the season of Advent, felt familiar and strangely comforting. The music invited him to relax and enjoy, and as he stood in the midst of the congregation each week, listening to the voices rise around him, letting the familiar words and tunes wash over him, he felt less and less a stranger.

Today in particular, the music had made the church feel almost like home. He imagined he could hear Katie's rich contralto rising to his seat high in the balcony as the congregation joined in singing Christmas carols. During the offertory, the handbell choir rang out the "Carol of the Bells," one of his mother's favorites. The choir's selection was the

"Hallelujah" chorus from Handel's *Messiah;* he remembered Katie practicing for it when she'd sung in the church choir years ago. When a mixed quartet wailed out "Go Tell It on the Mountain!" he was reminded of the Christmas album of spirituals and folk songs Mrs. Brannigan had played for him and Katie, over and over again because Katie wanted to learn all the words to the tunes.

A hunger began to build in him, a hunger he couldn't have defined if he tried.

A pair of teenagers, one a tall, good-looking, dark-skinned boy and the other a petite blond girl, rose from the front pew and climbed the stairs to the platform. Keith thought of himself and Katie at their age, mounting those same stairs to read Scripture or announce a youth activity together.

The girl stood back while the boy read a passage from the first chapter of Luke, the words of the angel announcing to Mary that she was to bear the son of God. As the boy finished reading, the girl stepped forward and lit the third candle in the Advent wreath on a stand next to the podium.

Turning toward the congregation, she said, "The Advent candle I light today stands for *hope.* The apostle Paul reminds us in Romans that hope is our salvation. Not hope in something visible, for why would we need to hope for something we already see? Real hope means waiting patiently for something *not* visible — as Mary waited for the birth of the child who would be her own salvation."

Keith was again prepared to tune out the sermon, but after the teenagers left the platform and he saw that it was Chappie who got up from the facing bench to speak, he decided to make an effort to pay attention. Surprisingly, it was no effort at all; he found himself listening with interest.

"And after the angel spoke to Mary, the power of almighty God overshadowed her, and so the Christ-child was conceived," Chappie said. "Mary was *expecting*, the word we use to describe a pregnant woman, as well as another word for hope. What did it mean to Mary to be expecting? How did she feel?"

Keith suddenly thought of his mother at seventeen, discovering she was pregnant. How must she have felt? *Expecting*. Not a love-child, but a hate-child, a child conceived in violence. *Expecting*. Not supported by a warm and caring family, but alone and afraid. Kicked out of her home.

How had she managed to survive?

Chappie continued, "As Carly suggested earlier when she lit the Advent candle, hope sometimes means simply *waiting* — something every expectant parent has to do. Waiting isn't easy; sometimes it can even be frightening. The angel told Mary not to fear, but I imagine she must have been anxious a time or two over those next nine months. I imagine she must have wondered in the dark of the night what the future held for her and the God-child she carried in her womb.

"I can empathize with Mary. Nine times another Mary, my dear wife, waited in the same way. I waited with her. Twice we waited for the birth of children who were never born. That made the sixty-three months we waited for the other seven anxious at best. Who knew what the future held? Whoever really knows? We hope, we expect, we wait — without knowing. Holding our breath, as it were, till the waiting ends."

The nine months of his mother's pregnancy must have been filled with anxiety, Keith thought, even dread at times.

Her future must have looked black. Maybe she'd hated him. Maybe she had even hoped he'd die....

"On the other hand," Chappie continued, "expecting can also mean *anticipating* — looking forward to something we're convinced is going to happen and we know is going to be good. Anticipation feels wonderful, doesn't it? This time of year it's in the air. It shines like colored lights reflected in the eyes of our children; it smells like hot cider with cinnamon and bread baking and turkey roasting. It sounds like laughter and bells and Christmas carols. It feels like the hugs and smiles of well-loved family and friends. Anticipation! My Mary and I felt it as we waited for our children to arrive. Mary of Nazareth must have felt it, too, when the baby stirred inside, when her belly jumped beneath her hands as if the child, too, could hardly wait to see what might happen. Oh, she had hopes for this child!"

Keith wondered if his mother had looked forward to his arrival with anticipation or only with dread. When had she come to terms with her fate and decided to love the child in her womb? He knew that somehow she had, for throughout his mother's life, he'd never felt less than adored. Had she harbored hopes for him as she felt him stir inside?

He focused again on Chappie's words. "Then again, expecting sometimes has little to do with hope. Sometimes it means *supposing*. When our oldest daughter was born, I remember a young couple we didn't know well bringing us a crib and a big cardboard box full of baby clothes. 'I expect you'll be needing these more than we will, now that our children are in school,' they said. We gratefully accepted, expecting we probably would be needing those things.

"In the same way, I imagine Mary expected her life would

change as the mother of a newborn, that her child would need her in the ways babies need their mothers. Whatever it is we expect in this context, we accept it as a given. No moral judgment as to whether it would be good or bad. It just *is*."

No moral judgment, Keith thought. *I expect Mama did what she thought was best for me when she lied about my father. I expect she saw it as her duty to protect me. She must have known I never would have understood the truth.*

He felt a headache coming on. Pressing his fingers against his temple for a moment, he wondered for the first time if he could accept his mother's deceit as an act of love instead of an act of betrayal....

Chappie's voice pulled Keith back from his musings once again. "Mary's response to the angel's announcement, her expression of hope, was simple and humble: 'I am the Lord's servant. May it be to me as you have said.'

"I'm sorry to say my response to God is not always so humble," the minister confessed. "While Mary's hope was grounded in humility, sometimes what *we* call hope is nothing of the kind. Sometimes it's arrogant, presumptuous — a kind of hope that may *appear* to wait, or anticipate, or suppose, but in reality *demands*. It focuses on *what we think we're owed*. We say 'expect,' but we mean 'insist on.'"

Keith furrowed his brow in concentration as Chappie continued. His head throbbed dully.

"Sometimes when we expect certain responses from our children, our friends, our spouse, even God — our expectations become requirements. We consider the person from whom we expect that particular response duty-bound to provide it for us — *obligated* to give us what we ask. If they don't, we become angry, resentful, bitter.

"We expect our children to help clean the house — we have, after all, provided them with a roof over their heads. We expect our friends to remember us at Christmas with gifts, or invitations to dinner, or at the very least a Christmas card — after all, we go out of our way to remember *them*. We expect our spouses to be understanding when we snap at them — we wouldn't have got stuck in traffic and been late for dinner if we hadn't been doing a favor for them in the first place. We expect God to make our lives easy and pain-less and happy all the time — we've done everything right, haven't we? Followed all the rules?

"In other words, we say to these persons who we feel are obligated to us, 'You had better respond the way I want you to — *or else!' Or else* you'll get grounded, *or else* you'll never get another gift from me, *or else* don't expect any more favors. *Or else,* in the case of God, I won't talk to you any-more. I won't worry about doing what's right. I won't even believe in you anymore."

Chappie paused for a drink of water from the glass on the pulpit before continuing. "There's nothing wrong with wanting mutuality in our relationships," he said. "Love is about both giving and receiving. To be happy and healthy, we need to do both. But as we approach Christmas, the day we celebrate the incarnation — God's longing for relationship with man made flesh and blood — I challenge you to think about your expectations of the people in your life. Are your interactions with your friends and family mere *transactions,* based solely on reciprocity? Do you give only because you expect some-thing in return?"

Did he? Keith asked himself. His mother had always told

him he had a generous heart, but how generous had he been in the last few years? How much had he withheld from Katie and Doc and other friends he'd known at Tomahawk? How much had he withheld from the players on the teams he'd been a part of overseas? How much did he withhold from the people he worked with?

But I'm getting better, he told himself. *I'm learning to be generous again. Doc and Danny and Katie are teaching me how.*

"I challenge you, too, to think about your expectations of God," the minister was saying. "Ask yourself this question: 'Is there something I expect of God he hasn't done for me? Something I deserve he hasn't given?'"

Keith's response to those questions in his sessions with Chappie had always been anger, automatic and vehement. This time he answered them without anger but with great sadness. *I expected you to protect my mother from evil,* he told God. *I expected good to be her reward for faithfulness.*

"Are you carrying a grudge against God?" Chappie asked. "Has he failed to live up to your expectations? Search your heart for anger, for bitterness, for resentment because God hasn't given you your due. What are you holding back from him because you feel as if he's holding back from you?"

Keith's head began to throb in earnest. The wall of resistance he'd been building for years was on the verge of collapse. He couldn't let it fall. It was his only protection.

Against what? a voice inside him seemed to ask.

He had no answer.

"It's part of the human condition that we long for spiritual connection," the minister continued. "For the feeling that we understand as we are understood, for relationships that transcend transactions. That kind of connection only happens when communication is open and honest, when you face yourself and share yourself as you really are.

"Do you have the guts to engage with God? To tell him how you feel? To forgive him for the ways you think he's failed you? To ask his forgiveness for your arrogant demands that life turn out the way *you* think it should?"

Forgive God? Now there was a concept....

"In the life transformed by God," Chappie said, "the act of giving becomes its own reward, a reward beyond all your expectations, all your hopes. You begin to offer your love freely, from a place of abundance and joy, rather than withholding it out of fear you won't get it back."

A moment of insight so bright and so piercing it felt like the stab of a silver blade to his heart caught Keith unawares. It was almost as if he heard God speaking aloud: *"You* were the reward for your mother's faithfulness. Her love for you was its own reward."

God had not wished for an evil man to commit an evil act against his mother. But in a world where man is free to choose, evil had intervened. God had not abandoned Keith's mother; he had comforted her, healed her, transformed fear and hatred and anger into the love she had so freely given him. Good had triumphed over evil in the life of Keith's mother after all — in her kindness, in her continued faith, in her love for the son she might easily have hated. Maybe it was time for Keith to forgive God.

For more than twenty years, Christine Castle had kept the secret of Keith's conception from him for his own sake, to protect him. She'd only broken her silence as she prepared to meet her Maker. How could he begrudge her for wanting to make her heart right before she died? Maybe it was time to forgive her as well.

Twenty-One

By the time Keith met with Chappie late Friday morning for his counseling appointment, the long-term struggle in his heart had nearly played itself out. Something was happening inside him. Surrendering his anger toward God and his mother had opened him to possibilities that had been outside his reach for years.

Chappie greeted him with a handshake, a cough, and a hoarse hello. "Hit me just this morning," he croaked as he offered Keith a chair. "Coffee?"

"Are you sure you want to go ahead with our appointment?" Keith asked, frowning. "We could reschedule."

The minister shook his head. "I had my secretary cancel all my appointments for today, but she couldn't reach you. Let's go ahead, since you're here." He poured coffee for Keith. "Cream, no sugar, right?"

"Can't believe you remember."

"It's the way I take mine." Chappie scooted the mug across his desk toward Keith and sat down. "I *feel* okay, I just *sound* miserable," he said, his voice cracking. "I'm counting on improvement by tonight — have to narrate a piece at the college Christmas concert for the chorale." He reached for the thermos on his desk and poured steaming liquid into his own mug. "Chicken broth," he explained as he screwed the lid back on. "Mary's cure-all."

Feeling a little embarrassed at first, Keith related the new insights and feelings he'd been experiencing with kaleidoscopic frequency since Sunday. When Chappie's delight became evident, Keith relaxed and grew almost excited as he continued to talk.

"It's as if nothing happened for me until I stopped trying to figure things out," he said.

Chappie nodded. "Reconciling the existence of evil in the world with the belief in a benevolent and omnipotent God isn't easy," he told Keith, his voice fluctuating between a croak and a loud whisper. "It's something every thinking person has to struggle with. If we don't, we're not being honest with ourselves. You have been, Keith. I've watched you for months. But there's a time to give up the struggle, too. It sounds as if you might have reached that place."

Keith wrapped his big hands around his warm coffee mug. "You're right. I've been fighting with God, blaming him even more than the man who raped my mother. Weird, isn't it? When I stopped fighting, things started to get clear. Somehow I've come to accept that sorrow and loss are part of living in a fallen world. I don't like it, but there it is."

He finished his coffee and got up to pour himself another cup. "Not that I have all the answers," he said over his shoulder. "But that's okay, too. I remember something you used to say when I was a teenager: 'Life is more about the journey toward the answers than it is about the answers themselves.'

It's a relief to know I don't have to have the whole thing figured out," he added as he settled back into his chair.

Chappie was nodding in agreement. "We'll never have the whole thing figured out. God is too big," he answered in a hoarse whisper. "The place I've come to in my own journey is the acknowledgement that evil infects every part of our world — *and* the faith that God can heal it. Love, healing, happiness, peace — I believe they're all miracles of God's grace."

"Hmm." Keith set his coffee on the corner of Chappie's desk to cool. "For the first time this week," he said slowly, "I've been looking back on my life and recognizing God's provision for my needs all along. After hearing my mother's story, I rejected the entire concept of a loving God. But now when I think about her life, I marvel. She was happy. She loved me without reservation. So did Doc — the father God gave me to make up for the one I didn't have. I had more as a child growing up than a lot of kids with two parents have."

I have more now than a lot of grown-ups have, he added to himself. *My health, a house, a job — a future. And most of all, people I love who love me back. Doc and Danny. Katie…*

"Have you told God what you're telling me?" Chappie asked gently.

Keith looked surprised. "I guess I haven't."

"I can't think of a better time."

Taking a deep breath, Keith nodded and bowed his head. After a short silence he prayed simply, "God, forgive me for my arrogance. You were with me all along — I just didn't know. Thanks for hanging in there." He paused, then added, "Teach me how to love again, God. Here's my heart."

"Amen," Chappie whispered.

A peace Keith hadn't known in years rushed through him in an overwhelming flood. He raised his head, and when his eyes met Chappie's they were wet with tears. He reached across the desk and gripped the minister's hand, unable to speak for a moment. "Thank you for walking through this with me," he finally said.

Chappie smiled and nodded. "Thanks for letting me," he said in a hoarse whisper. "It's been my privilege, Keith. Go in peace."

As Keith rose from his chair, the minister fell into a sudden fit of coughing that made his eyes water and his face turn red. He could barely speak when it was over.

Keith looked at him worriedly. "Is there something I can do?" he asked.

Chappie started to shake his head, then stopped. Minutes later Keith was on the phone with Myra Heimbach at Columbia River College, telling her the minister had lost his voice and volunteering to narrate the chorale number at the Christmas concert that evening in his place. Not surprisingly, his offer was quickly accepted.

The college was only minutes away from the church. After he'd picked up a copy of the music and narration from Professor Heimbach to look over that afternoon, Keith hurried to the cafeteria and then the auditorium, hoping to find Katie. Classes were over for the term, but he thought she might be on campus finishing grades before Christmas break or helping set up for the musical program. He had so much to tell her.

If she'd even listen to him, he mused, cringing as he thought about the way he'd treated her the last few weeks. He was sure he'd hurt her badly.

Katie wasn't to be found on campus, and when he called her apartment from the pay phone outside the cafeteria, she didn't answer. He hung up before her recorded message was finished. After he'd located a tuxedo for the evening and read over his part, he'd try again.

"Showtime in forty minutes."

Dr. Abercrombie's amplified voice cut through the mélange of sounds in the large, multipurpose auditorium: violins, trombones, flutes, trumpets tuning to the concert-master's pitch; a dozen or more conversations buzzing throughout the room; a pianist limbering up with scales on the grand piano; and a soprano sliding up and down the scale along with him.

Elgin Hall looked magnificent. All four corners of the huge room were filled with evergreen trees of varying heights — Douglas fir, pine, spruce — like a forest sprung up overnight. Thousands of tiny white lights twinkled on their branches like stars in a winter sky. Great swags of aromatic cedar tied up with huge red satin bows decorated the walls.

"Please clear the floor," Dr. Abercrombie continued over the state-of-the-art sound system. "The doors are opening in ten minutes."

"The program notes!" Katie panicked. "Where are they?"

"On the podium where we left them," Henry soothed. "Calm down, Katie. We're going to do fine."

"I don't know if it was such a good idea for us to sing as well as emcee, Henry," she fretted. "Especially the first number. What if it's awful and then we have to stand up there in front of everyone for the next two hours?"

"It won't be awful. Are you forgetting how much we've practiced?"

"What if I'm not in tune?"

Henry had arranged their song with the first verse to be sung a cappella, without accompaniment, which meant Katie had to be perfectly on pitch when the piano joined her for the second verse. She'd tended to be a little flat in practice, probably due to her depression over the last few weeks. Then the one time they'd rehearsed on stage earlier today, her nervous anticipation had raised her pitch a little too much.

"Listen, Katie, you know this song so well you could sing it in your sleep," Henry told her. "Don't even think about the technical stuff. *Feel* it. You'll do fine."

They were sitting at a table near the back of the auditorium, where Beau and Emily, who'd arrived early enough to hear them practice, would watch the program. Doc and Danny would be joining them before the concert began.

In the center of the table sat a large wooden star covered with gilt paper and adorned with bells and frills and colored ribbons, with a picture of the Holy Family painted in the center and illuminated from inside. A card penned in beautiful calligraphy identified the centerpiece as a Romanian *steaua*, which was traditionally carried on a pole by boys who went from house to house singing carols and reciting poetry and legends during the Christmas season.

"You sound like an angel," Emily assured Katie.

"And you look like one, too," Beau said admiringly. "Where'd you get that fabulous dress?"

"Very funny, Beau." She turned to Emily. "I do love the dress, Em." She smoothed a hand down one narrow sleeve, luxuriating in the feel of the soft silk jacquard. The style was simple and close-fitting, similar to a traditional Chinese silk dress, with a slit up one side to just above her knee, but with a jewel neck instead of a mandarin collar.

The brilliant emerald green was the perfect backdrop for Katie's ivory skin and auburn hair, pulled away from her face with mother-of-pearl combs and left to cascade in a mass of curls down her neck. A twisted strand of fresh-water pearls and matching drop earrings completed the elegant picture. "I can't believe all I had to do was tell you what I had in my head, and voilà! Here it is!" she said.

Emily laughed. "It took a little more than just voilà, girl-friend. But you do look —"

She stopped, an odd expression on her face. Then, shaking her head, she finished, "wonderful."

Katie threw her friend a curious look. "Thanks." She moved forward to perch on the edge of her chair. "I can't believe I'm so nervous," she added. "I've done this dozens of times."

"As a student. Not as a faculty member," Henry reminded her. "You've got more at stake."

"Thank you so much, Henry," she said dryly. "Just what I needed to hear. Em, how about coming backstage with me till the program starts? I can tell Gillette isn't going to give me any moral support."

"Maybe not, but he sure *looks* fine," Emily said, pulling at Henry's crimson cummerbund. "That has to count for some-thing!"

Henry reddened. Katie grinned at his discomfiture. Served him right.

"Go ahead, babe," Beau encouraged his wife, leaning over

to give her a quick kiss. "I'll hold down the fort till Doc and Danny get here."

Katie, Emily, and Henry made their way past a row of long tables lined up parallel to one wall, their feet crunching the dried leaves strewn on the floor. A pleasing fragrance rose into the air. Rosemary, Henry explained. Supposedly Mary had draped the Christ Child's garments across a rosemary bush, giving the herb its pleasing scent and, the myth had it, the power to keep those who breathed its perfume forever young. Rosemary leaves scattered across the floor at Christmastime commemorated the story.

"How do you *know* this stuff?" Katie teased him.

"I'm just a remarkable guy, Ms. Brannigan," he teased back.

The fragrance mingled with the strong but pleasant aromas of coffee and ginger as they made their way to the front of the auditorium.

"They're serving wassail," Henry noted, gesturing toward a huge crystal bowl filled with a steaming amber beverage. Slices of toasted apple floated on the surface. "It looks like the real stuff."

"Really?" Katie asked in delight, stopping to lean over the bowl and breathe deeply. "I've never had wassail. It smells like hot spiced cider."

"Originally it was made with ale, but sometimes cider or wine is used. Looks like they have all three tonight." He nodded to other large bowls farther down the table.

"I'd love to try some later. Want a cup to take backstage, Em?" She glanced at her friend. Catching the peculiar expression on Emily's blanched face, she grabbed her arm in concern.

"You all right, Em?" Alarm sharpened her voice. "Do you want to go back and sit with Beau?"

"Thanks, I'll be okay — it's all these strong smells." Emily tried unsuccessfully to smile. "They do things to you when you're pregnant. I'll be okay once we sit down backstage."

Katie kept her grip on Emily's arm and followed Henry through a maze of round, lace-covered tables toward the exit leading backstage. Each table featured a centerpiece representing traditional Christmas celebrations in different cultures: a colorful piñata donkey from Mexico; Dutch wooden shoes filled with hay for St. Nicholas's reindeer; a brightly painted, tree-shaped structure decorated with tassels, cones, and candles, with shelves containing candy and nuts, tiny gilt-wrapped packages, and a carved wood nativity scene. An Italian *ceppo*, Henry told them.

College students dressed in ethnic costumes were lighting candles throughout the room. Katie smiled at a handsome young man dressed in a red-and-green plaid kilt with knee-high argyle socks and a short black jacket, and admired a golden-skinned girl across the room wearing a beautiful purple-and-gold silk sari. During intermission, they would be serving plum pudding, *lebkuchen,* gingerbread, and other traditional ethnic Christmas desserts to the crowd already gathering in the lobby outside.

Henry guided them to the stage door nearest the podium where he and Katie would be announcing the program, and then through the crowd of milling performers backstage. He helped Emily into a chair near an exit, where a welcome draught of cool, fresh air filtered through to the backstage area. Her color was returning. She looked much better, Katie thought as she dropped into the chair next to her.

"Dr. Gillette —"

Katie looked up to see Dr. Abercrombie hurrying toward them. "There's been a change in the program you'll need to announce," he told Henry briskly. "Mark Lewis was going to narrate for the chorale number, but apparently he's lost his voice. Let's see, where's that paper?" He fumbled in his breast pocket for a moment and then reached into the pocket of his tuxedo pants. "Here it is." He unfolded the paper and held it at arm's length to read the print. "A Keith…Castle, it looks like, will be taking his place."

At the mention of Keith's name, Emily placed a calming hand on Katie's forearm, as if she knew her friend's heart had begun to beat in double time. Katie took a deep breath and slumped forward in her chair, dropping her head and rolling it in circles to try to relieve the sudden tension in her neck.

"Thanks," Henry was saying. "We'll take care of it."

What was she going to do when the mere mention of Keith's name turned her into a tangled mass of nerves, Katie thought? She couldn't afford this now. Not when fifteen hundred people were expecting her best performance.

Fifteen hundred people! She straightened and sucked in another deep breath, Keith Castle forgotten for the moment. This *wasn't* going to be like singing at the Lighthouse or even for her senior recital.

Henry, sensing her attack of nerves, took her hand and squeezed it. "We'll do great, Katie."

"Thanks, Henry." She gave his hand a quick return squeeze and left her hand in his. He felt secure, solid. She leaned back in her chair and closed her eyes, breathing deeply and listening to the distant, soothing medley of Christmas carols over the sound system in the auditorium.

"Katie." She opened her eyes at Emily's anxious voice and found herself staring across the stage at Keith, who gazed grimly at her.

His expression made her angry. *I don't like the idea any better than you do, mister,* she said in her mind as she met his eyes. *But here we are. Deal with it.* Almost immediately her anger melted into a suffocating weight of sadness that pressed down on her chest like a dozen layers of heavy quilts on a hot summer night.

"Katie!"

She broke her gaze with Keith and turned her head, then sat up with a start. Emily's face was pale and strained. What was she saying? She couldn't concentrate. Why did Henry release her hand so suddenly and shoot out of his chair like a clown from a cannon? He was heading straight for Keith.

In the next moment Emily forcibly hauled Katie up and dragged her out the door into the chill evening air. The cold wind felt like a slap across Katie's face. She wrapped her arms around herself and huddled against the wall.

"Come here, Katie."

Katie didn't know she was crying till she tasted the salt at the corner of her mouth. Silent tears trickled down her face as Emily awkwardly held her. Slowly Emily's calm strength seeped through Katie's cloak of misery and she stepped back, breathing deeply and feeling more in control.

Emily's face was pale but calm when her eyes met Katie's a moment later.

"All right?" she asked.

Katie drew in a long shuddering breath and exhaled slowly. "I'll be fine," she finally said. "Thanks, Em. You always know what to do."

The same odd look Katie had noticed earlier flickered across Emily's delicate features. Then all at once the alley behind Elgin Hall seemed crowded with people all talking at the same time. Katie looked around in a daze. Henry had returned. Doc and Danny were with him, Doc repeating over and over again, "Well, don't that beat all! Don't that just beat all!" Danny was jumping up and down with excitement. Keith looked over Doc's white head, and when the older man moved, Katie saw that Toni stood with him, dressed in a short, blue-sequined cocktail dress. Her heart stopped.

Before Katie could say a word to anyone, a white '65 Mustang careened around the corner into the alleyway and squealed to a halt in front of them. Leaving the engine running, a wild-eyed man leaped out, waving his arms and shouting. Beau? Beau! Had the whole world gone mad?

Then Emily was hugging Katie, saying something in her ear before Beau grabbed her hand and pulled her around the back of the car.

"What?" Katie stood with her mouth open. How had everything gotten so confused all at once? *What* did you say?"

"I said," Emily repeated in a calm voice over the roof of the car, "that I'm going to have my baby now." She smiled, her face suffused with joy for just an instant before another contraction hit.

Beau handed his wife into the passenger seat. "Not before we get to the hospital, I hope!" he shouted, panic-stricken. He closed her door and ran around the car to the driver's seat. As he jumped in, Emily leaned across the front seat and called, "Sorry we're missing your song, Katie. I know you'll do great. Come see me as soon as you're done?"

Speechless, Katie stared after the car as it tore down the alley and screeched around the corner.

Twenty-Two

❧

W hat's going on out here?" Dr. Abercrombie's disapproving voice cut through the excited buzz. "Gillette, Brannigan, we've got a concert to put on — get in here!"

His irritation galvanized Katie to action. Now that Emily was on her way to the hospital, she couldn't afford to be distracted by anything — or anyone — else. She was, after all, a professional. Dr. Abercrombie was right; they had a concert to put on.

Hurrying back inside, she motioned the others to follow. "Keith, get Doc and Danny back to their table. Toni, could you help me with my makeup? I'm afraid it's run. Henry, I'll be ready to go on in two minutes."

She caught Keith's lopsided grin before he turned away to say something to Doc. What was *he* smiling about, she wondered irritably?

"I wanna stay with Mama," Danny protested, leaning against Toni's side.

One look at his longing expression turned Katie soft inside. "Okay. You can help me with my breathing." She took a deep breath and let it out slowly to show him how.

"Can't you breathe by yourself?" he asked curiously.

Laughing, she bent down and gave him a hug, feeling herself unwind with the gesture. "It helps me relax when you do it with me," she told him. "So I can sing better."

She closed her eyes as Toni quickly and expertly repaired her makeup, smiling as she heard Danny inhale and exhale loudly. When Toni stepped back, Katie opened her eyes and for the second time that evening found herself under Keith's scrutiny from across the stage. Doc stood next to him. So much for any authority *she* had, she thought wryly. At least Keith didn't look so grim this time.

"You look beautiful, Kate," Toni said.

Breaking the connection with Keith, she turned to smile at the other woman. "Thanks to you, Toni. I lost it there for a minute or two."

"Understandably!"

Henry put an arm around her shoulders and gave her a quick squeeze. "Ready, sweetheart?"

She turned her head to search his face for a moment before nodding. "Henry — you are very special to me," she said quietly.

"Ditto," he grinned. Leaning over, he placed a chaste kiss on her forehead, then grabbed her hand and guided her toward the curtain. Tugging a cordless microphone from a stand, he handed it to her, then pulled a pitch pipe from his breast pocket. "As soon as I get to the piano the lights will go down. That's your signal to enter stage right."

Katie nodded, the faint note from the pitch pipe lodging in her mind as Henry hurried across the backstage area to enter on the opposite side, where the grand piano stood. A moment later, when the auditorium lights dimmed and the crowd's murmur faded, she switched on the mike and stepped around the curtain onto the stage. As soon as the spotlight found her she started to sing, her low voice the only sound in the silence of the big room: *"Some children see him lily white...."*

The spotlight followed her as she strolled across the platform, wandering and singing quietly, as if to herself, as if unaware of the listening crowd. And, indeed, the audience of fifteen hundred strangers faded from her mind as another formed there, a gallery of well-loved faces: her mom and dad, Doc and Danny, Beau and Emily and the baby who might even at this moment be entering the world. And yes, Keith. Her voice conveyed the mixture of happiness and wonder she felt as their images passed through her mind.

By the time she finished the first verse, she stood in the curve of the grand piano and Henry shared the spotlight with her. She smiled at his first notes; she was perfectly on pitch. Grasping the microphone with both hands, she lifted her head. Her voice echoed through the cavernous room, backed now by Henry's soft arpeggios. *"Some children see him almond-eyed...."*

Henry's fingers flew over the keyboard like butterfly wings. Katie felt such a surge of joy as she sang that she wondered it didn't catapult her off the stage. The depression she'd felt the last few weeks fell away like a tattered garment. God had so blessed her — with the gift of song, with work she loved, most of all with the people who'd always been there for her in her times of need. *Take care of Keith, God,* she prayed silently as Henry played an interlude. *The way you've taken care of me. I give him up to you.*

Katie's red-eye flight arrived in Phoenix at six o'clock the next morning, two days before Christmas. She was surprised and pleased to find both her father and mother waiting for her at the airport. Thomas Brannigan hadn't been exaggerating when he'd told her over the phone on Thanksgiving that her mother seemed healthier than she'd been in years. The golden glow of her skin was such a contrast to the pallor Katie remembered, she thought it was makeup until she realized her mother's arms and legs were as tanned as her face.

Her mother gave her a warm hug. "I'm so glad you're here!"

"Hello, baby," her father said, bending over to give her a quick peck on the cheek. "Wouldn't seem like Christmas without you. Wait till you see how your mama's decorated the house for the holidays!"

"How was the concert, honey?" her mother asked as they walked toward the baggage claim.

Katie shifted her carry-on bag from one shoulder to the other. "Really great! Henry and I had so much fun. Our number to open the show went well, too."

"Knowing you, that's probably an understatement," her father said, ruffling her hair.

Katie smiled at the compliment. She could always count on her parents for ego inflation. "I haven't even told you the Big News," she said.

"You and Keith?"

"Mom! No! Whatever gave you that idea?"

"I don't know. You've been spending a lot of time with him."

"Not lately." Before her mother could pursue the subject

further she said brightly, "Emily had her baby last night!"

"She did! Boy or girl?"

They stepped into the baggage claim area and jostled through the crowd toward the carousel where the first pieces of baggage were beginning to appear. "Girl."

"How much did she weigh? What did they name her? Is she healthy? How's Em? How did Beau hold up?"

Katie laughed. "I've never seen you so hyper, Mom! Hang on — let me get my bags and I'll tell you all about it."

On the way to the car, Katie described the frantic scene in the alley behind the stage at Elgin Hall. "It happened just a few minutes before the concert was supposed to start, and I was so engrossed in my own stuff, I didn't even know what was going on. Here she is, having *labor* pains, and she's got her arms around me to soothe my stage jitters! Doesn't that sound like Em?"

As soon as the concert was over, Katie had talked Henry, who'd been enlisted to take her to the airport later anyway, to drop by Emanuel Hospital. Anxious about Emily and still high from the concert, she'd raced up the steps to the birthing ward, holding her long dress up to her knees and giggling like a little girl. Henry's embarrassed attempts to quiet her down only made it harder to control her giggles.

Chappie and Mary had greeted them in the waiting room. Beau had been grinning like the Cheshire cat. "It's a girl! Mother and daughter doing fine!"

Emily hadn't wasted a moment after their arrival at the hospital: the delicate baby girl with one little tuft of blond, wispy hair and a tiny, whimpering cry that sounded more like a kitten than a baby had been born on a gurney in the hallway.

"Can you beat that!" Beau exclaimed. "First time Emily's ever been early for anything!"

"Enjoy it," Mary had told him. "This is the *last* time *either* of you will be early for the next eighteen years!"

"The voice of experience speaks," Chappie had agreed.

"At least I didn't have to deliver her in the backseat of the Mustang," Beau had said. He'd mopped his brow in exaggerated relief.

Katie had cried when they told her the name they'd chosen for the baby: Elizabeth Kathryn Leigh. "You didn't do that just because you felt sorry for me, did you?" she'd asked Emily. "I mean, knowing I'd had a *dog* named after me within the last month?"

Emily had laughed, shaking her head. "We named her after you because, after Beau, you're my best friend. And because we want her to grow up as loving and giving and honest and full of life as you are." Smiling at her friend, Emily had carefully raised the baby, who lay sleeping across her stomach. Katie just as carefully had reached for Elizabeth, instinctively placing a hand beneath her head, and lifted her from her mother's arms. Her heart had swelled as she pulled the baby close and gently rocked her.

"Promise you'll be part of her life?" Emily had asked.

Katie had stroked the baby's downy head and burrowed a finger into the tiny fist. Involuntarily the baby's fingers had curled around her own, shooting tenderness through Katie's heart. "I promise," she'd said gravely, as though taking a solemn oath. "I love her already, Em."

"You've had quite an exciting time the last twelve hours," Katie's father said, opening the trunk of the Taurus sedan to deposit her luggage. "You must be exhausted."

She considered the idea, then shook her head. "I rested on the plane, but I'm too keyed up to sleep. The concert, the baby, the flight — which was none too smooth over the mountains, by the way! The crowds. Seeing you for the first time in six months. Christmas. I may never sleep again!"

For the rest of the morning, her words seemed prophetic. They stopped for breakfast on the way home, where Katie consumed a gigantic serving of *huevos rancheros* and carried on an animated conversation with her parents, catching them up on hometown gossip and hearing about the changes in their lives since their move to Arizona. Leigh Brannigan was as lively as her daughter had ever seen her — more truly herself, Katie thought, than she'd ever been before, like a butterfly emerged from a cocoon. The difference was remarkable.

When they reached the Brannigans' hacienda-style ranch on the outskirts of Phoenix, Katie was happy to see they'd left the tree decorating till she came, although the rest of the house was festive with garlands, luminarias, nativity scenes, and candles everywhere. The three of them spent the rest of the morning stringing lights, hanging ornaments, and draping strands of tinsel over the branches of the artificial tree. Kathryn's allergies had excluded the use of a cut tree for years, and even though her asthma was much better in the dry Arizona climate than it had been in Portland, they hadn't wanted to chance having evergreens in the house.

While her father made a run to the store for replacement bulbs for the string of lights surrounding the living room window, Katie had a chance to talk to her mother alone. "Mom, it's great to see you doing so well. Daddy told me on Thanksgiving how much you'd improved." She took a deep breath. "Some things have happened lately to make me realize how *controlling* I can be. I'm sorry for the times that's happened with you. I want you to know I never meant to take over."

Her mother, perched on the edge of the sofa, sorting through a box of ornaments, shook her head. "Oh, honey! I know you didn't. I was just as much at fault for *letting* you do things for me I could have done myself."

"I always felt responsible for you, especially when Daddy was gone. I know it was being pregnant with me that made you so...fragile."

Mrs. Brannigan reached across the sofa, lightly stroking Katie's arm. "Is that what you think?" she asked sadly. I was *born* fragile, Katie. Being pregnant with you was a miracle, something I prayed for over the years after your daddy and I married. My health problems were *not* your fault."

"Really?"

"Really." Carefully pulling a Victorian angel from the box on her lap, Katie's mother smoothed its feathered wings. The angel had adorned the top of their Christmas tree since Katie was a child. Glancing at her daughter, she added, "Sometimes when people are as close as you and I have always been, we can't see the forest for the trees. There's no perspective at point-blank range, is there?"

She leaned forward and set the angel on the coffee table in front of her. "It seems silly to say this at my age, but I feel like being away from each other has helped us both grow up. It's wonderful to be able to do for myself. And you're making a good life for yourself in Portland. I'm proud of you, honey."

Katie sat down on the sofa next to her mother and put

her arms around her, resting her head against her shoulder. "I love you, Mama."

"I love you, too. I'm really glad you're here. Now — not to be nosy, but are you going to tell me what's going on with Keith?"

Katie laughed. "You haven't changed all that much, you know?"

While they hung the last ornaments on the tree, Katie briefly sketched the course of her relationship with Keith over the last few months. Her mother knew they'd been spending time together, but Katie hadn't talked much about her feelings. Neither had she talked about the breach between them since Thanksgiving.

"Even though I'm *furious* with him for disappearing from my life again, in a way it's a relief. It's too hard being around him when he's chosen someone else. But," Katie confessed after the story was told, "I have to admit a big empty place opens up inside me when I think about him. I feel like part of me is missing." She reached down from the top of the stepladder for the angel her mother held. "I know I'll get over him eventually. I know that God can heal the hurt and make me whole again." She slipped the angel over the top vertical branch of the tree and straightened its feathered wings. "But I have to say — it feels like it might not be for a good long time."

"I'm sorry, Katie. I know you've been in love with him for quite a while."

Katie was startled. "You do? I never told you. I didn't know it myself until a month ago."

Leigh held the ladder steady as Katie stepped down. "You'll understand when you're a mother," she said.

Jet lag and emotional fatigue finally caught up with Katie after lunch. In shorts and a T-shirt, she lay sprawled on her back on a lounge chair next to the pool in her parents' backyard, soaking up the pale December sun. Her eyes were closed. Her knuckles scraped the concrete patio as her arms dangled over the sides of the chair. The sun slanted through a palm tree, warming her face, and she felt herself drifting....

"Katie-Bug, Lady-Bug, Green Alligatey-Bug!"

Her eyes flew open. "Keith!" she gasped. He was squatting next to her, close enough to kiss. She sat up abruptly at the thought. "You have some nerve, ignoring me for weeks, then showing up on my parents' doorstep for Christmas!"

He sat with a thump on the patio, as if her words had knocked him off balance. Katie drew her knees to her chest and wrapped her arms around them protectively.

"Katie, I know you're mad. I know I hurt you."

She compressed her lips, refusing to respond or even look at him.

He sighed. "Once again, 'Love means saying you're sorry every single time you screw up.' I'm sorry, Katie. At least *think* about forgiving me. Please?"

She stole a glance at him, eyeing the dark stubble on his chin and the rumpled clothes — a tuxedo shirt and pants, she realized with a start. He looked as if nothing more than his fingers had combed his hair for days. "How *did* you get here?" she asked, curious in spite of herself.

"Paid some unscrupulous college kid four times the ticket price for his seat to Phoenix."

"I'm supposed to feel *sorry* for you?"

"Please, Katie —"

"Look," she said, swinging her legs over the edge of the lounge chair and bouncing up. "I'm sure it must have been a trial getting here. You certainly look the worse for wear. But I don't know why you bothered. Go back to where you're wanted." She took a deep breath and lied, with only a trace of guilt: "You're not wanted here."

"No?" He unfolded himself from his position on the concrete and gazed down at her, his hands in his pockets, looking far too vulnerable and endearing in his rumpled clothes.

Don't look at me that way, Keith, she told him in her mind, feeling her defenses weaken. Suddenly it felt dangerous to be this close. Turning away with a flip of her ponytail and her chin thrust out, she started toward the house.

Keith grabbed her arm before she'd taken two steps. "That's not what your mother told me."

Katie stiffened. "My mother?"

"She said you'd be happy to see me. And *she* seemed happy that I'm here. She invited me to stay for Christmas. I think she's getting the guest house ready now."

Her *mother!* Katie felt betrayed.

She didn't resist as Keith turned her around. His eyes held hers for a brief moment before she snapped her head away and stared back toward the house.

"Why did you come?" she finally asked.

He didn't respond for a moment, then said quietly, "Because something important happened and I wanted to tell you about it. Because you're the most important person in my life. Because I saw you with Henry last night and I thought —" He stopped. "Because I love you."

Her mouth opened, but not a sound came out.

"Are you in love with Henry?" he asked anxiously. "He

isn't right for you, Katie —"

"Aren't you in love with Toni?" she interrupted, finding her voice.

"Of course I'm not in love with Toni! I hardly know her!"

Katie stared at him. "What's this important thing you wanted to tell me?"

"It's about…getting my heart settled, even if things aren't entirely settled in my mind. About feeling like I've finally come home. I don't mean physically, I mean — oh, it would take me hours to explain. Days. Weeks, maybe."

Her eyebrows rose. "Years, perhaps?"

"Years." He nodded emphatically. "Years, I'm certain."

Narrowing her eyes, she asked, "You *promise* to take years to explain it to me?"

"Absolutely." He grinned his familiar, wonderful, lopsided grin. "The rest of my life."

She plopped down on the lounge chair and pulled him down next to her. "Starting now?" she asked, taking his hand.

"Right this minute."

"Well, then!" A smile lit her face. "Okay! But before you get too involved…" Waggling her eyebrows, she paused dramatically.

"*What*, Squirt?"

She tossed her head and threw out her arms. "Kiss me, you fool!"

Laughing, he did.

Epilogue

❧

Toni knelt to straighten Danny's bow tie. He looked adorable in the little tuxedo, his dark hair slicked back from his scrubbed and shiny face. Pop was looking fine, too, she thought, glancing across the gazebo to where her father stood to one side with Chappie Lewis. Doc had a new haircut, and his snowy beard and mustache were neatly trimmed; he looked quite dapper in the gray tuxedo.

Not, however, as dapper as he'd looked in the Santa outfit he'd donned six months ago on Christmas morning for Danny's sake. Danny had known it was his "Grumpy," of course, but she'd convinced him to play along so as not to hurt Doc's feelings.

Pop and Danny. Christmas had been magical with them — her first Christmas clean and sober in years; the first opportunity she'd had to truly experience her son's incredible sweetness and her father's forgiving love. Her first inkling of what "family" meant, what made a house a home came during those days. The only thing that marred her happiness over the holidays was her sorrow at all the years she'd already lost. *I'll make it up to them,* she'd vowed.

The quiet sound of plucked violin strings broke into her musings. The members of the string quartet, their chairs and stands set up near the back of the tile-roofed gazebo, had begun tuning their instruments. Toni looked at her watch. Good. Twenty minutes before the ceremony was scheduled to begin, right on time. She could relax for a few minutes.

Turning, she leaned against the brick and concrete parapet overlooking the sunken rose gardens at Peninsula Park. When Katie had decided she wanted a garden wedding in June, all Toni could think of was the fact that the Rose Festival got rained on every year, and she should at least reserve an alternate location for the ceremony. True to form, the festival had once again been a soggy celebration, but the clouds seemed to have rained themselves out in the last couple weeks. The only water visible now was leaping into the air from the fountain at the center of the formal gardens, where it cascaded gracefully back into the pool, glistening like a shower of brilliant diamonds in the sun.

Danny pressed close to Toni's side, and her arm automatically went around him. "Which are your favorite roses?" she asked him.

"Mmm…" He tugged at his lower lip in the gesture she knew by now meant he was thinking very hard.

"The dark red ones that smell so good?" she prompted. "Or the gigantic yellow ones? Or the miniatures?"

"They're *all* my favorites," he finally said.

She laughed. "Mine, too. Who says we have to choose, when God made them all?"

Danny tugged at her hand. "I'm thirsty, Mama," he said.

She looked around. "I think I saw a drinking fountain.…

Oh, there it is, sweetheart," she said, pointing. "I'd like a drink, too."

They made their way through the gathering crowd, Danny holding tightly to his mother's hand.

"Toni!"

Turning, she saw that Keith was hailing her from the gravel walkway. She whistled, then grinned as he reddened. "Between you and Pop and Danny, you'll have some hearts palpitating around here for sure," she said.

"Thanks, I think. I hate to say it, but I don't remember where I'm supposed to be."

"A little nervous, are you?" she teased.

"Who, me?" Keith reached to run his fingers through his hair, but Toni grabbed his arm before he could do damage. He grinned sheepishly.

"Take a deep breath. You'll be fine," Toni soothed. "Just do what you did in rehearsal." She nodded toward the far side of the gazebo. "Pop and Chappie are over there. If you could chase Pop out to the street to wait for the rest of the wedding party, I'd appreciate it. I'll give you a signal as soon as the cars pull up on Albina. Let the string quartet know, wait for them to start the piece Katie chose for the processional, then come around the side with Chappie and stand to the left of the steps. Got that?"

"Sure. Okay. Simple."

"Good."

Originally, Emily Bradley had planned to coordinate the wedding for Katie, but having a new baby in the house was more exhausting than she'd expected. She was also making her own matron-of-honor dress, as well as the flower girl's dress. Emily had gratefully accepted Toni's offer of help, and when Katie asked Toni if she could possibly take over the coordinating entirely, she'd agreed without hesitation. It seemed a good way to tell Katie thank you for all the help she'd given Doc with Danny the last few years.

In fact, working on the details of Keith and Katie's wedding had given Toni an advantage at the stationery store where she worked part-time. Within a month of starting as a sales clerk, she was managing the wedding department. The job didn't pay much, but the owner liked her and little by little was teaching her the nitty-gritty of running a business.

"Okay, baby, go on with Kee now," she told her son when he'd finished drinking from the water fountain, swatting him gently on the bottom. "Remember how we practiced last week? Carry the pillow nice and straight so the rings won't fall off."

"They're sewed on, Mama — you silly!"

Keith raised his eyebrows. "You call your mom a *silly?*"

Toni laughed. "He got it from me, I'm afraid. We both get pretty silly sometimes, don't we, Danny?"

Grabbing Keith's hand, the little boy nodded happily. "Let's go, Kee! We gotta chase Grumpy out to the street!" Toni followed them with her eyes till they reached Doc and Chappie, a smile playing on her lips.

She'd been back in Portland since the end of January, her rehabilitation program successfully completed. She knew she'd be in recovery the rest of her life, but the work she'd done at the ranch had given her a solid foundation. Where she was still weak, she knew God was strong and would continue to heal her.

It felt wonderful to be taking care of her son and helping out her father in ways she'd never done before. In the everyday chores of laundry, cooking, and keeping house, she saw fresh opportunities to express her love for them. She'd also been able to negotiate her work schedule so she arrived home by the time Danny got out of school. His hello-I'm-so-happy-to-see-you hug and his daily recital of the joys and tribulations of first grade were the highlight of her day.

Seeing a black Taurus pull up to the curb at the end of the walkway, followed by a white limousine, Toni located Keith and waved her hand. Thank goodness he stood head and shoulders above the rest of the crowd, or he'd never have been able to see her signal. As soon as he acknowledged her wave, she hurried toward the street, snagging the usher who would escort Mrs. Brannigan to the one chair at the stand-up wedding — a colleague of Katie's, Henry something. Distinguished-looking, he was, with his trim beard just beginning to silver and touches of gray at his temples.

Doc was helping a small woman in a stylish, pale blue dress out of the car as a ruddy-faced man with faded red hair walked around from the driver's side. Katie's parents, a lovely couple. The chauffeur of the limousine, meanwhile, opened the door for his passengers: first a little girl with long blond hair in a floral print dress with a white collar and a big pink bow — the flower girl, Emily's little sister Isabel; then Emily, in a softly draped dress of the same fabric; then Katie. Toni's breath caught in her throat.

Katie was radiant. Happiness seemed to exude from her pores, its indisputable glow lighting her face from within. Her soft white dress was simple — tea-length chiffon with a tucked bodice and a flowing skirt over a slim underdress and a pale pink ribbon around her waist. Her beautiful chestnut hair had been French-braided and looped at the nape of her neck. Instead of a headpiece and veil, pink and white rose-buds and wispy baby's breath had been tucked into the plaits. She wore a twisted strand of fresh-water pearls around her neck, with matching earrings. Danny suddenly reappeared and danced around her with excitement. Her dress billowed around her legs in the June breeze as she bent to give him a big hug.

Quickly taking charge, Toni directed Leigh Brannigan down the walkway on Henry's arm. When they disappeared around the crowd toward the gazebo, she sent Emily and Doc after them, and then, kneeling to give him one last hug, Danny, with Isabel literally in tow. She and Katie exchanged an amused look.

When she'd first learned, in a letter from Pop right after the New Year, that Keith and Katie were engaged, Toni had been more than a little disappointed. She knew she wasn't in love with Keith, but he'd seemed like such a good choice to complete the circle of her family. When she'd visited at Thanksgiving, she'd set her mind on convincing him they should be together.

By the time she'd come home for good, though, she'd worked through her disappointment and was pleased to find that Keith and Katie had every intention of staying in Pop's and Danny's lives — and hers, by extension. It was obvious, seeing them together over the last few months, that they shared something between them that was very special.

The string quartet paused, and all eyes swung back to the street where Katie waited with her father, a beautiful bouquet of pink and yellow roses and white stephanotis in her arms. When the music began again — an exuberant piece of classical music Toni recognized only because she'd heard it on CD at last week's rehearsal — she nodded to Mr. Brannigan.

Toni didn't follow until the two had disappeared around the crowd, and when she did, she stood a little apart. As soon as the ceremony was over, she had to race over to the church where the reception was being held to make sure the caterers had everything under control before the guests began to arrive from the park. The wedding party, standing on the brick steps leading up to the gazebo, was clearly visible from her position.

In consideration of the guests, who were standing, the ceremony was short. Emily's sister Abigail read what Pop called the love chapter from the Bible. Chappie spoke briefly to Keith and Katie about sharing all of themselves with each other. "Now Katie has something very special to share with Keith before they say their vows," he finished.

Toni heard the pluck of an acoustic guitar rippling a complicated sequence of notes. Pressing closer, she craned her neck and found a narrow gap through which she could see the guitarist, Katie's friend Henry.

An unmistakable voice, rich and low, rose in song. Toni watched Keith's face while Katie sang:

Walk with me
I want you to walk with me
We'll travel with the sun
Two becoming one
Together walk through life and love.

Hold my hand
I need you to hold my hand
We'll face whatever comes

Two becoming one
Together stand for life and love.

Take my love
Everything I offer you
We'll love till life is done
Two becoming one
Together drink of life and love.

I know
You know
God knows
how I love you.

Take my love
Let me show you that it's true
I love you.

Toni found when the song was done that she'd been holding her breath. She let it out in a heavy sigh and was startled to hear the sigh echoed around her. Others had sensed the same thing, then. In Katie's voice and on Keith's face.

Toni tiptoed away as Katie and Keith exchanged their rings and vows. She didn't know everything about what she wanted in this new life she'd begun, but she knew without a doubt she didn't want to marry anyone unless she shared with him what Keith and Katie shared.

The vitality. The intense awareness of each other. The joy. Most of all, the profound belief that God had brought them together, that in each other — no matter where they went — they'd found their home.

Dear Reader:

It came as a shock, a number of years ago now, when I first realized my life wasn't turning out the way I'd expected it to. I'd always been a "good girl," I tried hard, I strove to do right. Why, then, were uninvited, unwanted, unhappy experiences knocking at my door?

I can't tell you I've discovered the answer to that question — only that the asking of the question itself was a milepost in my spiritual journey. Like the cast of characters in *Coming Home*, I approached the puzzle from different perspectives and dealt with my feelings in many ways.

At first, like Katie, I tried to "fix" things. When that didn't work, like Danny, I simply withdrew. Then, like Keith, I blamed God. Later, like Doc, I accepted my lot in life philosophically. Finally, like Chappie, I saw that the experiences I had so resisted had served a purpose after all: I'd learned, I'd grown, I'd become more intimate with God — I'd become less arrogant and more human. Now, I can be an Emily to others in ways I never could before — listening, loving, sympathizing, sometimes even challenging.

I was delighted when a friend who read the manuscript for *Coming Home* told me my characters had inspired her to reevaluate her life and her relationship with God. My prayer is that Keith and Katie and the others who stroll, skip, march, and meander through the pages of this book might inspire you to do the same — that as you journey with them, you might refresh your faith and hope in a God who waits with open arms for all his children to come home.

Barbara Jean Hicks

Write to Barbara Jean Hicks
c/o Palisades
P.O. Box 1720
Sisters, Oregon 97759

❧

Look for Barbara Jean Hicks' next novel,
Snow Swan, in April 1997.
Toni had come through so much — could she get
past the guilt and feel worthy of love again?

PALISADES...PURE ROMANCE

THE PALISADES LINE

Reunion, Karen Ball (July, 1996)
ISBN 0-88070-951-0
There are wolves on Taylor Sorensen's ranch. Wildlife biologist Connor
Alexander is sure of it. So he takes a job as a ranch hand to prove it. Soon he
and Taylor are caught in a fierce controversy—and in a determined battle
against the growing attraction between them...an attraction that neither can
ignore.

Chosen, Lisa Tawn Bergren
ISBN 0-88070-768-2
When biblical archeologist Alexsana Rourke is handed the unprecedented
honor of excavating Solomon's Stables in Jerusalem, she has no idea that she'll
need to rely heavily upon the new man in her life—CNN correspondent Ridge
McIntyre—and God, to save her.

Refuge, Lisa Tawn Bergren
ISBN 0-88070-875-1 (New ISBN)
Part One: A Montana rancher and a San Francisco marketing exec—only one
incredible summer and God could bring such diverse lives together. *Part Two:*
Lost and alone, Emily Walker needs and wants a new home, a sense of family.
Can one man lead her to the greatest Father she could ever want and a life full
of love?

Firestorm, Lisa Tawn Bergren (October, 1996)
ISBN 0-88070-953-7
In the sequel to Bergren's best-selling *Refuge, Firestorm* tells the romantic tale
of two unlikely soulmates: a woman who fears fire, and the man who loves it.
Reyne Oldre wasn't always afraid, but a tragic accident one summer changed
her forever. Can Reyne get beyond her fear and give her heart to smoke
jumper Logan Quinn?

Torchlight, Lisa Tawn Bergren
ISBN 0-88070-806-9
When beautiful heiress Julia Rierdon returns to Maine to remodel her family's
estate, she finds herself torn between the man she plans to marry and unexpected feelings for a mysterious wanderer who threatens to steal her heart.

Treasure, Lisa Tawn Bergren
ISBN 0-88070-725-9

She arrived on the Caribbean island of Robert's Foe armed with a lifelong dream—to find her ancestor's sunken ship—and yet the only man who can help her stands stubbornly in her way. Can Christina and Mitch find their way to the ship *and* to each other?

Cherish, Constance Colson
ISBN 0-88070-802-6

Recovering from the heartbreak of a failed engagement, Rose Anson seeks refuge at a resort on Singing Pines Island, where she plans to spend a peaceful summer studying and painting the spectacular scenery of international Lake of the Woods. But when a flamboyant Canadian and a big-hearted American compete for her love, the young artist must face her past—and her future. What follows is a search for the source and meaning of true love: a journey that begins in the heart and concludes in the soul.

Angel Valley, Peggy Darty
ISBN 0-88070-778-X

When teacher Laurel Hollingsworth accepts a summer tutoring position for a wealthy socialite family, she faces an enormous challenge in her young student, Anna Lee Wentworth. However, the real challenge is ahead of her: hanging on to her heart when older brother Matthew Wentworth comes to visit. Soon Laurel and Matthew find that they share a faith in God...and powerful feelings for one another. Can Laurel and Matthew find time to explore their relationship while she helps the emotionally troubled Anna Lee and fights to defend her love for the beautiful *Angel Valley*?

Seascape, Peggy Darty
ISBN 0-88070-927-8

On a pristine sugar sand beach in Florida, Jessica has a lot to reflect upon. The untimely death of her husband, Blake...and the sudden entrance of a new man, distracting her from her grief. In the midst of opening a B&B, can Jessica overcome her anger and forgive the one responsible for Blake's death? Loving the mysterious new man in her life will depend upon it.

Sundance, Peggy Darty (August, 1996)
ISBN 0-88070-952-9

Follow Ginger Grayson to the wilds of British Columbia, Canada, where she meets Craig Cameron, a widowed rancher with two small sons who desperately need a mother. Is free-spirited Ginger ready to settle down in the 1990's last wild frontier? And can Craig risk his heart again, all the while wondering if Ginger can handle his rugged lifestyle?

Love Song, **Sharon Gillenwater**
ISBN 0-88070-747-X
When famous country singer Andrea Carson returns to her hometown to recuperate from a life-threatening illness, she seeks nothing more than a respite from the demands of stardom that have sapped her creativity and ability to perform. It's Andi's old high school friend, Wade Jamison, who helps her to realize that she needs inner healing as well. As Andi's strength grows, so do her feelings for the rancher who has captured her heart. But can their relationship withstand the demands of her career? Or will their romance be as fleeting as a beautiful *Love Song*?

Antiques, **Sharon Gillenwater**
ISBN 0-88070-801-8
Deeply wounded by the infidelity of his wife, widower Grant Adams swore off all women—until meeting charming antiques dealer Dawn Carson. Although he is drawn to her, Grant struggles to trust again. Dawn finds herself overwhelmingly attracted to the darkly brooding cowboy, but won't marry a nonbeliever. As Grant learns more about her faith, he is touched by its impact on her life and slowly begins to trust.

Echoes, **Robin Jones Gunn**
ISBN 0-88070-773-9
In this dramatic romance filled with humor, Lauren Phillips enters the wild, uncharted territory of the Internet on her home computer and "connects" with a man known only as "KC." Recovering from a broken engagement and studying for her teaching credential, her correspondence with KC becomes the thing she enjoys most. Will their e-mail romance become a true love story when they meet face to face?

Secrets, **Robin Jones Gunn**
ISBN 0-88070-721-6
Seeking a new life as an English teacher in a peaceful Oregon town, Jessica tries desperately to hide the details of her identity from the community...until she falls in love. Will the past keep Jessica and Kyle apart forever?

Whispers, **Robin Jones Gunn**
ISBN 0-88070-755-0
Teri Moreno went to Maui eager to rekindle a romance. But when circumstances turn out to be quite different than she expects, she finds herself spending a great deal of time with a handsome, old high school crush who now works at a local resort. But the situation becomes more complicated when Teri meets Gordon, a clumsy, endearing Australian with a wild past, and both men begin to pursue her. Will Teri respond to God's gentle urgings toward true love? The answer lies in her response to the gentle *Whispers* in her heart.

Coming Home, Barbara Hicks
ISBN 0-88070-945-6

Keith Castle is running from a family revelation that destroyed his world, and deeply hurt his heart. Katie Brannigan is the childhood friend who was wounded by his sudden disappearance. Together, Keith and Katie could find healing and learn that in his own time, God manages all things for good. But can Katie bring herself to give love one more chance?

Glory, Marilyn Kok
ISBN 0-88070-754-2

To Mariel Forrest, the teaching position in Taiwan provided more than a simple escape from grief; it also offered an opportunity to deal with her feelings toward the God she once loved, but ultimately blamed for the death of her family. Once there, Mariel dares to ask the timeless question: "If God is good, why do we suffer?" What follows is an inspiring story of love, healing, and renewed confidence in God's goodness.

Diamonds, Shari MacDonald (November, 1996)
ISBN 0-88070-982-0

When spirited sports caster Casey Foster inherits a minor league team, she soon discovers that baseball isn't all fun and games. Soon, Casey is juggling crazy promotional events, major league expectations, and egos of players like Tucker Boyd: a pitcher who wants nothing more than to return to the major leagues...until Casey captures his heart and makes him see diamonds in a whole new way.

Forget-Me-Not, Shari MacDonald
ISBN 0-88070-769-0

Traveling to England's famed Newhaven estate to pursue an internship as a landscape architect, Hayley Buckman looked forward to making her long-held career dreams come true. But upon arrival, Hayley is quickly drawn to the estate and its mysterious inhabitants, despite a sinister warning urging her to leave. Will an endearing stranger help her solve the mystery and find love as well?

Sierra, Shari MacDonald
ISBN 0-88070-726-7

When spirited photographer Celia Randall travels to eastern California for a short-term assignment, she quickly is drawn to—and locks horns with—editor Marcus Stratton. Will lingering heartaches destroy Celia's chance at true love? Or can she find hope and healing high in the *Sierra*?

Westward, Amanda MacLean
ISBN 0-88070-751-8

Running from a desperate fate in the South toward an unknown future in the West, plantation-born artist Juliana St. Clair finds herself torn between two men, one an undercover agent with a heart of gold, the other a man with evil intentions and a smooth facade. Witness Juliana's dangerous travels toward faith and love as she follows God's lead in this powerful historical novel.

Stonehaven, Amanda MacLean
ISBN 0-88070-757-7

Picking up in the years following *Westward, Stonehaven* follows Callie St. Clair back to the South where she has returned to reclaim her ancestral home. As she works to win back the plantation, the beautiful and dauntless Callie turns it into a station on the Underground Railroad. Covering her actions by playing the role of a Southern belle, Callie risks losing Hawk, the only man she has ever loved. Readers will find themselves quickly drawn into this fast-paced novel of treachery, intrigue, spiritual discovery, and unexpected love.

Everlasting, Amanda MacLean
ISBN 0-88070-929-4

Picking up where the captivating *Stonehaven* left off, *Everlasting* brings readers face to face once more with charming, courageous—and very Irish—Sheridan O'Brian. Will she find her missing twin? And will Marcus Jade, a reporter bent on finding out what really happened to Shamus, destroy his chances with her by being less than honest?

Betrayed, Lorena McCourtney
ISBN 0-88070-756-9

As part of a wealthy midwestern family, young Rosalyn Fallon was sheltered from the struggles brought on by the Depression. But after the collapse of her father's company and the elopement of her fiancé and best friend, Rosalyn unexpectedly finds herself facing both hardship and heartbreak. Will her new life out West and a man as rugged and rough as the land itself help her recover?

Escape, Lorena McCourtney (September, 1996)
ISBN 1-57673-012-3

Is money really everything? The winsome Beth Curtis must come to terms with that question as she fights to hold on to guardianship of her nephew, even facing her deceased sister-in-law's brother. Sent to collect the boy, handsome Guy Wilkerson has no idea that he will fall for Beth, and come to see his own family's ways of living in a new light. Can the two overcome such diversity to be together, beginning their own family?

Voyage, Elaine Schulte (August, 1996)
ISBN 1-57673-011-5
Traveling via ship to the Holy Land, Ann Marie is on a pilgrimage, discovering things about faith and love all the way. But will a charming man who guides her—among the romantic streets of Greece and elsewhere—distract her from the One who truly loves her?

A Christmas Joy, MacLean, Darty, Gillenwater
ISBN 0-88070-780-1 (same length as other Palisades books)
Snow falls, hearts change, and love prevails! In this compilation, three experienced Palisades authors spin three separate novelettes centering around the Christmas season and message.
By Amanda MacLean: A Christmas pageant coordinator in a remote mountain village of Northern California is reunited with an old friend and discovers the greatest gift of all.
By Peggy Darty: A college ski club reunion brings together model Heather Grant and an old flame. Will they gain a new understanding?
By Sharon Gillenwater: A chance meeting in an airport that neither of them could forget...and a Christmas reunion.

Mistletoe: Ball, Hicks, McCourtney (October, 1996)
ISBN 1-57673-013-1
A new Christmas anthology of three novellas...all in one keepsake book!

❧

Also look for our new line:
PALISADES PREMIER
More Story. More Romance.

Chase the Dream, Constance Colson
ISBN 0-88070-928-6, $11.99
Alison Austin's childhood dream of being a world-champion barrel racer leads to problems at home and in the arena. Rising rodeo star Forrest Jackson, wounded from the death of his father and abandonment of his mother, is Alison's ideal—and her cousin Jenny's boyfriend. Ultimately, Alison must decide how much she is willing to give up...and to take.

Raised on the circuit, Jenny's love for Forrest is mixed with her love for barrel racing, while bull rider Tom Rawlings rodeos with much different motives.

As the time runs down and the competition heightens, the destinies of these four entwine, leading to a breathless climax. It's rodeo: the rough-and-tumble sport propelled by dreams; where love, life, and death are separated by mere seconds; and where meeting the Master Rider is inevitable.

Promise Me the Dawn, Amanda MacLean (September, 1996)
ISBN 0-88070-955-3, $11.99

Set in turn-of-the-century San Francisco and Monterey, *Promise Me the Dawn* weaves the tender love story of spirited English beauty Molly Quinn and Zachary MacAlister, an immigrant who came to America to flee his family's titles, wealth, and influence. During the dark days that follow the 1906 earthquake, Molly and Zachary plan a future rendezvous in the Pacific cliffs.

After they separate, Molly makes a name for herself and becomes the glamorous, new toast of the town. When Zach proposes, Molly decides that she hasn't lived enough yet, and lets him go. But when she later realizes that she may have lost him for good, Molly must reexamine the desires of her heart and turn back to her God before rediscovering the love she nearly lost in *Promise Me the Dawn*.

⌘

AND ESPECIALLY FOR YOUNG ADULTS:
Announcing the exciting new
Pacific Cascades University Series!

Come and meet nine college students and witness their trials and tribulations as they discover more about relationships, college life, and their world.

Freshman Blues, Wendy Lee Nentwig, ISBN 0-88070-947-2 (July 1996)
Homeward Heart, Lissa Halls Johnson, ISBN 0-88070-948-0 (July 1996)
True Identity, Bernie Sheahan, ISBN 0-88070-949-9 (September 1996)
Spring Break, Wendy Lee Nentwig, ISBN 0-88070-950-2 (September 1996)

Titles subject to change.